Creative technological change

'Professor McLoughlin has managed to span a number of disciplines in an excellent coverage of current research and perspectives and clearly illuminates the complex problems involved in managing technological change processes.'

Professor Richard Badham, *University of Wollongong, Australia*

Modernist notions of technology appear to dominate much past and contemporary organisational practice. *Creative Technological Change* thoroughly examines the theoretical and conceptual basis of our understanding of technology and the nature of the relationship between technological change and its organisational outcomes. By drawing together diverse and prominent literature on technological and organisational transformation, together with a detailed survey of new 'virtual' technologies, this book serves to illustrate the contrast between both modern and emergent post-modern images of technology, and distinct conceptualisations of the interaction between technology and organisations. This approach ultimately offers the possibility of developing new insights, lessons and creative responses to the organisational challenges posed by technological change in contemporary society.

This book will be of interest to those studying in the fields of management and technology studies, organisational theory and change, and the sociology of technology.

Ian McLoughlin is Professor of Management at the University of Newcastle-upon-Tyne. He is co-author of *Enterprise Without Unions: Industrial Relations in the Non-Union Firm* (Open University Press 1994), *Technological Change at Work* (Open University Press 1988, 1994) and *The Process of Technological Change* (Cambridge University Press 1988). He is co-editor of *Innovation, Organis~~~ ~~d Technology* (International Thomson Business Press 1997).

The Management of Technology and Innovation
edited by David Preece, University of Portsmouth, UK

The books in this series offer grounding in central elements of the management of technology and innovation. Each title will explain, develop and critically explore issues and concepts in a particular aspect of the management of technology and innovation, combining a review of the current state of knowledge with the presentation and discussion of primary material not previously published.

Each title is designed to be user-friendly with an international orientation and key introductions and summaries.

New titles in this series include:

Teleworking: International Perspectives
From Telecommuting to the Virtual Organisation
Edited by Paul J. Jackson and Jos M. Van Der W'elen

The Management of Technology and Innovation
Edited by David Preece and John Bessant

Technology in Context
Technological Assessment for Managers
by Ernest Braun, Emeritus Professor and former Head of the Technology Policy Unit, Aston University, UK

Creative technological change

The shaping of technology and organisations

Ian McLoughlin

London and New York

First published 1999 by Routledge
2 Park Square, Milton Park, Abingdon, Oxon, OX14 4RN

Simultaneously published in the USA and Canada
by Routledge
270 Madison Ave, New York NY 10016

Transferred to Digital Printing 2006

Typeset in Sabon by Routledge

British Library Cataloguing in Publication Data
A catalogue record for this book is available from the British Library

Library of Congress Cataloguing in Publication Data

ISBN 0–415–17999–8 (hbk)
ISBN 0–415–18000–7 (pbk)

Publisher's Note
The publisher has gone to great lengths to ensure the quality of this reprint
but points out that some imperfections in the original may be apparent

Printed and bound by CPI Antony Rowe, Eastbourne

For Sue, Ellen, Marie and Patrick

Contents

Illustrations

Figures

Tables

Acknowledgements

Books, like life, get done against a 'soundtrack'. This one is no exception: the birth of children, new work responsibilities, career moves, relegation struggles (thanks Jürgen for four of the best), and so it goes on. Because of this, and despite some of it, I would like to acknowledge the following: Miles for the music, the publisher for patience, Chris Payne for covering-up and keeping the show on the road in my many absences, Elinor McClelland for last minute word processing help, Richard Badham, Dave Buchanan, Patrick Dawson, Martin Harris, John Howells, Christian Koch and Dave Preece for variously, inspiration, discussions, ideas and reading and comments on earlier drafts of some of the material in this volume. Finally, and most importantly, those who have suffered most through the whole project: thanks to Ellen, Marie and Patrick for all the 'huggles' and to Sue – for Ellen, Marie and Patrick.

Ian McLoughlin
Newcastle, October 1998

Permissions

Permission has been granted to reproduce the following material: Figures 2.1, 7.1 and 7.2 by the Open University; Figure 3.1 and Table 7.1 by Allen and Unwin Pty Ltd (Australia) and ILR Press (USA); Figures 4.1 and 8.3 by International Thompson Publishing Services Ltd; Figure 7.3 by the European Commission; Figure 8.2 by MITOC, University of Wollongong; Table 2.1 by Edward Elgar Publishing Limited; Table 4.1 by John Wiley & Sons Ltd.

Introduction
Shaping technology and organisation

From automation to 'cybernation': finding the 'human centre'

In the 1990s the Internet and related information, computing and telecommunications (ICTs) technologies have emerged as perhaps the key technological developments of the twentieth century. Whilst the 'microelectronics revolution' based on the silicon chip prompted concerns in the late 1970s and 1980s about its social impact in the workplace, in particular in relation to the quantity and quality of work (see e.g. Forester 1980, 1985, 1989b), new hardware and software which enhance the connectivity and capacity to capture, distribute and display information have, more recently, highlighted other issues (see e.g. Barnatt 1995a, 1995b). These new technological developments are seen by many as enabling hitherto unimagined levels of electronic-mediation of human interaction and the embodiment of much business communication and activity in the realms of 'cyberspace'. At the same time the notion of work as something that occurs between particular times, within a detailed division of labour and bureaucratic hierarchy, normally at a given place – an organisation physically manifested in offices, factories and the like – is being challenged. Ideas such as 'flexibility', 'team-based' and 'tele'-work, 'holonic' and 'agile' factories, and 'network', 'distributed' and 'virtual organisations' (Davidow and Malone 1992; Kidd 1994; Grenier and Mates 1995; Birchall and Lyons 1995, Upton and McAfee 1996, Castells 1996) all point to what appears to be the radically new ways of working and organising enabled by current technological developments.

Taken together, these possibilities seem to point to a new phase in the automation of work where, instead of disparate elements of organisational functioning and activity being automated, the totality of an organisation's automated operations are electronically integrated and linked together. Bryn Jones has recently termed this the 'automation of automation' or 'cybernation' (Jones 1997: 19).

Moreover, these ICTs are increasingly thought of as underpinning the transformation of organisations which is said to be taking place with the decline of 'Fordist' production paradigms and the rise of new 'post-Fordist' production concepts such as 'lean production' and 'flexible specialisation' (Badham and Mathews 1989). As Harris (1998) has observed, it has become increasingly common for the advance of ICTs to be linked to some kind of 'paradigm shift' whereby technological change 'triggers' a fundamental transformation of organisations, if not a 'radical break' in terms of the continuity of the economic, social and political order as a whole. Numerous variants on this theme are evident (see Table A). These range from Piore and Sabel's (1984) flexible specialisation thesis which they claim is the harbinger of a 'second industrial divide', through Freeman and Perez's (1988) notion of the emergence of a new 'techno-economic paradigm', the 'Japanese' concept of 'lean production' as the only alternative to 'Fordism' (Womack *et al.* 1990), and more recent renditions such as 'business process engineering' (BPR) (Hammer and Champy 1993) and Quinn's arguments concerning 'intelligent' organisational forms (Quinn 1992). As Harris notes, the idea of 'virtual organisation' represents a further addition to this lengthening line of 'oppositional' typologies which, although frequently overstating the extent of actual techno-organisational change, do highlight emergent discontinuities in the way technology and organisation interact.

Indeed, despite the apparent certainties associated with the predictive and prescriptive models that the above typologies embody or have spawned, the direction that new technological and organisational developments may take remains open to fundamental questioning and broad debate. Kohn (1997) sees many parallels between contemporary techno-

Table A New organisational paradigms

Paradigm shift	*Role of technology*	*'Moral fabric'*
'Second industrial divide' (Piore and Sabel 1984)	Programmable machines allow flexible specialisations	Craft ethos Multiskilling High-trust relationships
New techno-economic paradigm (Freeman and Perez 1988)	ICTs signal end of Fordism and 'hard growth'	'Creative destruction' of old practices
Lean manufacturing (Womack *et al.* 1990)	Technology signals end of mass production	Consensus at work
BPR and the 'disaggregated organisation' (Quinn 1992)	IT allows control of processes	Control of labour and value chains creates responsive organisational forms
Virtual organisation (Handy 1995)	ICTs allow organisations to be dispersed in time and space	Fragmentation offset by high-trust relationships

Source: Harris 1998: 80.

logical innovations with those of the camera and projection technology in the 1890s which ultimately led to the cinema as we know it today. Indeed, in the early years of its development cinema technology was perceived in the popular imagination as a scientific and technical wonder just as new technologies such as the Internet and cyberspace tend to be represented for popular consumption today. Notably, the earliest uses of the cinema were simple demonstrations to audiences of the capabilities and capacity of a new technology which could make images move. Quickly the cinema progressed beyond novel demonstration and became a technological and organisational medium for the communication of information about current events. Further experimentation quickly followed and spawned increasingly sophisticated rearrangements of images and new techniques of narrative editing. These created visual experiences beyond those that could be experienced in real life. Cinema began to come of age as an art form, industry and culture. Metaphors and models were drawn upon from other art forms (for example the theatre) and directors developed new languages of expression which audiences learnt to read; audience reactions, in their turn, taught directors to try new cinematic devices to get their story across. In this way a 'new paradigm' of artistic, cultural and popular representation and expression was established with fundamental implications for thought and action.

At one level one might interpret such developments as an example of social change being driven by technological innovation. But Kohn makes a more subtle and profound point. It was, he suggests, the collective development of the 'new language of expression' which was crucial to the success of the cinema as an innovation rather than its invention, adoption and subsequent technological and organisational development. To date, the success of technological and organisational innovations involving ICTs has similarly been facilitated by the creation of new languages in the form of appropriate metaphors such as those of 'menus, desktops and windows'. These have enabled humans to interact with computers in a manner which resonates with their everyday experience of work and organisational life.

At the same time it can equally be argued that the widely reported failures of ICTs and related production techniques to deliver planned improvements in work and organisational performance reflects the inadequacy of much of what Weick terms our 'reasoning' in relation to the 'deep structure of new systems'. Unlike previous technologies, he suggests, making sense of, and with, these systems requires the creation of 'mental models' that 'represent an imagined technology that people assume parallels the actual technology' (1990: 35). Managerial choices made in the design, implementation and operation of new systems frequently rest on assumptions which generate a more deterministic model. Here technology is seen as a replacement for informed 'mental' action and intervention by humans.

This point has resonated frequently in recent critiques of contemporary technological developments. For example, a range of recent work – which taken together constitutes a 'new wave' in socio-technical theory and practice (see Chapter 7) – suggests that productive efficiency is no longer exclusively served by design objectives which seek to eliminate as far as is possible the need for informed, or even any, human intervention in work or organisational processes. What is needed, it is argued, is a 'human-centred' approach which seeks ways of finding a complementary or 'symbiotic' relationship between the technical and the human in the way work, organisation and technical systems are designed, implemented and used (see e.g. Benders *et al.* 1995; Mathews 1997). Arguments such as these suggest that not only might technology be seen as shaping work and organisations but that in a more profound and subtle way organisations – for example through the design philosophies which generate particular technological innovations and lines of technological development – shape technology.

The objective of this book is to pull together around these themes a wide range of thinking from organisational theory, innovation studies, evolutionary economics, feminist theory and the social shaping of technology. The aim is to explore and evaluate the different ways in which the interaction between technology and organisation can be framed and understood. Following Morgan (1986, 1993, 1997) this will, in part, involve an examination of the metaphors which lay behind various perspectives and the way these can be used to capture the differences between, and strengths and weaknesses of, different ways of conceptualising the technology–organisation relationship. The central argument will be that creative approaches to technological change increasingly rest upon the collective creation of intuitive and serviceable metaphors which allow humans to make sense of and learn from experiences in the workplace, organisation and beyond. However, both generating new images of the relationship between technology and organisation and translating these into practice raise fundamental questions concerning the nature of the process of technological innovation and organisational change. This, as will be suggested, is the crux of the challenge that is faced in developing new ways of thinking about and ultimately responding creatively to the way in which technology and organisation are currently shaped in order to redirect them towards a more 'human centre'.

The problem of technology and technological determinism

Any attempt to review and develop our theoretical and analytical understanding of the relationship between technology and organisation must wrestle with the issue of what, if any, definitive independent influence technology has in shaping organisational behaviour and the organisational outcomes of technological change. This question has long exercised students of organisations and, more broadly, sociologists of technology and a host of others. A long-standing and overriding concern in most of this literature has been to avoid and counter 'technological determinist' analysis of the capabilities of and characteristics of technology and their effects on work, organisations and society. By the same token, the notion that effective policy and practitioner responses to organisational and other problems are either wholly or mainly embodied in technological solutions or 'fixes' has also been strongly contested. Such concerns have arguably become even more important as the pace of technological innovation has increased and determinist images of technology and their supposed trans-formative effects on organisation have remained dominant in some academic, and much practitioner and popular thinking.

However, theory and research on the question of alternative models of the technology–organisation relationship remain at best 'ambiguous and conflicting' (Orlikowski 1992); prone to the very 'technicism' that they frequently claim to avoid (Grint and Woolgar 1997); have as their central analytical focus a term – 'technology' – which has been defined and opera-tionalised in so many ways that the 'development of common conceptual models is...difficult' (Roberts and Grabowski 1996) such that as a term it is now 'barely useful' (Fleck and Howells 1997); and whose contemporary characteristics 'organisational theorists have yet to grapple with' (Weick 1990). Perhaps, not surprisingly, the guidance for those seeking to shape and/or intervene to redirect the outcomes of technological change is simi-larly confused. As Orlikowski has correctly observed:

> the divergent definitions and opposing perspectives associated with technological research have limited our understanding of how tech-nology interacts with organisations....What is needed is a reconstruction of the concept of technology, which fundamentally re-examines our current notions of technology and its role in organisations.
>
> (Orlikowski 1992: 398)

What is technology and what does it do?

If a reconstruction of the concept of technology is needed in order to improve our understanding of the technology–organisation relationship, what broad options do we have in its definition and conceptualising in order to make sense of its effects on organisations? Grint and Woolgar make a useful distinction between approaches to defining technology in terms of seeking to distinguish between its 'non-human' and 'human' elements and those which seek to recast the relationship between tech-nology and humans 'as a network rather than as parallel but separate systems' (Grint and Woolgar 1997: 10).

In the first approach the significance of technology and its effects is understood through attempts to draw a boundary between 'technology' and its manifestation in particular social contexts, for example as a determinant of organisational variables or in shaping the organisational outcomes of technological change. A key analytical issue here is where this boundary is to be drawn. The broader or more expansive the definition of 'technology' the more significant an explanatory variable or category it becomes. The narrower or more restrictive the definition the more the independent effects of 'technology' become relatively insignificant, or not significant at all, when compared to the influence of social factors. From this vantage point the critique of technological determinism can be seen as one where unnecessarily expansive definitions of technology are challenged by much more restrictive notions which seek to minimise or even, for analytical purposes, totally disregard the possibility of technology having 'effects' on organisational variables and outcomes.

An excellent example of this line of reasoning is provided by Orlikowski, who distinguishes between two aspects of analytical definitions of technology (Orlikowski 1992: 398–9). First, the 'scope' of the definition – that is, what is defined as technology – and thereby the boundary between the 'human' and the 'non-human'. Second, the 'role' ascribed to technology – that is, the nature of the interaction between 'technology' and human and organisational variables – and thereby the independent effect of technology itself. Orlikowski suggests that approaches to the definition of the scope of technology range from the restrictive view as 'hardware' through to those which embrace 'social technologies' in the form of the tasks, techniques and know-how needed by humans to use 'hardware'. Differences in the definition of the role of technology range from those which suggest the strong determining influence of technology on organisational variables, through to those which posit a 'softer' determinism viewing technology as a 'reference point' whose effects are more or less strongly 'mediated', or more or less strongly mediating, during the shaping of organisation by human agents (Orlikowski 1992: 401–2).

In the second approach, identified by Grint and Woolgar, the notion of technology having independent 'effects' is challenged. The starting point here is the social constructivist point that 'technology does not have any influence which can be gauged independently of human interpretation' (Grint and Woolgar 1997: 10). In this sense what a technology is and is not and what it can and cannot do are all socially constructed. In other words, there is no boundary between the technical (non-human) and the social (human) other than that which is socially defined.

> Technologies, in other words, are not transparent; their character is not given; and they do not contain an essence independent of the nexus of social actions of which they are a part. They do not 'by themselves' tell us what they are or what they are capable of. Instead, capabilities – what, for example, a machine will do – are attributed to

the machine by humans. Our knowledge of technology is in this sense essentially social; it is a construction rather than a reflection of the machine's capabilities.

(Grint and Woolgar 1997: 10)

A key objective of this book is to explore these two apparently competing accounts and to examine ways in which they might together contribute to a more creative conceptualisation of technological change and its relationship to organisational outcomes.

Metaphors, technology and organisation

Metaphors, in Morgan's famous phrase, are 'a way of thinking and a way of seeing'. They are the way in which – by drawing upon areas of pre-existing knowledge (the 'source domain') – we can 'make sense' of and act in relation to organisational situations with which we have relatively little familiarity or which we do not fully understand (the 'target domain'). As such, metaphors have a 'generative capacity' which permits the possibility of bringing new perspectives into existence and modes of action onto the organisational agenda (Grant and Oswick 1996: 2). This 'generative' capacity leads directly to a much debated aspect of metaphors – the notion that their use is in some sense liberative, freeing, for example the organisational theorist or practitioner from the 'trap' of current images of self and organisation and instead permitting a creative reshaping of organisation – what Morgan refers to as 'imaginisation' (Morgan 1993).

This liberative and creative potential makes the use and exploration of metaphor highly attractive as a means of gaining new purchase on the relationship between technology and organisation. According to Grant and Oswick, the liberative and creative properties of metaphor manifest themselves in at least three ways. (Grant and Oswick 1996: 3–4). First, metaphors can help 'generate alternative social realities' in that pre-existing conceptions concerning an organisational situation – in particular the conception that reality is inevitable, rigid and determined – may be transformed and understood in a more informed way by the application of a new metaphor. Second, metaphors can facilitate the acquisition of new knowledge and enable individual, group and organisational learning when practitioners, and for that matter organisational theorists, are confronted by entirely novel and unfamiliar organisational phenomena. Third, metaphor can be used as an 'investigative tool', either in the understanding of organisational theory, or in the diagnosis of and search for solutions to organisational problems.

How, though, do we establish the usefulness of a metaphor in organisational analysis? Morgan's own response to this question is not that we should seek to establish the 'truth' or otherwise of a particular metaphor but rather that we should seek to establish the specific strengths and weaknesses that its use brings to our perspective on organisations or an aspect of them (1996: 230). At best a metaphor can be regarded as a 'partial truth' which excludes 'partial truths' made available by other metaphors. Metaphors can generate new images in relation to an organisational phenomenon – the relationship between technology and organisation for example – which allow for a more creative understanding and more creative action. At the same time metaphors have limitations which, if not recognised, can undermine their utility.

Against this positive view of the role of metaphor must be put more negative arguments as to their utility (Grant and Oswick 1996: 5–6). First, from a positivist perspective metaphors hardly accord with the basic tenets of social 'scientific' practice. They are imprecise and potentially misleading linguistic devices which cannot be subjected to empirical test and verification. The extent to which a metaphor works, i.e. how useful the source domain is when applied to the target domain, is not measurable. Rather, it is purely dependent upon cognitive processes. Moreover, as frequently observed, metaphors can be 'pushed too far' where their use is uninformed and pays little regard to limitations and contextual relevance (Døving 1996). Second, from a radical perspective metaphors can serve as ideological devices that conceal social inequalities and political domination. In the same way, the 'generative' qualities of metaphors can serve only the interests of the powerful with little liberative intent for those who are exploited in and by organisations. The value of metaphors from this viewpoint is, therefore, strongly related to their capacity to enable critical social analysis and challenges to the dominant views of organisational reality and the metaphors which underpin them (Tinker 1986). Such criticisms notwithstanding, the core argument of this book is that in both analytical and practical terms, the use of metaphor offers a useful device which can aid a rethinking of the relationship between technology and organisation in a more creative and beneficial way. As Clegg and Gray observe, 'metaphors are inevitable and useful' and 'without them we would be nowhere that we could know' (1996: 91).

Creative technological change – book structure

In each of the chapters of this book we will examine how the technology–organisation relationship has been understood in terms of a range of different metaphors.

In Chapter 1 we consider analyses which seek to understand this interaction in terms of 'machine', 'organism' and 'information processing brain' metaphors. As we will see, each of these tends towards a technologically determinist view of the relationship between technology and organisation. The 'machine' metaphor, for example, seeks to promote models which equate efficiency with machine-like organisational design and behaviour. The 'organism' metaphor, in contrast, promotes a view of satisfying human needs by adapting organisations to their environment, where technology is seen as the most, or one of the most, significant such contingencies. The 'information system' metaphor locks onto the transformative potential in ICTs, noted above, for revolutionising our concepts of organising and organisation through the electronic mediation of human communications and interaction. In so doing images of organisation become increasingly technological as 'information' is seen as their defining characteristic.

Chapter 2 considers a similar set of issues but from a different starting point. That is, the attempt to use evolutionary metaphors to explain technological innovation and change, in particular the nature of the interaction between environmental selection on the one hand and the strategic activities of organisations on the other, as they seek to influence their survival possibilities through 'mutation', i.e. engaging in technological and related organisational innovation. Again this perspective appears to carry with it strongly deterministic overtones, in particular when it is suggested that evolutionary developments follow 'natural' technological trajectories.

In Chapter 3 a broad range of mainly critical analyses is discussed around the theme of new production concepts, in particular the idea noted above of a transformative shift from 'Fordist' to 'post-Fordist' production and organisation. These ideas seek to avoid the technological determinism of concepts such as the 'information society' and 'technological trajectories' by focusing on the 'relations' rather than 'forces' of production. Three strands of this debate are considered: the radical critiques of positive images of the effects of advanced technology on work and organisations; the thesis that new production concepts are emerging to transform the hitherto predominant 'post-Fordist' paradigm; and the view that new forms of technology and organisation constitute a more negative reality of increased electronic surveillance. The predominant metaphors in these debates point to contradictory outcomes. On the one hand are images of organisations where technology is a means of ever more sophisticated management control and organisational surveillance. On other are transformative images which point to new possibilities for autonomy and flexibility in the pursuit of productive and competitive advantage.

The debate concerning new production concepts retains a strong flavour of change *within* organisations as being determined by broader economic and technological imperatives. In Chapter 4 an approach intended as a corrective to such determinism is introduced. The essence of this view is that environmental and contextual factors which have been the focus of much of the discussion in the previous three chapters act only as 'reference points' for the choices, decisions and negotiating activity of 'power-holders' and other groups within organisations. This usefully highlights the micro-political role of change agents in shaping the organisational outcomes of technological change. It also raises the question of what, if anything, technology does since the effects of technological change are presented as entirely socially negotiated.

The following three chapters focus more directly on technology. If the effects of technology are socially shaped, what of technology itself? In Chapters 5 and 6 social constructivist perspectives on technology are considered. These deploy a variety of metaphors, technology as a 'seamless web', 'actor-network', 'socio-technical ensemble' or 'text' in attempts to 'open the technology black box' to show that not only its effects but the actual content of technology is a social construct. That is, what a technology is, what it can do, what constitutes its effective working and so forth are all subject to 'interpretative flexibility' in the context of its production and consumption. Whilst there are disputes between constructivists and others concerning whether there are material limits to interpretation of this kind, the fundamental insight from this perspective is that the term 'technology' is a mere shorthand for a complex set of socio-technical relationships. It is change in these relationships, rather than changes 'caused' by technology in any deterministic sense, which provides the arena for organisational and broader social transformation.

In Chapter 7 another variant of the social shaping perspective is considered. This looks 'inwards' at technology to show how it is socially shaped in interaction with organisations rather than 'outwards' from the technology itself. Metaphors of 'embodied interests' and 'crystallised contingency' are evoked to capture this mutual shaping of technology and organisation over time in complex interactions between internal organisational actors, suppliers, vendors, customers, users and other social institutions. A key insight from this position is to show how innovation cannot be adequately understood if it is seen as a purely technological phenomenon occurring up to but not beyond the point of first successful adoption. Rather, 'post-adoption' innovation and reinnovation become the key dynamic in the mutual shaping of technology and organisation were new technology, new organisational forms and new production concepts and paradigms become inextricably intertwined.

The concluding chapter seeks to exploit the generative and liberative properties of metaphor in order to identify ways in which advances in both thinking and action in relation to technological change can be creatively enhanced. This, it is suggested, requires a willingness to 'mix metaphors' in the search for new ways of making sense of and enacting contemporary technological and organisational complexity.

1   Machines, organisms and virtual realities

Introduction

Technology has consistently played a dominant role in our images of modern, and now 'post-modern', organisations. But exactly what role technology plays and how in analytical terms it should be defined have been a matter of continuing controversy. In particular, from around the start of the 1970s it has been almost obligatory for academic studies of the relationship between technology and organisations to begin with a refutation of 'technological determinism'. This refutation has focused on a variety of issues which we will explore in detail in this and following chapters but it relates at its core to the problems that arise in much organisational analysis through the use of metaphors of the organisation as a 'machine', 'living organism' and, most recently, as an 'information processing brain'. This chapter is primarily concerned, therefore, with a discussion of the strengths and weaknesses of metaphors of organisation which give a primacy to technology as a key factor explaining organisational structure, behaviour and change.

The machine and its organisational dysfunctions

Gareth Morgan in his highly influential book *Images of Organisation* (1986, 1997) draws our attention to the fact that much of the theory and prescription of management and organisation, and indeed practitioners' own perceptions of their managerial role and its organisational context, have been dominated in the twentieth century by a metaphor which views organisations 'as if' they were machines.

> Consider...the mechanical precision with which many of our institutions are expected to operate. Organisational life is often routinised with the precision demanded of clockwork. People are frequently expected to arrive at work at a given time, perform a predetermined set of activities, rest at appointed hours, then resume their tasks until work is over. In many organisations one shift of workers replaces

another in methodical fashion so that work can continue uninterrupted twenty-four hours a day, every day of the year. Often the work is very mechanical and repetitive. Anyone who has observed work in the mass-production factory, or in any of the large 'office factories' processing paper forms such as insurance claims, tax returns or bank cheques will have noticed the machinelike way in which such organisations operate. They are designed like machines, and their employees are in essence expected to behave as if they were parts of machines.

(Morgan 1986: 29)

The appeal of the machine metaphor clearly relates to the historical context in which initial ideas concerning the nature of management and organisation were developed in the late nineteenth and early twentieth century. Industrialisation and technological change were proceeding apace in both Europe and the USA. At the same time the evolution of the nation state and centralised government were also leading to the development of complex administrative processes.

Thus, Frederick Winslow Taylor and a succession of followers made the short step from acknowledging the productive potential of the science of machines to insisting that a 'science of management' was required to turn this potential into actual improvements in employee and organisational performance. Similarly, Max Weber's concept of bureaucratic organisation was taken up by early management theorists such as Henri Fayol as the basis of a science of rational administration (for discussion of these developments see Rose 1988). Classical administrative theory and scientific management provided 'one best way' approaches to management and organisation. In effect they argued that the most effective/efficient performance followed from adopting a structure close to the 'rational', bureaucratic ideal-type of hierarchically arranged command and control structures or work design based on the principles of a detailed division of labour. In both cases the basis of these prescriptions was deemed to be the imperatives of industrial and administrative technology.

In order for these systems to work efficiently, their human counterparts had to be made to function in a machine-like manner as well. In fact, the less human-like the work of the humans and as a result, the less human-like the humans themselves, the better. Thus jobs were designed so that they were deskilled, fragmented, machine-paced and routinised, whilst human motivation was sought through relatively high material rewards in the form of pay and job security. At the same time, employees were required to bring little of their humanity to the workplace:

The lightest jobs were again classified to discover how many of them required the full use of faculties, and we found that 670 could be filled by legless men, 2,637 by one-legged men, two by armless men, 715 by one-armed men, and ten by blind men. Therefore, out of 7,882 kinds of job...4,034 did not require full physical capacity.

(Henry Ford 1922 quoted by Salaman and Littler 1984: 75)

The problem with such mechanistic images is that this model of organisation results, from a human and social viewpoint, in serious dysfunctions. Workers experience their jobs as boring and alienating which gives rise to grievances and conflictive relations with management. These relationships were, and still are, manifested in such 'dysfunctional' phenomena as poor labour relations, high levels of industrial disputation, absenteeism, accident rates, labour turnover and even industrial sabotage. The spread of scientific management and the mass assembly-line, whilst undoubtedly the basis for huge leaps in productive efficiency and overall improvements in economic well-being, has repeatedly been seen by critics as extracting too high a price in human terms (see e.g. Blauner 1964; Braverman 1974; Ritzer 1996).

One origin of this critique was 'human relations theory'. This stemmed from the work, conducted over 15 years during the 1920s and early 1930s, of Elton Mayo and his collaborators in the Hawthorne plant of the General Electric Company in Chicago (Roethlisberger and Dickson 1964). The Hawthorne studies reached the telling conclusion that workers were not primarily motivated by material rewards alone. Rather, work was seen as a means of satisfying social needs. Thus in engaging in apparently dysfunctional behaviour workers were not, as assumed by Taylor and his followers, motivated by monetary gain but by the need to exercise some social control over their work environment. In fact, the presence of Mayo's experimenters in the Hawthorne plant over long periods of time was to tap this need by creating an environment in which the workers' cooperation was required in order to conduct the experiment – the famous 'Hawthorne Effect'. The prescriptions drawn from this were that in order to raise worker output management had to change their approach to the motivation and reward of employees. Attention had to be given to satisfying the workers' social needs at work and to developing less authoritarian and more human orientated modes of supervision. Humans had to be regarded as 'living systems' with 'needs' rather than as inanimate 'machine-like' objects.

Technology and organisations

The insight of human relations theory was to challenge ways of thinking about technology and the organisation as if the latter, and its human inhabitants, were themselves machines. Instead it encouraged thinking about organisations and technology in terms of biological metaphors. Organisations can be thought of in these terms, as *natural living organisms* or systems. In order to survive organisations have to find ways of satisfying the *needs* of their members. To do this they must adapt to the environmental context in which they operate where technology can be seen as one such key contingency. The organism metaphor thus permits a more subtle understanding of the relationship between technology and organisation. This insight was developed by what has become known as 'contingency theory'. This had as 'an assumption', usually demonstrated, 'that technology and work behaviour are intimately related' (Rose 1988: 176).

Views over the way in which the relationship between technology and behaviour takes effect differ within contingency theory. In particular, drawing on the distinctions made in our Introduction, there are differences in how contingency theorists view the 'role' that is played by technology in shaping organisation and in their view of the 'scope' or definition of technology itself. Thus, in some views technology is seen as having a direct influence on organisational behaviour but in others this is seen as mediated by factors such as the way work is organised. Similarly, in some views behaviour is seen as a direct response or 'reflex' to a particular technology–organisation relationship and in others a product to some degree of individual interpretations of that situation. Further, the definition of 'technology' itself is variable, sometimes embracing only physical artefacts and systems and in others extending so far as to cover the organisation of work and more. These differences can be illustrated by briefly reviewing some of the key landmarks in attempts by contingency theorists to analyse the technology–organisation relationship.

Technology was first identified as a key variable shaping organisations in research published in the USA in the 1950s. This suggested, contrary to the inferences of human relations theory, that it was the nature of technology, if not directly, then mediated to varying degrees by forms of work organisation, which determined human behaviour. Thus managers keen to improve organisational efficiency were encouraged, not only to pay attention to matters of management style and communications, but also to take account of the way in which technology generated certain requirements in terms of organisational structure, or enabled and constrained choices over work organisation (Rose 1988: 175–6).

For example, in their study of the attitudes of car workers in Detroit, Walker and Guest (1952) observed that assembly-line technology acted to constrain the formation of work groups and, to use Rose's words, 'frustrated' what was assumed to be a 'natural urge for social attachments' (Rose 1988: 185). In other words, technology could play a crucial role in 'determining the character of the social relationships for any individual or for a group of individuals' (Walker and Guest 1952: 145). Sayles (1958) took this line of argument further by suggesting that actual patterns of behaviour – specifically grievance behaviour – could be seen as strongly related to the technology in a particular work setting rather than to variables such as management policy, labour turnover or style of supervision.

In these studies 'technology' was largely taken to be physical artefacts or systems which had an apparently direct and readily observable effect on behaviour. Thus Sayles makes the observation that, 'we recognize that many persistent industrial relations problems have their roots in the technology of the plant' and '...the social system erected by the technological process is also a basic and continuing determinant of work group attitudes and actions' (Sayles 1958: 119) although elsewhere the argument is made more subtle by the suggestion that technology has an enabling and constraining, rather than determining, effect on behaviour. Nevertheless, the identification of technology as one factor in shaping grievance behaviour, and by inference the nature and pattern of industrial relations in a workplace more generally, questions the human relations assumption that grievance and other conflict orientated behaviours are best dealt with by attending to the individuals seen as its cause or by seeking to improve management–labour communications. Rather, if technology is part of the cause of such 'problems' then organisational practitioners need also to bear this in mind in seeking to manage 'dysfunctional' grievance and other troublesome behaviours, perhaps by using Sayles' analysis to anticipate trouble and target managerial efforts to potential problem areas in anticipation of rather than in response to worker actions.

Other contingency theorists have been less concerned with the relationship between technology and employee behaviour and have focused on the relationship with organisational structure and performance (see Hatch 1997). In so doing they have proposed a number of taxonomies which allow the characteristics of different types of production technology to be identified and the implications for 'fit' with different types of organisation structure to be assessed. Typically, these approaches adopt a more 'expansive' definition but the role of technology is still viewed as having relatively deterministic effects on organisation structure and behaviour.

The work of Joan Woodward (1970, 1980) provides a widely known illustration of such an expansive definition of 'technology'. At the same time her conception appears to be highly determinist insofar as the room for interpretative action, albeit recognised, is limited and the effects of technology, albeit mediated by organisational variables, are seen as ultimately decisive in determining organisational efficiency. In fact, Woodward's celebrated research in Southern England in the late 1950s and 1960s provides a classic illustration of the working through of the organism metaphor. Her analysis led to the conclusion – frequently cited as an example of technological determinism – that given technologies require management to adopt particular forms of organisation if their enterprises are to be commercially successful. At the same time, the starting point for her analysis was the problematic nature of the 'one best way' models of management and organisational design that are necessarily produced when the organisation is construed as a machine.

Woodward defined the scope of 'technology' as being more than just physical artefacts. Rather she focused on the broader 'production system' employed by an organisation, that is, 'the collection of plant, machines, tools and recipes available at a given time for the execution of the production task and the rationale underlying their utilisation' (Woodward 1970:4). From her empirical studies Woodward identified eleven different types of *production system*, so defined, which she subsequently grouped into three main categories of unit and small batch, large batch and mass, and automated continuous-process production systems. Further, the effects of different types of production system on managerial and employee behaviour were seen as mediated by the organisation's structure, or more precisely, the management control system which varied according to whether they were: 'integrated/fragmented', i.e. control was centralised or spread out across several divisions or departments; 'personal/mechanical', i.e. control over employees was exercised directly by supervisors and managers; or built into the production system itself, e.g. the pace of work was controlled by direct supervision or was machine-dependent.

The degree of fit between the type of production system and management control system was seen as the key factor in determining the commercial success of an organisation. Woodward found a strong statistical correlation between type of production system, type of management control system and commercial success. Thus her analysis suggested that unit or small batch production systems were best served by 'integrated personal control systems' (e.g. a small business producing single or small runs of products where all aspects, functions and employees are controlled by the owner manager). Large batch or mass production systems were best served by fragmented control systems of a personal or mechanical type (e.g. larger organisations where management functions are distributed across departments and where employees are controlled either by direct supervision or through machines). Finally, process production systems were seen as best served by integrated mechanical control systems (e.g. as in organisations such as oil refineries or chemical plants where management functions are highly centralised and where the consequences of employee task performance can be monitored and regulated through machinery designed to monitor the production process itself).

Woodward's overall conclusion was that: 'there is a particular form of organisation most appropriate to each technical situation' (Woodward 1980: 72). However, other contingency theorists have come to a more limited conclusion than Woodward about the determining influence of technology on organisations. For example, the Aston School (a team of researchers headed by Derek Pugh and based at Aston University, Birmingham, UK) began work in the 1960s and identified seven types of organisation structure. The researchers argued through a complex statistical analysis that variations in organisation structure were principally explained by the contextual factors of size and national context/culture rather than just technology (see e.g. Pugh and Hickson 1976). Other taxonomic approaches to the relationship between technology and organisation also give less emphasis to technology as the principal determinant of organisational behaviour but continue to employ and refine an expansive definition of 'technology' where the nature of the work task is the principal defining element. For example, Perrow (1967) recognised that organisations rarely have one type of 'technical situation' to respond to and that a range of technologies, rather than just one type of 'production system', are likely to be involved in production or service provision. It follows that the technological shaping of organisations is much more multifaceted than envisaged by Woodward (see also Thompson 1967; Galbraith 1973).

In summary, since the 1950s technology has been seen as a key variable in the analysis of organisations and, if not the key determinant, then one of the major contingencies shaping both structure and behaviour. However, there is no consensus over the analytical definition of technology, although the tendency has been to adopt ever more expansive definitions, in particular as attempts have been made to analyse non-manufacturing organisations. It is also unclear how much the actual effects of 'technology', whatever the definition, are mediated by human interpretation. At worst human behaviour appears to be a reflex response to given technological conditions. What is clear, however, is that technology is seen as an important driving force in organisational design and development. This core idea has led to much broader theoretical and analytical constructs concerning the relationship between technology, organisational change and the structure of society as a whole.

From industrial to post-industrial organisations

So far we have examined the interaction between technology and organisation as represented through the machine and organism metaphors in static terms. However, it is clearly also necessary to focus on the dynamic relationship between technology and organisation. If we take the view that technology is a key, if not the key, variable shaping organisations, then changes in technology – in particular those which lead to its greater sophistication and complexity – can be expected to have a profound effect on organisations and beyond.

Of course this is a familiar, almost common sense view. Technology is a pervasive feature of advanced industrial societies and to raise the significance of technological change by suggesting it as a causal or determining variable of organisational and broader socio-economic change seems almost natural. Clark Kerr *et al.* in their highly influential *Industrialism and Industrial Man* (1960) referred to the 'logic of industrialism' and the 'technological imperative' which they claimed was driving industrial and industrialising societies to adopt similar economic, political and social structures apparently regardless of their history and own cultural identities. As we will see in a moment, new information and computing technologies have frequently been identified as the source of a new 'technological revolution' to rival those of the past and as ushering in a major transition from a manufacturing-based industrial society to a post-industrial 'information society' with wide economic, political and social ramifications (see e.g. Forester 1985).

Such arguments are usually inextricably linked to positive, optimistic and progressive views of the long term consequences of the technological shaping of organisations. Indeed, they were clearly reflected in the work of many organisational analysts who focused on the consequences of automation in the 1950s and 1960s. For example, Woodward took the view that technological advance involving computer-based systems enabled increasing automation of the control of work operations as distinct from the transformation of, and transfer of, raw materials and part-finished products enabled by previous electro-mechanical technologies. This new technology would mean production systems in an increasingly diverse range of industrial sectors could, in the future, take on the characteristics of continuous process production systems. That is, key managerial goals and objectives could be designed into the technology itself and the plans to execute these – and related monitoring and corrective mechanisms – embodied in the layout and configuration of the physical hardware and systems.

Given such developments the predicted effects on organisational behaviour were:

- Insofar as the key operations involved in transforming and transferring raw materials are incorporated within the technology itself, the work tasks of employees will become ones of monitoring the operation of the process.
- Since such monitoring tasks are best accomplished by employees working as multiskilled teams (e.g. in a control room or as a maintenance crew) the logic of designing work organisation around a rigid low skill division of labour would cease.
- These teams would become self-supervising since the key managerial decisions which might require direct management control (e.g. what work to do, when to do it, how fast to work) are in effect 'built-in' to the technology.
- The absence of the need to engage in the direct supervision of the workforce through personal supervision would eliminate a major source of industrial conflict – visible managerial authority – thus rendering industrial relations more harmonious and employee contributions much more valued.

Woodward's predictions, although prescient in many ways, predate the microelectronics and information technology 'revolutions' of the last quarter of the twentieth century. These have given the computer-based systems upon which she based her view of a long term trend towards continuous process production systems and associated management control systems far greater technical capacities and capabilities than could have been imagined, outside the realms of science fiction, at the time.

In combination with the globalisation of economic activity, advances in ICTs have prompted a much more radical reassessment of the technology–organisation relationship than Woodward envisaged. In particular, changing global competitive conditions and technological advance have increasingly been seen by some observers as requiring a redefinition of the concepts of work, organisation and the economic structure as a whole. This not only goes far beyond the prescriptions of 'one best way' and traditional contingency approaches but also questions the notion of 'industrialism' which gave rise to them.

According to Daniel Bell capital and labour began to be replaced by information and knowledge as the organising principles of economy and organisation in the 1950s. This marked, in the USA at least, the emergence of post-industrial forms of organisation and economy which, as technology advanced, would replace industrial capitalism. Here the computer began to emerge as the 'analytical engine' of change, organisations started to become increasingly characterised by their orientation towards the provision of services rather than production of goods, and work was increasingly accomplished by a professional and technical rather than a low-skilled and manual labour force (Bell 1973). Subsequently, with the further advance of ICTs, information has been identified more centrally as the driving force of these changes which have been seen as more accurately described as leading to 'knowledge-based' rather than 'post-industrial' forms of organisation and economy (see e.g. Toffler 1981; Bell 1980; Stonier 1983; Masuda 1985).

For these theorists, change and transformation in organisations is seen as driven by the convergence of computing and telecommunications technology. This has created a global economy based on instantaneously shareable information. This information is not just increased in quantity but since it can now be segmented, customised and sourced into specific locations and temporal spaces as required by users in qualitative terms as well. As a result organisations and work within them are no longer bound by time or space. These technological imperatives bring about changes in the activities of organisations which are increasingly orientated towards the production of information-related goods or information services. These come to define and dominate economic activity as a whole. Related to these trends is the growth in the occupational structure of 'information' or 'knowledge' workers to outnumber 'non-information' workers (Kumar 1995: 8–15). The overall effect is to question the conventional concepts of both 'work' and 'organisation'.

From post-industrial to 'virtual' organisations

The technologically determinist themes, expressed in notions of post-industrialism and the information society have now found a further incarnation in concepts of 'virtual organisation' (see e.g. Grenier and Mates 1995; Davidow and Malone 1992; Barnatt 1995a, 1995b). The driving forces behind this latest technological transformation of work and organisations are reminiscent of those of previous variants of this idea. That is, further hardware and software advances in the capabilities of ICTs and the coupling of these to a restructuring of organisations make them more flexible and responsive to rapidly changing and unpredictable global market, customer and technological conditions.

This adds further emphasis to the view that the relationship between technology and organisation is increasingly best understood, not in terms of metaphors of 'machines' or 'organisms', but rather in terms of the information processing requirements of systems akin to 'brains' (Jackson 1996). According to Morgan for example,

> every aspect of organisational functioning depends on information processing of one form or another. Bureaucrats makes decisions by processing information with reference to appropriate rules. Strategic managers make decisions by developing policies and plans that then provide a point of reference for the information processing and decision making of others...we are finding that organisations are becoming synonymous with the decisions, policies and data flows that shape day-to-day practice.
>
> (Morgan 1997: 78)

From this perspective advances in ICTs – which increasingly embody information processing activities and functions previously accomplished by organisational means – make the distinction between the 'technology' and the 'organisation' appear ever more difficult to draw and in fact increasingly meaningless. Thus, 'organisation in such circumstances increasingly rests *in* the information system. Indeed microprocessing technology has created the possibility of organising without having an organisation in strictly physical terms...information technology is used to dissolve the constraints of space and time' (Morgan 1997: 81–2, original emphasis).

Indeed, technological advances are now claimed to have reached a level where it is not convergence between computing and telecommunications which is the 'engine' of technological development. Rather it is the medium in which the capture, process, display, storage and networking of information is increasingly taking place (see Figure 1.1). That is the 'cyberspace', 'where electronic communications flow and computer software operates' (Barnatt 1995b: 83). According to Barnatt, whilst all computers embody 'cyberspace' the real significance of this concept has come from the linking of computers through global communications networks – the so-called information 'super highway' of the Internet, 'intranets' and local and wide area networks (LANS, WANS), the interactivity and information carrying capacity of which is increasingly enhanced by the broader bandwidths offered by technologies such as optical fibres. Such developments, Barnatt argues, will ultimately create 'a single nexus of electronic data and communications upon which all business operations will be dependent' (ibid.). In addition, whilst computers will be communicating with each other more through electronic data interchange (EDI), the basis of human–computer interaction (HCI) will also change. In particular the way the capture (input) and display (output) of information is accomplished will be radically altered (Barnatt 1995a: 42). For example, humans will no longer need to directly input most information through keyboards. Instead it will be captured through such means as voice-recognition, graphical and textual scanning systems and devices able to record three-dimensional movements such as 'data gloves' (Barnatt 1995a: 46).[1]

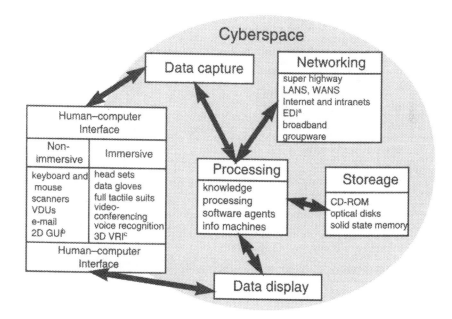

Figure 1.1 Cyberspace and human–computer interaction

Notes:
[a]Electronic data interchange
[b]Graphical interface
[c]Virtual reality interfaces

Moreover, as the function of computing systems shifts from calculation to communication and knowledge processing, the nature of human interface with them will also alter. That is, it will change from a 'non-immersive' level experienced by most computer users at present to an 'immersive' level where the user seemingly 'enters' the virtual world of cyberspace (Barnatt 1995a: 14). For example, existing two-dimensional graphical interfaces (2D GUIs) such as the ubiquitous Windows operating system (itself a replacement for the distinctly non-user friendly command line, text-based interface offered by the DOS operating system) will, it is suggested, be replaced as part of this process by three-dimensional 'virtual reality' interfaces (3D VRIs) and increasingly sophisticated software (groupware) which will permit collaborative working in cyberspace. According to Barnatt these developments will allow users to work together with three-dimensional representations of 'real-world phenomena' and increasingly enable users to become 'immersed' in a 'virtual world'.[2]

The case for virtual organisations rests on the way these new technological capabilities allow organisations to cope with the increasingly turbulent environments that they face. For some, contemporary technological advances will permit organisations to be designed in ways which allow knowledge of the whole to be built into their constituent parts. Such 'virtual' forms will be intelligent, self-organising networks able to 'learn to learn' and thereby peculiarly suited to turbulent conditions (Morgan 1997: 89–94). For example, computer-based information systems enable access to be gained widely and remotely by users. Organisation members can thus 'become full participants in an evolving system of organisational memory and intelligence' and be creators and sustainers of a 'shared organisational mind' (Morgan 1997: 104). Information which, in the past, might have been 'shaped, manipulated and controlled through organisational hierarchies in an exclusive manner', can, 'become widely assembled and disseminated and used as a new source of intelligence and growth throughout the enterprise' (ibid.). We will explore these ideas further in Chapters 2 and 3; suffice it to say that the idea of 'virtual organisation' offers a technological embodiment of models of the 'innovative' or 'learning' organisation and in some eyes appears also to be the archetypal post-modern or post-Fordist organisational form.[3]

Assessment: technology as a contingent variable

It should be clear from the above that the metaphors of 'machine' 'organism' and 'information processing brain' can readily lend themselves to what we have termed technologically deterministic modes of explanation of changes in organisational structure and behaviour. For example, the definitions of technology in terms of its scope and role which we have considered, at least at first sight, fits neatly with the notion that technological innovation is an exogenous and autonomous development which coerces and determines social and economic organisations and relationships. Technological determinism appears to advance spontaneously and inevitably, in a manner resembling Darwinian survival, in so far as only the most 'appropriate' innovations survive and only those who adapt to such innovations prosper.

(Grint and Woolgar 1997: 11)

Thus, 'technology', however defined in terms of its scope is frequently ascribed a determining influence in terms of its role, sometimes as the principal causal variable, but more often as one of a number of features of the organisation's environment which have a decisive bearing on the internal form and structure of the organisation itself. As we will see in subsequent chapters, support for at least crude 'technological determinism' of this type is hard to find in contemporary academic writing on the relationship between organisation and technology. Indeed, arguably it is not a feature of the work of some of the writers considered in this chapter. Even Woodward who perhaps comes closest of the writers considered above to such a position, modified her view in later work on the subject to stress that whether and how an organisation adapted itself to the requirements of its production system was a matter of management choice (Dawson and Wedderburn 1980). Moreover the *expansive* definitions of 'technology' employed by many of the writers considered above make the charge of 'determinism' hard to be precise over, whilst the introduction of mediating and other causal variables, and the albeit modest amount of recognition that some form of interpretative rather then reflex action on the part of organisational members is involved, all serve to 'soften' the degree of determinism involved.

However, leaving aside such qualifications for the moment, it is worth noting some of the apparent strengths of adopting a view which sees 'technology', perhaps not as the main causal variable, but certainly as one key contingency shaping organisations and that a key to organisational survival is the capacity to adapt and learn to cope with new competitive and increasingly novel technological circumstances. As Winner (1977) points out, if technology did not 'determine' in some sense then it would be of little analytical interest and certainly of no practical import. Moreover it would, as Kumar observes, be 'foolhardy to deny' the kinds of advances in information and computing technology which appear to have transformed the world of work and organisations and much more (Kumar 1995: 15). The contemporary emergence of metaphors of the organisation as a 'virtual' entity that appear to collapse the organisational into the technical is also testament to the continuing resilience of ways of thinking about the relationship between technology and organisations where the former determines the shape of and change in the latter. Thus, whilst such ideas 'may be a partial and one-sided way of expressing contemporary social reality' they are for many in contemporary organisations 'an inescapable part of that reality' (Kumar 1995: 34). What then are the strengths of seeing the technology–organisation relationship in these terms?

First, it might be argued that by identifying the importance of the relationship between the organisation and its competitive environment (including its technological environment) a dynamic view of the technology–organisation relationship is made possible. Here technological innovation and organisational change can be understood as a process of adaption to environmental conditions. Following from this, the commercial success and ultimate survival of the organisation rests on the capacity of management and others to respond appropriately to changing technological and other environmental circumstances. Having said this, the success of the machine metaphor as the dominant basis of organisational design for much of the twentieth century arguably owes itself to the fact that this particular formulation of the technology–organisation relationship has been particularly well suited to the stable and largely predictable environmental conditions which most organisations faced.

Indeed, there are strong arguments that in many circumstances a 'machine-like' understanding of the interaction between technology and organisation continues to be the most likely source of productive efficiency for many organisations. For example, according to Adler and Cole:

> It would be wonderful if we lived in a world where every job could be an opportunity for Maslovian self-actualisation. But when products are fairly standard and mass-produced, and when automation is still not cheap enough to eliminate labour-intensive methods of production, then efficiency requires narrowly specialised job assignments and formalised standard methods – a form of work organisation that precludes the very high intrinsic work satisfaction that would, for example, stimulate workers to come in without pay on a day off to tackle a production problem.
>
> (Adler and Cole 1993: 91)

In fact, rather than viewing machine-like bureaucracy as an exclusively coercive effect on the behaviour of organisation members, it is suggested that bureaucratic dimensions such as formalisation have an enabling characteristic which employees like and find desirable (Adler and Borys 1996). Thus, the performance of straightforward tasks to produce goods and services in high volume to stable product markets, where the human 'machine' parts are compliant and behave – more or less – as the designers of organisations intended, can, taken together, be viewed as a remarkably enduring and still relevant model. If more turbulent environmental conditions are requiring some organisations to adopt non-hierarchical organisational forms enabled by new technology this does not mean all organisations will need to. Moreover, where they do aspects of bureau-cracy and 'machine imagery' will still be highly relevant (Badham and Jürgens 1998).

Second, where adaptation *is* required the organism metaphor reminds us that this is not only a technical issue of new hardware and systems, but also a human and organisational concern as well. In this sense human and organisational elements might readily be regarded both as a feature of 'technology' and as a core element of any process of successful technolog-ical innovation. The 'organism' metaphor usefully focuses attention on the need to ensure an appropriate fit between the technical and social. The metaphor acts as a strong antidote to mechanistic thinking and action which can treat technological innovation purely as a technical matter and see attendant problems as readily resolved through technological means. It also provides a potential means of tackling some of the dysfunctional human and organisational consequences of viewing organisations as 'machines' such as: the problem of obtaining employee commitment to the achievement of organisational goals; mindless and unquestioning bureau-cracy; low flexibility and creativity; and unanticipated outcomes, for example the pursuit of sub-goals which are at variance with overall collec-tive goals by organisational interest groups (empire building, careerism, defence of departmental interests and pet projects). Most notably of all, the dehumanisation of the work of employees which may follow from forcing them to do deskilled and alienating jobs where motivation is provided by extrinsic monetary rather than intrinsic job content-related factors can, and has been, forcefully challenged by those seeking to reshape technology and organisation. This is a point we will return to in Chapter 7.

Third, increasingly such 'adaptation' is best understood as a process of organisational learning where the capabilities of both individuals and organisations to 'learn to learn' appears to be key. As Morgan (1997: 116–17) notes, this offers an insightful way of understanding the implica-tions of information and computing technologies. It offers an escape from the narrow mechanistic metaphors which tend to see new technologies as a means of enhancing the centralisation of bureaucratic control. It also updates the 'organism' metaphor in a way more consistent with the rapidly changing nature of organisational environment and the need to constantly rethink what are appropriate organisational forms in these circumstances. In particular, it raises questions concerning the salience of setting clear goals and objectives, hierarchical organisational structures, and top down forms of change management. Instead it suggests that leadership should be diffused to teams, that goal setting and objectives should set boundaries for action not define action itself, and that organisational change should be regarded as a self-regulating and emergent phenomenon. In this view information becomes the basic resource necessary for exchanges between organisations and their environments and the adequacy of available infor-mation the basis for control and organisational survival (Wiener 1968).

Finally, metaphors which stress environmental adaptation and learning, as we will discuss in the following chapter, provide a useful starting point for attempts to understand both how technological innovations are generated and the relationship between these organisational processes and broader trends and dynamics in the economic environment.

Against these positive observations we must note on the one hand the almost unremitting optimism in relation to, and an uncritical acceptance of, the view that technological development is progressive and positive in its social consequences. On the other, we must also observe a fatalistic acceptance that the negative consequences of such progress is taken as inevitable and unavoidable. One result is a vision of technological development as leading to 'computopia' (Masuda 1985 cited by Kumar 1995: 15). Another is dystopian visions of an unavoidable 'rationalised' future (see e.g. Ritzer 1996). We will examine the criticism of deterministic models of the consequences of technological development for organisations in more depth at the end of the following chapter.

Conclusion

The machine, organism and information processing brain metaphors clearly give technology an important, if not the most important, role in shaping organisation. As we have seen, considerable confusion arises because of varying definitions of technology – there is no definitive analytical understanding of what this causal variable actually is. This is emphasised by the lack of consensus in contingency theory over the relative significance of technology *vis-à-vis* other contingent variables and whether 'technology' is part of the organisation's 'environment', or a structural property of the organisation itself or both. Having said this, exactly how technology shapes organisation is unclear. At its crudest the analysis suggests an almost automatic link between a given technical situation and human adoption, almost as a reflex action, of certain behaviours and attitudes. However, the point that technologies have effects and in some sense 'determine' the need for machine-like organisation cannot be ignored. At the same time, the notion that technological development requires organisational adaptation and learning resonates strongly with contemporary organisational experiences of the increasing importance of information and the technological media through which this can be communicated and controlled. This leads us in the next chapter to a closer consideration of the processes by which new technologies are generated, adopted and diffused and the ways in which processes of adaptation and learning can be seen as the basis of the innovative organisation.

Notes

1 One example of this given by Barnatt is the development of 'virtual reality head sets'. These contain sensors to capture the user's head movements thus indicating the direction of their gaze and provide visual displays from small in-helmet LCD screens mounted in front of the wearer's eyes (Barnatt 1995a: 50–1). A bizarre sounding extension of this idea is to enhance the reality of virtual worlds by providing non-visual outputs, for example to permit users to 'feel' virtual objects. One potential development is the 'full tactile data suit' to accompany the virtual head set. Whilst apparently much discussed in the literature on teledildonics (virtual sex systems!), Barnatt points out that such technologies would have less exotic but nevertheless beneficial applications in engineering and medicine, for example in permitting surgeons to conduct operations remote from the patient and operating theatre (1995a: 52).

2 Morath suggests that a model of organisational/social forms constituted within such 'immersion' is provided by the 'virtual communities' which have grown up on the Internet in recent years around 'MOOS' (Multiple Object Orientated) and 'MUDS' (Multi-User Domains/Dungeons) which provide interactive electronic gaming, adventure and fantasy for their users. Whilst in technical terms no more than computer programs which allow distant individuals to interact, MOOS and MUDS 'have a life of their own' since they exist 'because people want to build their personal world and realize their vision within it. They log-in and become their virtual character, their personae. And with it they and their virtual friends build their virtual community' (1997: 59).

3 For a useful insight into the 'leading edge' of virtual technology and virtual working see the web site of Peter Cochrane, Head of Research at BT laboratories, Martlesham, UK. http://www.labs.bt.com/people.cochrap/index.htm.

2 The evolution of the innovative organisation

Introduction

In this chapter we explore the relationship between technology and organisation from the perspective of innovation economics. This will involve a discussion of the factors shaping long term trends in technological development, the relationship of innovation to economic progress and the role of organisations as sources of innovative activity. Underlying the innovation economics perspective are metaphors that draw upon and extend the machine-like and, in particular, the biological ways of thinking about technology and organisation discussed in the previous chapter. This line of reasoning leads to particularly interesting conceptualisations of the interaction between technology and organisation in terms of an evolutionary process. Here technological innovations are viewed as mutations which if successful result in variation in the economic environment. Success is in part a function of environmental selection by consumers and users. However, unlike living organisms, organisations can play an active role in developing strategies that strengthen their innovative capacity and enable them to learn from their environment. When institutionalised, these processes constitute the unique 'knowledge base' of the organisation – in effect its genetic make-up. The new organisational forms that will thrive most readily in the emergent economic and technological environments of the late-twentieth century, it is argued by proponents of this perspective, are precisely those which are able to innovate through such learning.

Evolutionary economics and technological innovation

Evolutionary economics has emerged in response to perceived deficiencies in the way in which orthodox or neo-classical economists conceptualise technology, organisation and innovation. For the latter, technology is regarded as an exogenous variable which is of interest only insofar as it has effects on economic variables such as profits, productivity and prices (Coombs *et al.* 1987: 4). In this perspective there is no concern for the processes through which new technologies are generated nor the organisational circumstances in which innovative activity takes place (Coombs *et al.* 1992: 2). Similarly, the behaviour of firms is conceptualised purely in terms of profit-maximisation, in the context of perfect information concerning market opportunities, where the organisation and control of the enterprise is assumed to be embodied by the concept of the individual owner (Coombs *et al.* 1992: 3). In effect, for orthodox economics, both technology and the organisation are analytical 'black boxes' whose content is regarded as of little importance in explaining economic variables.

However, for evolutionary economists such conceptual starting points provide little purchase on key policy questions such as why particular technological innovations are successful and why others are not. Similarly, at the organisational level little guidance is offered in relation to strategic questions such as which products to develop and where to invest expenditure in research and development (Coombs *et al.* 1992: 3). The economics orthodoxy has, therefore, increasingly been challenged by economists and others who have been concerned to provide a more adequate explanation of how change occurs in the economic system (see e.g. Rosenberg 1982; Coombs *et al.* 1987; Dosi *et al.* 1988; Saviotti and Metcalfe 1991; Boisot 1996; Soete 1996).

The principal starting point for the evolutionary perspective is the work, conducted during the 1930s, of economist Joseph Schumpeter (1934, 1939, 1942) who saw innovation as a key driver of economic development. For 'neo-Schumpetarians' – as many followers of the evolutionary approach have become known – technical change viewed as a 'crucial factor in the explanation of business cycles and the dynamics of economic growth' (Freeman 1988: 1), rather than as a phenomenon separate from the economic system.

According to Allen (1988), what is in fact at stake here is a debate over the most appropriate metaphors to guide economic enquiry. Neo-classical economics has drawn on the machine and mechanistic metaphors associated with the physical sciences. They have sought to identify the key parts of the economic system and the causal connections between them and in so doing built models of the economy which are akin to a giant 'clockwork mechanism'. Here efficiency is defined in terms of a natural state of equilibrium between component elements and analytical interest, is focused on how the system works to maintain this state. The evolutionary perspective, on the other hand, challenges this 'Newtonian' paradigm and seeks to place the questions of 'how the system became what it is' and 'how it will evolve in the future' at the centre of analysis. As such the latter approach can be regarded as 'fundamentally about the origins of qualitative change in things, and how the "parts" of a system came into being, and are maintained' (Allen 1988: 96–7). For evolutionists' the 'natural' state of affairs is one of change and disequilibrium and as such 'those who can adapt and learn will survive' (ibid. 117).

Soete defines the key elements of the evolutionary approach to

understanding the linkage between technology, organisation and innovation in the following terms (Soete 1996: 42–8). First, economic
development can be thought of as taking place through the generation of
new products, processes, markets, forms of organisation and so on.
Innovations, especially 'radical' innovations (see below) can thus be
regarded in the same way as 'mutations' are in biology. It is this process
that generates variety in the economic system (see Table 2.1). However, the
generation of variety is also checked by the failure of some innovations to
survive and the replacement of old innovations by new ones, the former in
effect becoming 'extinct'.

Second, the shape of economic development can be understood in terms
of the way selection mechanisms work alongside processes of variety
generation. As in nature, selection is 'determined by the differential adaptation of different species to their environment' (Soete 1996: 43). Thus the
survival of an organisation can be seen as in part determined by the willingness of customers or users to buy or adopt its innovations: in other
words, in much the same way as Darwinian models of evolution see the
fate of living organisms as dictated by random processes of natural selection. However, evolutionary economists deviate from Darwinian models in
that they do not see the production of variety and environmental selection
as entirely random events beyond the influence of organisations themselves. Here a Lamarckian model of evolution is preferred. This suggests
that organisms can attempt to improve their characteristics and thereby
mutate in order to adapt to their environment (Soete 1996: 44; see also
contributions to Saviotti and Metcalfe 1991).

In similar fashion, the mechanistic models of orthodox economics that
see the firm as a theoretical 'moment' of rational decision-making driven
by a profit-maximising imperative, are also regarded as inadequate by
evolutionists. Rather, drawing upon behavioural theories of the firm (see
e.g. March and Simon 1958), it is argued that the innovative behaviour of
organisations is best understood in terms of the concept of 'bounded rationality' (Nelson and Winter 1982). Here actors follow 'routines, recipes
and rules of thumb' whilst monitoring a small range of environmental
variables to judge 'feedback'. Provided such feedback is deemed satisfac-
tory then the routines will continue to be followed. If they are not, then
adjustments will be made on the basis of a similarly 'bounded' review of
alternatives.

Thus the capacity of the organisation to innovate can be seen as influenced by search activities – conducted within the confines of bounded
rationality. These activities – for example seeking new technological and
product market opportunities – aim to differentiate the organisation from
rivals whilst, at the same time, adapting its innovations to the environment
or even seeking to shape the environment itself. Similarly, a bounded but
conscious process of planning and strategic adjustment by the organisation
will influence the pace at which organisations adapt to environmental

Table 2.1 The growing variety of telecommunications technology

1847	1877	1920	1960	1975	1984	2000
Telegraphy	Telegraphy	Telegraphy	Telegraphy	Telegraphy	Telegraphy	Telegraphy
		Telex	Telex	Telex	Telex	Telex
						Broadband data
			Data	Medium speed data	Packet switched data	Packet switched data
				Low speed data	High speed data	Circuit switch data
					Circuit switched data	Telemetry
					Telemetry	Teletex
		Photo Facsimile	Photo Facsimile	Photo Facsimile	Facsimile	Textfacsimile
			Facsimile	Facsimile	Teletex	Facsimile
					Facsimile	Colourfacsimile
					Videotex	Electronic mail
						Telenewspaper
						Videotex
						Speechfacsimile
	Telephony	Telephony	Telephony	Telephony	Telephony	Telephony
						Hifitelephony
						Telephone conference
					Videoconference	Videoconference
						Videotelephony
	Sound	Sound	Stereo hifi sound	Stereo hifi sound		Stereo hifi sound
				Stereo hifi sound		Quadraphon
		Television	Colour television	Colour television	Stereo television	Colour television
				Colour television		Stereo television
						High def. colour television
			Mobile telephony			Mobile video
			Mobile telephony		Mobile telephony	Mobile telephony
						Mobile text
						Mobile facsimile
						Mobile data
						Mobile video
				Paging	Paging	Paging

Source: Soete 1996: 97.

change. This will be governed by such factors as the speed of the search activities required to produce innovations that result in better adaptation; the readiness of management culture and the existing organisational knowledge base to accept and absorb change; and the capacity of the organisation to both 'unlearn' existing practices and 'learn' new ones (Soete 1996: 44).

This points to a further key element of the evolutionary model, the capacity of organisations to reproduce what has been learnt over time. That is, whilst organisations do not need to engage in sexual reproduction as living organisms do to survive, their longevity is related to the development of means through which information concerning adaptive behaviour can be transmitted to subsequent generations of organisation members. This takes place through decision rules and routines that ensure continuity in behaviour. In this sense organisations can be considered as having a 'genetic make-up' embodied in the notion of 'know-how' captured by these rules and routines (Soete 1996: 44–6).

Finally, whilst one way of construing evolutionary metaphor would be to see it as suggesting a market in which only the fittest can compete to survive, it also serves as a reminder to economists that collaboration may also be a means to this end (Soete 1996: 47). This point is elaborated by Morgan (1986: 69–71). He points out that increasingly schools of biological thought influenced by ecological and environmentalist concerns suggest that environments and organisms, rather than living in a state of constant tension, are in fact part of a total 'eco-system'. Here environments are recognised as being constituted by other organisms (organisations). Thus, instead of competing against each other to survive, organisations may find a more effective mode of survival in collaboration (see e.g. Inkpen 1996).

Technological innovation and organisations

For the evolutionary approach, innovation is a key 'milestone' in the linear process which begins with the invention of a new product, process or system and concludes with the diffusion of an artefact within a given population of 'users'. In the most often cited version of this view Freeman defines 'innovation' as the point of 'first *commercial* application of a new process or product' (Freeman 1982).[1]

A key set of initial questions, therefore, concern: first, how innovative activity is initiated; second, what form the process by which inventions are turned into successful products or processes takes, and; third, how innovations are subsequently diffused through the economy. Intuitively, innovation seems to be the result of the successful technological application of new scientific knowledge. This 'technology push' view is supported by the growth of large-scale productive organisations and the advent of specialised research and design (R&D) departments tasked with developing new products and processes. R&D departments, in this purely descriptive sense, can be regarded as a key source of innovation. However, it has also been argued that innovation owes less to the brilliance of inventors, their organisation and management, in turning science into technology and rather more to the way in which the market generates demands for the new products and processes in the first place (see Langrish *et al.* 1972).

For Freeman (1982) neither the 'technology push' nor 'market pull' explanation alone is convincing and both fail to account for the view that technological capabilities and market needs may be 'matched' together within the innovation process. Thus Freeman argues that innovation is 'essentially a two-sided or coupling activity' requiring a matching of technological development to market requirements. No matter what levels of organisational or institutional sophistication are involved, 'this remains a groping, searching and uncertain process' and the coupling of technological development to changing market needs raises key issues concerning the nature of the innovation process *within* organisations (Freeman 1982).

At its simplest the process of technological innovation within organisations has also been represented in terms of models which stress either 'technology-push' or 'market-pull' factors as 'drivers' of a simple linear process. Here different organisational functions are engaged in innovative activity in sequence. These basic models have been developed with varying degrees of complexity (for discussion see Forest 1991). However, they have been found to be poor representations of innovation in practice. According to Forest (1991): they fail to take into account the concurrent and iterative nature of innovation, the overlaps between stages and feedback relationships between functions within organisations, and the influence of contextual factors outside of organisations such as the nature of markets, the supply of scientific and technological expertise and other resources; in addition, they treat what actually goes on in functional areas of the organisation during innovation as a 'black box' and that suggest innovation can be understood as a rational and orderly process in which the possibility of alternative developments and the need for decision-making are ignored (Forest 1991: 441).

Such issues have been addressed more effectively in subsequent theories of the innovation process. These have taken the basic 'building-blocks' identified in early linear-sequential models and sought to develop a more interactive, iterative, context contingent and open-ended representation of the process of innovation (see Figure 2.1). Rothwell, for example, provides a model which represents innovation as 'logically sequential, though not necessarily continuous' and as involving a 'series of functionally separate but interacting and interdependent' phases. The 'overall pattern' of the innovation process is thus embodied in a complex web of communication paths within and between organisations which link functional areas such as R&D and marketing to the scientific and technological community outside of the organisation and critically to the market place. In subsequent variants of this idea Rothwell points to the importance of

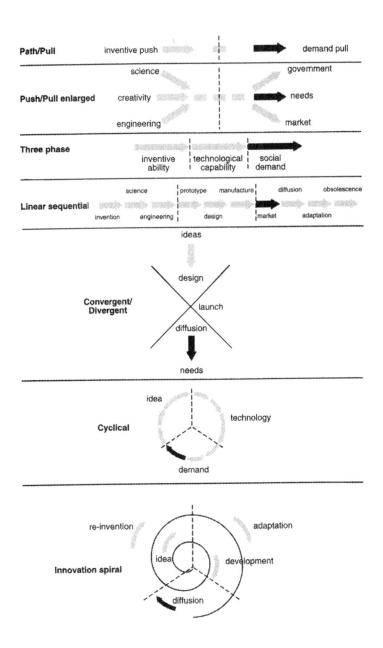

Figure 2.1 Models of the process of technological innovation
Source: Open University T362 Course Team 1986a: 5.

integration at the firm and inter-firm level to enable these complex innovation networks to function – a process which, incidentally, he sees as significantly aided by the electronic mediation facilitated by ICTs (Rothwell 1992). We will return to this notion of technological innovation as a networking phenomenon below.

Trajectories, techno-economic paradigms and ICTs

The concept of innovation as a 'coupling activity' points again to the view that technological innovation is not – as a Darwinian evolutionary model might have it – entirely random in terms of its sources and outcomes. Rather it is a function of the constraints placed by an organisation's current knowledge and cognitive capabilities on its capacity to exploit the opportunities which are opened up by technological advances (Tidd *et al.* 1997: 105). To extend existing technical knowledge organisations have to learn, but learning is of necessity incremental since radical leaps in knowledge involve both risk and, if attempted on too many fronts, can reduce learning capacity. The innovative behaviour of an organisation can therefore be said to be 'path-dependent' with its direction, 'strongly conditioned by the competencies accumulated for the development and exploitation of their existing product base', and with major restrictions on the capacity to 'jump' from one path to another (ibid.: 106).

The notion of path-dependency provides the starting point for the concept of *'technological regimes'* or *'trajectories'* (Nelson and Winter 1982; Dosi 1982). This idea seeks to provide an explanation of the persistent rather than random patterns of technological development found in the economic system as a whole, but also at the sectoral and organisational level (Pavitt 1984). These concepts suggest that innovation unfolds along 'pathways', derived partly from the possibilities inherent in the technology itself, and partly from the technological strengths of innovating firms. Nelson and Winter go as far as to argue that, 'natural trajectories particularly in industries where technological advance is very rapid, seem to follow advances in a way that appears somewhat inevitable and certainly not fine tuned to the changing demand and cost conditions' (Nelson and Winter 1982: 57).

The pathways along which technological development might occur, therefore, can be seen as involving a series of *incremental* innovations, that is, more or less continuous marginal changes to existing products or processes. New trajectories might be expected to result from discontinuous events, such as the application of new ideas generated through R&D, which produce *radical* innovations – entirely new products or processes. One cause of such shifts has been identified as the product lifecycle which can give rise to relatively short periods of radical product and process innovation that are subsequently followed by a longer period of incremental innovation (Abernathy and Utterback 1978). However, this explanation has frequently been found wanting in practice (Clark and Staunton 1989).

Freeman and Perez (1988) suggest that two further types of innovation occur. First, changes of *technology system*. These are based on a combination of related radical and incremental innovations accompanied by organisational innovations. Their effects are felt across several existing economic sectors and can result in the emergence of completely new sectors (Freeman and Perez 1988: 46–7). Second, where such changes exert an influence on the behaviour of the economy as a whole then the effect can be 'revolutionary':

> Some changes in technology systems are so far-reaching in their effects that they have a major influence on the behaviour of the entire economy. A change of this kind carries with it many clusters of radical and incremental innovations, and may eventually embody a number of new technology systems. A vital characteristic of this fourth type of technical change is that it has *pervasive* effects throughout the economy, i.e. it not only leads to the emergence of a new range of products, services, systems and industries in its own right; it also affects directly or indirectly almost every other branch of the economy, i.e. it is a 'meta-paradigm'.
>
> (Freeman and Perez 1988: 47)

Changes in 'techno-economic paradigm', therefore, not only have pervasive effects throughout the economy but may embody a 'quantum jump' in potential productivity gains whilst offering 'an unusually wide range of investment and profit opportunities' (Freeman and Perez 1988: 47–8).

The notions of technological trajectory and techno-economic paradigm provide a way of linking such patterns of technological development and innovation to the dynamics and growth of the economic system as whole. Underpinning this view is the theory of 'long waves' of economic development first outlined by Kondratief in the 1920s. 'Long waves' of innovative activity are related to long term economic cycles of boom and slump occurring every forty or so years. Four such 'waves' have been identified in the world economy during the twentieth century. In the mid-1980s the world economy was at the bottom of the fourth of these waves and experiencing a severe economic recession.

According to 'long wave' theory, whilst inventions are occurring all of the time, they are only transformed into successful innovations in very specific historical periods. It is at these points that new techno-economic paradigms can emerge and new technological trajectories develop that become the engine that drives to the next long term upturn in economic activity. Many contemporary observers view the microelectronic revolution of the 1970s as the starting point for such a burst of innovative activity (Freeman 1994). However, as was the case with previous examples of 'heartland' technologies the full assimilation of microelectronics into the economic and social system 'is a matter of decades, not years' (Freeman and Soete 1997: 184). Initially the new technology has found application in rapidly growing sectors of the economy, most notably the electronics industry itself (i.e. firms whose products or processes already contain electronic subsystems), and those already operating continuous flow production systems the control of which, as noted in Chapter 1, is already highly automated. However, diffusion to more mature sectors of the economy, where growth is slow or even declining, has been less rapid (Freeman and Soete 1997: 185–6). This points to the 'inertia' in social institutions and structures and the need for these to be adapted and changed before the full economic benefits of this new technology can be felt (Freeman 1996; Freeman and Perez 1988). If such adjustments can be achieved, then contemporary developments in ICTs may be the precursors of the onset of the 'fifth wave' and a new techno-economic paradigm based on information technology (Bessant 1991). However, as the need for institutional and structural adjustments suggests, the nature of this paradigm is not just technological. Rather, the paradigm shift in the underlying techno-economic system is closely associated with the new concepts of the relationship of organisational, managerial and institutional responses to changing market and technological conditions. These are factors which we will discuss in more detail in the following chapter but for the moment we can focus on some of the organisational level adjustments which are implied in this analysis.

The innovative organisation

Concepts of trajectories, paradigms and long waves point to the need for organisations to increasingly be able to 'mobilise knowledge and technological skills and experience'. Such capabilities are required in order exploit future technological opportunities such as those offered by contemporary developments in ICTs (Tidd *et al.* 1997: 16). This raises questions concerning the strategies which organisations need to follow in a given set of circumstances in order to maximise their innovative potential. In particular, it focuses attention on; the organisation's position in relation to its external environment; the evolution of its own existing technological trajectory; and how well key organisational processes and aspects of organisational design operate in providing the integration and learning required both to generate innovation in producer firms and achieve successful implementation in user firms (ibid.).

These issues have provided a specific focus for innovation theorists in recent years. They have borrowed insights from the organisational studies literature, some of which was addressed in the previous chapter. In particular, although not exclusively, they have drawn on those models of the organisation and its relationship to the environment developed within contingency theory in order to further develop the evolutionary perspective at the level of organisational strategy, structure and behaviour.

A key reference point in the organisational literature is provided by Burns and Stalker's classic study *The Management of Innovation* (1961). This suggested that organisations could be placed on a continuum according to whether they had *mechanistic* or *organic* structures. Organic organisation structures were best suited to highly unpredictable environments, in particular in relation to change in product markets and the complexity of technology. Mechanistic structures were most appropriate, in contrast, to stable product markets and relatively simple technological conditions. Other variants of contingency theory developed in the 1970s suggested that the survival of organisations could best be explained, not by the organisation selecting the appropriate organisation structure to suit its environment, but rather in terms of processes of environmental selection. Pfeffer and Salancik (1978), for instance, argued that organisations are, in effect, controlled by their environments since they are dependent upon resources outside of the organisation for survival. Technical knowledge and expertise, as well as technology in a 'hardware' sense, are likely to be amongst the critical resource dependencies of many organisations. In a similar vein 'population ecology' theories emphasised the process of natural selection as a key to understanding how some organisational *species* survive and others do not. The key to survival was the capacity of an organisational species to identify and retain the resources which allow it to gain sustenance from the environment when its competitors cannot (see e.g. Aldrich 1979; Hannan and Freeman 1977).

Such considerations have a direct bearing on the capacity of firms to engage in and appropriate the results of technological innovation. This links directly to the concern of innovation economists to identify the characteristics of innovative organisations. First, viewing innovations as mutations which generate economic variety results in a focus on the search activities of organisations as they seek to initiate innovations which customers and users will want to buy or adopt. Corporate innovation strategies can be seen as the embodiment of these activities. A key aim of such strategies, according to Tidd *et al.* (1997: 72), is to position the organisation in a differentiated way from its competitors in terms of the products it makes, the processes it uses to produce them and the technologies that are used. To a large degree the positioning of the organisation in this way will be dependent upon its existing technological trajectory and the possibilities that this accumulated knowledge base gives for exploiting new opportunities, and perhaps even embracing new technological paradigms. However, the 'national system of innovation' in which firms operate is also a key contextual factor since this, through its effects on demand and competition, the supply of human resources, forms of corporate governance and so forth, provides a framework which both enables and constrains corporate options (Tidd *et al.* 1997: 99).

Second, seeing the survival of organisations as determined by environmental selection turns attention to the factors within the organisation which enable and constrain adaptive behaviour. This highlights the organisational processes which exist to enable and integrate learning across the organisation (Tidd *et al.* 1997: 72). At the strategic level these include internal structural design considerations such as the degree of centralisation–decentralisation and geographical concentration–dispersion of core innovation functions. Decisions here have a direct bearing on technological learning within the organisation through to the development of effective external linkages which enable knowledge to be appropriated from the market place, competitors, suppliers and other external repositories such as universities and government agencies. At the operational level the processes concerned are those which enable the implementation of innovation such as scanning the environment for possible inputs to the innovation process (e.g. a new technology) and selecting appropriate projects in which to use them; managing product innovation projects in producer organisations; and managing change programmes when implementing process innovations in adopter organisations (Tidd *et al.* 1997: 239).

Third, the idea of reproduction highlights the mechanisms through which the continuity of an organisation's capacity to innovate is ensured. Sustaining innovation in this way increasingly requires the capacity to review and capture learning from innovation projects for transfer to future projects (Tidd *et al.* 1997: 305). Willman (1997) argues that competitive advantage is dependent upon securing the internal appropriation of such learning from innovation whilst at the same time preventing it being transferred to competitors (i.e. externally appropriated). However, internal appropriability can be highly problematic where tacit (as opposed to formal) knowledge about technical processes or products/customers accumulates in an organisation – say amongst employees – but is inaccessible to management because its possessors have no incentive or motivation to share it. The success of Far Eastern firms can be attributed, Willman suggests, to providing such incentives and motivation to their workforce, thus enabling the full appropriation of the benefits of innovation. These observations have profound implications for the management of a firm's knowledge base since they suggest that the reproduction and enhancement of know-how through the capture of learning may require organisations to adopt fundamentally different employment contracts and forms of work design (Willman 1997: 47).

Finally, the problem of appropriability also points to how organisations might link together more effectively in order to engage in innovative activity. Increasingly, it has been argued, innovative capacity is dependent upon building linkages through collaborative relationships (Coombs *et al.* 1996). Amongst other things this enables learning which adds to an organisation's existing knowledge base and the creation of completely new knowledge (Inkpen 1996), and also contributes to 'novelty and variety in the economic system' by creating 'new economic resources which otherwise simply would not exist' (Coombs *et al.* 1996: 12–13). Such collaboration might involve sub-contracting, strategic alliances or joint ventures organised on regional or industrial lines and involve linkages with government or other public agencies (Freeman 1991). A further form of collaboration that has gained considerable currency in recent years is what has been termed 'innovation networks'. These are seen as possessing many of the benefits of internal development in respect to enabling learning and the internal appropriation of innovation, whilst avoiding the conventional problems of collaboration such as concerns over quality, the appropriation of knowledge by partners and the 'cultural mismatch' of collaborators.

There is considerable definitional divergence concerning the nature, formation, content and consequences of networks in general (for discussion, see Freeman 1991; Coombs *et al.* 1996). However, one argument is that innovation networks increasingly constitute hybrid forms of organisation which are more 'technology-intensive'. Freeman attributes this to the pervasiveness of ICTs across sectors of the economy and the manner in which they create new 'technological complementarities' and change intersectoral relationships as well as relationships between firm functions, suppliers, customers and so on. In fact, networking behaviour appears to be a key organisational concomitant of the emergence of the information technology paradigm outlined above (Freeman 1991: 509–10). Indeed, the effectiveness of this mode of organising as a means of generating variation, adapting to environmental change and sustaining learning over time is likely, argues Freeman, to be a key factor in the consolidation of any new 'techno-economic paradigm' as we move into the twenty-first century.

Assessing evolutionary and biological models

For evolutionary economists biological metaphors provide a key source of understanding and explanation of innovative activity, its relationship to economic progress and the role of the organisation as a source of innovation. In this way organisations are seen as both a source of variation in the economic system through the innovations that they produce and, at the same time, themselves subject to shaping by the techno-economic environment. However, unlike Darwinian organisms, organisations are not hapless victims of random environmental events. Rather, they can do much in terms of their strategies for both producing and adopting innovations to influence their own fate in the broader process of technological development and economic progress. In particular, by making appropriate adaptive responses they may be able to overcome the constraints of existing path-dependencies and be able to exploit emerging technological opportunities to the benefit of themselves and the overall economic system.

What then are the strengths of conceptualising the relationship between technology and organisation in terms of this evolutionary model of the role of innovation? First and foremost the approach redirects orthodox economic analysis towards the dynamics of economic development and to the 'creative processes' – the actions of actors in specific historical and institutional contexts – which drive them (Allen 1988: 98). Thus a model of economic development is suggested which places technological change at the explanatory core rather than periphery of analysis. As such the 'black box' of technology is opened for economists and assumptions – for example that firms choose technology purely on the basis of profit maximisation – are opened up for scrutiny (Rosenberg 1982; MacKenzie 1996: 50).

At the same time key issues such as the existence of long term trends in technological development – the miniaturisation of microelectronic components, the increasing speed of microprocessors, the replacement of analogue technologies by digital for example – are admitted and subject to analysis. This goes beyond a simplistic notion of a 'logic of industrialism' and 'technological imperatives' that have been given contemporary manifestation in ideas such as the 'information technology revolution' discussed in Chapter 1. In particular, the notion of 'technological trajectories' and the related concept of 'technological paradigms' reveals the complex relationship between the bursts of innovative activity which give rise to them and the subsequent diffusion of new products and processes and the consequent structural effects on the economy. Moreover, the relationship between technological change and structure is not a simple determinate one. Rather, a 'crisis of adjustment' is involved in the development of new technological trajectories and paradigms. This involves a search for appropriate policy, institutional, managerial and organisational responses, themselves mediated by 'local' conditions such as the nature of national innovation systems, if new trajectories are to be 'latched on to' and sustained (see e.g. Freeman and Perez 1988). Indeed, since the successful adoption and diffusion of new technological systems is ultimately dependent on innovations at the level of policy, institutional frameworks, management strategy and practice, as well as on new organisational forms, it makes more sense to speak of the contingent emergence of new 'techno-economic' rather than merely 'technological' paradigms.

Such arguments not only open the black box of technology but also inevitably lead to an opening of the black box of organisation. The faltering steps of the 'information technology revolution' for example, represented most blatantly in the high levels of investment but low levels of productivity improvement associated with the adoption of ICTs, are not to be explained simply by the inability of organisations to read economic signals or the constraints of existing institutional arrangements (Freeman 1996). Rather, they point to the complex nature of the linkages between technology, innovation and organisation and the fact that it is at the organisational level, supported by appropriate policy initiatives and adjustments to institutional frameworks, that the strategic moves necessary to seize new market and technological opportunities have to be made. Comparative analysis of Western and Far Eastern organisations, for example, suggests that innovative behaviour at the level of the firm, both in terms of technology strategy and organisational innovation, have been key to the relative success of the Japanese and others over their Western counterparts (see e.g. Womack *et al.* 1990; Nonaka and Takuchi 1994).

Indeed, the focus on the strategic behaviour of organisations in relation to positioning and adaptation to environmental contingencies provides insights into the factors both inhibiting and facilitating innovative behaviour. Or to put it another way, new purchase is given by the evolutionary approach on the old problem of explaining why some organisations do, and others do not, adapt to changes in their competitive and technological environments. Indeed, the evolutionary model points to 'inertial pressures' such as fixed organisation structures and skill distributions amongst the work force, adherence by managers to outmoded assumptions and values, barriers to change posed by trade unions and industrial relations structures and so forth, which go some way to explaining why many organisations find it so difficult to escape from the constraints of their existing knowledge base and path dependencies. Indeed, the approach can offer explanations as to why whole populations of organisations (industries/sectors) may develop or decline because of such factors.

Increasingly, as we have seen, the evolutionary approach has placed organisational learning at the centre of explanations of what generates innovative capacity, enables it to be sustained over time, and permits the appropriation of its benefits by the organisation. Indeed, models of learning in evolutionary studies have become more sophisticated as interactions with the organisational studies literature have developed. For example, for innovation economists, organisational learning initially referred to the capacity of firms to become aware of and assess the cost-benefit of adoption at a particular point in time (Attewell 1996: 208). However, such a view is regarded as increasingly inadequate when advanced technologies such as ICTs are considered. For example, whilst the adoption of such technology is increasingly relatively easy, acquiring the know-how necessary to use it is increasingly difficult. Moreover, finding better mechanisms to permit the transfer of such knowledge from supplier to user does not significantly reduce this problem. Rather, much of the learning required in how to use these technologies can only be produced in the adopting context. Thus, adoption of such systems cannot be viewed as a 'one off' decision-event. Rather it is a complex organisational process where the transfer of technical know-how is problematic and possibly incomplete (Attewell 1996: 211).

From this viewpoint 'learning' becomes an altogether more complex phenomenon which 'can be described as the way firms build, supplement and organise knowledge and routines around their competence and within their cultures, and adapt and develop organisational efficiency through improving the use of these competencies' (Dodgson 1996: 55). Such learning is a defining characteristic of the innovative capacity, and ultimately competitive advantage, of the organisation. This is especially so in periods of significant environmental turbulence:

> In turbulent environments learning can be seen as a purposive quest by firms to retain and improve competitiveness, productivity and innovativeness. The greater the uncertainties facing firms, the greater the need for learning. Learning can be seen to have occurred when organisations perform in changed and better ways, when competencies are better defined, more appropriate and effectively implemented. The goals of learning are useful outcomes, which in the present industrial context include, at best, improved comparative performance; at worst, survival.
>
> (Dodgson 1996: 55)

Evolutionary models of the innovative organisation, it should now be clear, increasingly share a great deal of common ground with the organisational theories reviewed in Chapter 1 which also stress the need for organisations to adapt and learn if they are to survive. We are now at a point therefore where the drawbacks of viewing the interaction between technology and organisation in this way can be considered.

First, biological metaphors and evolutionary thinking encourage a view of organisations and their environment as 'objective' phenomena in the same way that living organisms, brains and the natural world are typically viewed as objective realities. The environment, including the technological environment, is therefore seen to determine organisation structure by requiring behaviour from organisation members which enables the organisation to adapt in order to survive. As we have already indicated in Chapter 1, mechanistic, organic and brain metaphors are all ways of thinking about the relationship between technology and organisation which, in different ways and to different degrees, are prone to such deterministic representations of the role of technology, and the almost reflex behavioural response of humans to it. One facet of this is the uncritical acceptance of accounts of the characteristics and capabilities of technology in bringing about a transformation in the nature of work and organisation. This is often allied to historically short-sighted attempts to identify new technologically driven radical breaks or departures in organisational practice (Kumar 1995: 15–18).

Such observations apply no less to the evolutionary approaches considered in this chapter. For example, the ideas of technological trajectory and paradigm are particularly troublesome in these regards of, especially where the adjective 'natural' is evoked, they convey strong overtones of an 'autonomous technology'. As MacKenzie notes, 'the notion of "technolog-ical trajectory" can... very easily be taken to mean that once technological change is initially set on a given path (for example by the selection of a given "paradigm") its development is then determined by technical forces' (1996: 55). The point being that whilst lines of technological development can develop momentum, this is not momentum of its own, even if that is how it appears or is presented (Hughes 1987). The fact that particular technological developments – the 'information technology revolution' for example – have the appearance of their own logic and inevitability, is to be explained in terms of the manner in which technologists and others are able to get their beliefs accepted and institutionalised (MacKenzie 1996: 58).

By the same token, it is a also a misconception that the manner in which new technologies are generated, adopted and diffused appears, albeit with considerable qualification and attenuation, to be a linear process. Such perceptions are rather a product of how technologists and others reconstruct and make sense of the innovation process after the event, rather than as a literal account of how it was experienced at the time (Bijker and Law 1992: 17). Finally, the lack of any attempt to view what technology is and what it can do in any interpretative sense tends to result in 'technical know-how' being portrayed as an unproblematic entity determined by the characteristics and capabilities of the technical system concerned. Or to put it another way, the genetic make-up of the organisa-tion is taken as a 'given' and as independent of the social, political and cultural systems upon which it is deemed to act.

Second, the social systems of the organisation are seen as cohesive with a norm of all elements operating in harmony (like any efficient machine, or healthy organism or brain). This ignores the possibility that in organisa-tions different elements will operate over time with different degrees of harmony and conflict. When this happens in practice biological metaphors, just like their mechanistic counterparts, have a tendency to see such conflict as harmful to the system and, like an unwanted ailment or disease, something to be treated and 'cured'. Thus for example, the problem of innovation is frequently constructed in terms of 'barriers' to effective communication between the suppliers of technology and end-users who have to work out ways to absorb and apply it. Similarly, resistance to change by trade unions or employees can too readily be construed in terms of communication barriers between them and manage-ment rather than as something which analytically might better be understood in its own terms as a rational response to a contingent set of social, economic and political circumstances (Wilkinson 1983).

Taken together these criticisms can be applied to the way in which evolutionary models have become increasingly concerned with organisa-tional learning. For instance, they tend to depend on a crude 'stimulus/response' metaphor whereby 'given' turbulence in organisational environments is deemed to induce attempts at adaptive behaviour within organisations in response to 'given' goals of 'efficiency' and 'survival'. Learning by, and presumably within, organisations is deemed to be a reflex response to a set of external circumstances which are in no way viewed as problematic in their meaning or significance. In short, little or no account is given of the interpretations of organisational actors in this process, for example in deciding when, what and how 'environmental' conditions are 'uncertain' and what constitute 'useful' knowledge which needs to be acquired, developed and reproduced. Similarly, as Clausen and Nielsen (1997) point out, what constitute a problem and an appropriate solution within an organisation are politically informed preconditions for learning and organisational learning is all part of the organisational 'political game'. In whose interests is it for firms to improve productivity and efficiency and how are these benefits to be shared by organisational members and other stakeholders; how are definitions of effective change and organisational improvement decided and who by; and who sets the goals that organisations seek to achieve through developing their competencies? These are all questions begged in the evolutionary approach. As we will see in Chapters 3 and 4, the consensual or unitary view of organisations is the focus of critique from those who seek to emphasise the conflictual nature of relationships, in particular those between employer and employee, as a key factor shaping the organisational outcomes of technological change and even the nature of technology itself.

Conclusion

Evolutionary approaches move us beyond the view of technology as an exogenous variable that is held in orthodox economics. Thus, rather than technology being presented as something which is shaped by the 'all-knowing hands of market forces' (MacKenzie 1996: 58), it is seen as the key source of dynamism in economic development. However, this approach tends to render 'technology' exogenous in another sense. That is, its content is taken as 'given', 'natural' and 'inevitable' and 'inherent' within the 'black box' which has so carefully been prised open by the evolutionary perspective. This inevitably leads to an endorsement of the view that change in the social systems of organisations is ultimately driven by the requirements of technology embodied in concepts such as technological 'know-how'. Ultimately, to survive, it is increasingly the case that organisations must adapt to radically new and emergent technological and market conditions ('techno-economic paradigms'). To do this they must learn how to assimilate and apply the new knowledge required to bring about and sustain innovation. It is this that will enable a shift from current pathways of technological development onto the completely new trajectory offered, for example, by ICTs. Whilst organisations may have choices in how they do this, for example in relation to strategic positioning or organisational design, the parameters within which they operate appear tightly defined by the concepts – such as linear models of innovation, path-dependencies, trajectories, and prevailing paradigms – favoured by this perspective. As we will see in subsequent chapters, from other vantage points the evolutionary approach serves only to embellish the 'black box' and to conceal rather than illuminate the social nature of its constitution.

Notes

1 In the 'neo-Schumpetarian' approach, a distinction is normally made between *product* and *process* innovations. The former involve the incorporation of new technology into new or existing products (or services), whilst the latter involves the adoption of new technology in the actual production of new products (or services). In practice, however, this distinction has proven increasingly difficult to draw and it probably makes more sense to regard them as opposite points on a continuum rather than as mutually exclusive categories of innovation (Gattiker 1990: 20).

3   Fordism, post-Fordism and the electronic panopticon

Introduction

In this chapter we consider a broad range of mainly critical analysis that has sought to counter what it sees as the unacceptable technological determinism of the approaches outlined in the previous two chapters. These discussions subject ideas such as the emergence of a post-industrial information society and techno-economic paradigms to critical scrutiny and a radical re-interpretation. This is accomplished as part of a broader debate concerning the nature of a supposed transformative shift from, or 'radical break' with, Fordist organisational forms consequent of the emergence of new 'post-Fordist' production concepts. Three strands of this debate are considered. First, radical critiques of positive images of the effects of advanced technology on work as exemplified in ideas such as the 'information society' and 'information technology paradigm'. Second, the argument that new production concepts are emerging to transform the hitherto predominant 'post-Fordist' mass production paradigm. Finally, the view that the post-modern forms of technology and organisation implicit in such ideas bring with them a new reality of increased electronic surveillance.

The predominant metaphors in these debates are contradictory. On the one hand they are negative insofar as technology is presented as a means of management control, or as part of a broader set of forces of domination or panoptic power. On the other hand they are positive in the sense that transformative potential is identified in notions such as 'flexibility' and 'leanness' which promise both productive efficiency and more humane forms of work and organisation. In most, though not all, renditions of these types of argument ICTs play a key enabling role supporting either the development of new production concepts or the continued vitality of existing ones.

Labour process theory and the critique of post-industrialism

As we rehearsed in Chapter 1, the rapid diffusion of ICTs has given new life to earlier theories of the 'post-industrial' society under the guise of the concept of the 'information society' and most recently 'virtual organisa-tion'. The critiques of this position point strongly to the deterministic role given to technology in explaining and accounting for social change, including that in the form of work and organisation. To boot, the tone of the discussion is overwhelmingly optimistic pointing to the liberative effects of technology, for example in terms of creating highly skilled and enriching jobs, more autonomous and less alienating forms of work, and more harmonious and consensual relations between management and labour. The trouble with this position from a critical perspective is that technology is characterised, 'as a neutral input to individual production systems, the motivation behind its introduction being purely competitive, and its effects, apart from the improvement of the competitive position of the firm or nation-state, being largely incidental' (Wilkinson 1983: 9).

Many of these points have been addressed most effectively by those influenced by Harry Braverman's (1974) seminal work *Labor and Monopoly Capital*. This sought to revive and develop Karl Marx's theory of the labour process and to locate the kinds of technological and organi-sational trends identified by proponents of post-industrialism and the like within the dynamics of the development of capitalism. For writers working in this tradition, technological innovation is not driven by its own internal logic but is shaped by the social and economic characteristics of capitalist societies – particularly by the need to generate profits through the control of labour (see e.g. Knights *et al.* 1985; Knights and Wilmott 1988; Thompson 1989).

One consequence of such imperatives is that management seek to find progressively more effective ways of ensuring control over employee behaviour and productive efficiency. Underlying this argument is the view that there is a fundamental and structurally determined conflict underlying the relationship between capital and labour arising from the concentration of the ownership of the means of production in private hands. In order to get the maximum return on their 'investment' in human labour employers have to maximise their control over the behaviour of employees and production. Indeed, for Braverman, 'the essential function of management in industrial capitalism' was 'control over the labour process' (1974: 63).

For labour process theorists, relations between management and work-force, and the question of the relationship between technology and organisation, both need to be seen in the light of this basic fact. Thus, notions of an expanding stratum of information and knowledge workers misses the point that professional and technical sounding job titles (the growth in which is readily recorded in economic statistics) ignores the fundamental fact that the nature of the work such occupations undertake is in fact shaped by the need for management control. In essence 'skilled' job titles frequently mask deskilled jobs.

According to Braverman, such control has been sought in the twentieth century in increasingly sophisticated ways. Thus, initially the adoption of the techniques of scientific management pioneered by Taylor and Ford, involved a separation of 'conception' (the mental labour of planning and decision-making) from 'execution' (exercise of manual labour) in the accomplishment of work tasks primarily through organisational and disciplinary means. However, subsequently, technological development has increasingly offered to management a more effective means of control over the labour process. This reduces reliance on the direct personal supervision of labour normally required under Taylorist methods. Taylorist ideas have thus found new expression in the use of new technology to deskill operators' work, either by 'automating out' the need for direct human intervention, or by using new technologies to break jobs down into fragmented tasks which require little or no conceptual ability, or autonomous intervention, on the part of workers. ICTs, therefore, rather than being harbingers of a 'radical break' with the past, actually represent a further stage in an established long term historical development. That is, they encourage the further extension of the centralisation of the functions and activities of management and the embodiment of control in technological means, beyond the factory into the office. Even, it is noted with some irony, designers and computer programmers themselves are ultimately subject to the same Taylorisation of their work as those for whom they produce deskilling technology (see e.g. Cooley 1980b). Thus, whilst technological change enables improvements in productive efficiency, it also facilitates 'the progressive elimination of the control functions of the worker, insofar as possible, and their transfer to a device which is controlled, again in so far as is possible, by management from outside the direct process' (Braverman 1974: 212). It is this dynamic which defines the relationship between technology and organisation in capitalist society.

The theoretical consistency and empirical accuracy of Braverman's thesis has been hotly disputed, not least from within the labour process perspective itself. The principal focus of criticism has been his apparent confusion of 'a particular system of control with management control in general' (Thompson and McHugh 1995: 115). One consequence has been to suggest that the motivations for technological change and the inevitable organisational effect of its introduction has been to deskill work. However other labour process theorists, and those sympathetic to this position, have pointed to:

- a range of control strategies that might be deployed by management in pursuit of the broader goal of securing and increasing profitability (see e.g. Edwards 1979; Friedman 1977, 1990);
- the way that such strategies are in practice contested and resisted by employees (see e.g. Burawoy 1979; Zimbalist 1979); and
- the historically specific and culturally mediated way in which the Taylorist/Fordist paradigm has spread through the world economy (see e.g. Littler 1982).

The consequence of this reformulation is to suggest a more contingent view of the nature of the relationship between technology and organisation, which is less universalistic and 'culture-free' and a more open-ended understanding of variations in the actual effects of technological change on organisations. Thus, many labour process theorists have pointed out, and empirically demonstrated, that in particular product and labour market conditions, technology is introduced by management with the intention of securing control by redesigning work to give employees more discretion and autonomy (see e.g. Friedman 1977). At the same time, where such 'responsible autonomy', or for that matter, 'deskilling' strategies are pursued, it has been increasingly recognised that empirically outcomes are mediated by a range of factors such as the capacity of workers to resist and modify management intentions. The upshot is that an adequate labour process theory of the relationship between technology and organisation needs to be able to take account of the way factors such as the condition of labour and product markets, the strength of trade union organisation, and varying historical and cultural conditions, limit the capacity of management to engage control through deskilling (Thompson 1989: 111–17).

A further criticism of labour process theory, in particular Braverman's version, is the inadequate analysis of gender and the position of women (for discussion see Thompson 1989: 180–209; also Beechey 1982; Knights and Willmott 1986). Over recent years some feminist writers have argued that conflict at work occurs not only between labour and capital, but also reflects inequalities and antagonisms in the wider sexual division of labour between men and women. On this analysis technology needs to be viewed, not only as a means by which management seek to control labour, but also as a means by which the subordinate position of women may be maintained by men (see e.g. Barker and Downing 1985; Cockburn 1983, 1985; Wajcman 1991).

Webster (1996) draws attention to the following effects of technology used as a means of control in this way. First, there is the social definition of what are 'skilled' and 'unskilled' jobs, insofar as work traditionally performed by women is frequently labelled as 'low skilled' and accordingly paid at lower rates. Thus a management, for example, introducing new technology which replaces traditional 'male skills' might seek to accomplish deskilling by recruiting an alternative, cheaper, female labour force. Second, male workforces may well evoke traditional images of what is 'man's' work in an attempt to retain their employment in skilled status in the face of such management strategies (see e.g. Cockburn 1983, 1985; Crompton and Jones 1984). Finally, existing gender-based definitions of 'skilled' and 'low-skilled' work may be reinforced and reproduced by the adoption of new technology.

Considerable attention has been paid by feminist researchers to the effects of ICTs in office employment where women are disproportionately

represented in routine and lower-grade administrative, clerical and secretarial occupations. However, Webster's own summary of the factors
influencing the effects of word processing technology on the work predominantly done by women, reveal the manner in which a simple recasting of
Braverman's deskilling thesis as a means of patriarchal control is also too
simplistic. In fact, the outcomes of the introduction of such technology on
labour processes conducted primarily, if not exclusively, by women have
been shown to be highly varied and not confined to an organisational
outcome which deskills their work. Webster suggests the following reasons
for this (1996: 119). First, word processors are introduced into workplaces where the nature of the task performed varies in terms of its
relationship to the principal activity of the organisation and the scale of
the operations performed. Second, the content of the jobs of clerical,
administrative and secretarial labour varies, in particular with respect to
the degrees of autonomy and discretion that they incorporate. Third, even
within these occupational groups the actual content of jobs and their
organisation varies from office to office according to local situational
factors. Fourth, the technology introduced varies in terms of its capabilities
and characteristics, in particular whether it is 'stand alone' equipment or
part of a 'networked' system, and this affects the nature of the new tasks
to be performed by office staff.

Finally, the nature of the effects of the new technology is mediated by
variations in, and the coherence of, management strategies which themselves reflect financial market, product market, labour market and labour
cost factors. Indeed, it is only in the specific conditions where 'clerical
work is the business of the organisation, where clerical costs are a large
proportion of office costs, or where management strategies for work reorganisation are highly developed in relation to market conditions or
pressure from shareholders' that the use of new office technology to deskill
work is likely to be perceived by management as a viable option (Webster
1996: 119). Again, nation-specific factors are an additional influence and
countries where Taylorism/Fordism have long been established (e.g. USA)
are more conducive to such a deskilling approach than those where traditions of the autonomy, status and role of secretarial labour in particular
are rather different (e.g. as in Germany and France) (Webster 1996: 121).

From the foregoing, it should be clear that labour process theorists do
not see the use of technology to deskill or upskill jobs as an expression of
the inevitable impact of the technology itself. Rather, the organisational
effects of technological change are entirely a product of the need to control
the labour process in order to increase profits, although how, why and if
this is actually done is increasingly seen as highly contingent upon a
complex of situational and contextual factors. Having said this, under a
different social system, it might still be argued that new technologies such
as ICTs would open up the possibility of different forms of job design and
work organisation which would benefit the workforce. For example, for

Braverman this would have involved workgroups possessing the engineering knowledge required to operate and maintain the technology, and a rotation of tasks to make sure everyone had opportunities to work on both highly complex and routine jobs (Braverman 1974: 230). Thus, rather than being deskilled, they would retain autonomy and control over the labour process, and advanced technology would be used as a complement to, rather than substitute for, human skills and abilities. However, for Braverman at least, such a form of work organisation and control is not conducive to the interests of management in a capitalist society, and therefore could not be brought about without a major political, economic and social transformation. However, the emergent debate on the replacement of Fordist by post-Fordist organisations suggests that precisely such a transformation is underway.

Post-Fordist production concepts: flexible specialisation and lean production

The relevance of the labour process critique has been severely challenged by arguments which have suggested that the Taylorist/Fordist production paradigm, even in its contingent and modified formulation, is being replaced by new production paradigms or concepts. Thus, whilst the criticism of technologically determinist ideas such as the post-industrial information society are all very well, to conclude as a result that there is an essential continuity in the way technology is used as a means of control in organisations is to miss the point. Rather, important transformations are afoot, but it is not an inherently 'neutral', 'progressive' technology which is driving change in organisations and beyond. Rather, changes in technology are 'put instead within a matrix of social relations that determines [their] use and application' (Kumar 1995: 37). These matrices are usually represented, as we noted in the Introduction to this volume, by the idea of new production paradigms or concepts which, it is argued, offer an increasingly viable alternative to Taylorism and Fordism. Two such 'post-Fordist' paradigms are most frequently identified: 'flexible specialisation' and 'lean production'.

According to proponents of the notion of new production concepts, the Fordist paradigm flourished in the context of particular market, technological, organisational and job/employment characteristics (see Sabel 1982; Piore and Sabel 1984; Wood 1989). Mass production required large investments in dedicated plant and equipment. For this to be profitable the markets for mass produced products had to be both large and have a stable pattern of demand which allowed them to absorb high volumes of standardised products over time. The large-scale organisation, utilising Taylorist/Fordist methods of work design and managed through an adversarial industrial relations system, was the dominant organisational form. Technology, as we have already seen, was a means through which management could exercise control and ICTs a means through which such control could be extended into hitherto unreachable areas of organisational activity and over organisational members who, in the past, had exercised skill and enjoyed a degree of autonomy in the execution of their work tasks.

There is general agreement amongst such theorists that Fordism (a concept based on a much broader set of factors than just those defining social relations within work organisations e.g. stable growth rates, corporatist industrial relations, welfare capitalism and mass consumption) began to unravel from the early 1970s onwards (Harvey 1989). The capacity of large organisations to maintain high levels of productive efficiency started to be fatally undermined (Piore and Sabel 1984; Lash and Urry 1987; Hall and Jaques 1989). Domestic demand for consumer goods had been saturated in the advanced industrial nations, leaving the home market unable to absorb further increases in output. Corporations sought to respond by seeking out new markets in both developed and developing nations. However, these efforts to engage in global competition failed to restore productive efficiency. Instead, the growth points of national economies – often small and medium sized enterprises which clustered together in particular geographical regions – turned out to be those which eschewed the Fordist approach. These organisations had, it was claimed, taken advantage of the flexible capabilities and characteristics of new ICTs to cut the cost of producing customised – as opposed to mass market – goods and services.

According to proponents of such ideas, what was taking place here was an innovatory organisational response to a set of new global product and technological conditions. In a situation where product markets are increasingly characterised by instability and uncertainty, organisations are motivated to seek to use new technological opportunities to generate product and process innovations which will meet the new 'fragmented' pattern of demand. The organisational forms associated with the pursuit of this objective are typically small-scale producers linked to each other and to larger producers who they supply in tightly knit industrial networks. Such networks embody what has been termed the principle of 'flexible specialisation':

> Flexible specialisation is a strategy of permanent innovation: accommodation to ceaseless change, rather than an effort to control it. This strategy is based on flexible – multi-use – equipment; skilled workers; and the creation, through politics, of an industrial community that restricts the forms of competition to those favouring innovation. For these reasons, the spread of flexible specialisation amounts to a revival of craft forms of production that were emarginated at the first industrial divide.

> (Piore and Sabel 1984: 17)

As similar product market conditions have confronted larger organisations they too, it is argued, have sought to exploit new technological innovations in this way. As a result, similar organisational forms to those of their smaller counterparts have been adopted. Increasingly, it is claimed, large 'Fordist bureaucracies' are being transformed through a 'downsizing' and delayering of managerial structures; the reskilling of workers through team-based systems which increase autonomy and 'empowerment'; the 'democratisation' of work through involvement and participation; and the development of networked forms of intra- and inter-organisational relationships (see e.g. Mathews 1989a, 1989b, 1994).

The outcome is a new post-Fordist model of organisation based, not on the principle of control, but rather that of flexibility:

> Where modernist organization was rigid, postmodern organisation is flexible. Where modernist organization was premised on technological determinism, postmodernist organization is premised on the technological choices made possible through 'de-dedicated' microelectronic equipment. Where modernist organization and jobs were highly differentiated, demarcated and de-skilled, post-modernist organization and jobs are highly de-differentiated, de-demarcated and multi-skilled. Employment relations as a fundamental relation of organizations upon which had been constructed a whole discourse of the determinism of size as a contingency variable increasingly give way to more complex and fragmentary relational forms, such as subcontracting and networking.
>
> (Clegg 1989: 181)

An important dimension of the 'matrix of social relations' in which such changes are embedded is the role of national context in shaping the use and application of these ideas. For example, according to Piore and Sabel some national economies will be more disposed to move towards this new production paradigm of 'flexible specialisation' than others. Those with adversarial industrial relations systems will find it harder than those where the basis of cooperative employer–employee relations already exists to develop post-Fordist organisational forms and exploit the full flexibility of ICTs.

Piore and Sabel argue that, 'the balance of power between labour and capital' will in fact 'have to be fought out country by country' (1984: 277). As a result the diffusion of the new production paradigm can be expected to be both uneven and variable across national boundaries. The spread of lean production presents a particular illustration of this point. The concept of lean production itself emerged on the back of the success of Japanese organisations in the post-war period in penetrating overseas markets with high quality products and a distinctive approach to, *inter alia*, the organisation of production and the management of labour. In essence, lean production presented a completely new paradigm for organising production, developing new products, managing supply chains, and dealing with sales and service.

The identification of 'lean production' as a revolutionary way to organise production and service operations in the West has been popularised following the publication of the book *The Machine That Changed the World* (Womack *et al.* 1990) and its startling claim that:

> Lean production is a superior way for humans to make things. It provides better products in a wider variety at lower cost. Equally important, it provides more challenging and fulfilling work for employees at every level, from the factory to headquarters. It follows that the whole world should adopt lean production, and as quickly as possible.
>
> (Womack *et al.* 1990: 225)

However, whilst the performance improvements claimed for 'lean production' appeared, in the eyes of these authors at least, to constitute an imperative which would, or should, result in the universal application of the concept, other observerse have pointed to the way in which nation-specific factors shape the application of these techniques and cast doubt on many of the 'efficiency' and 'humanising' claims that are made (see e.g. Dankbar 1988; Berggren 1993; Lane 1989; Garahan and Stewart 1992; Schumann 1998).

More generally, other post-Fordist theorists are also less certain about the nature of the organisational and other outcomes of the shift away from Fordism apparently promised by new production concepts. For Lash and Urry (1987), for example, the 'disorganisation of capitalism', which they discern as the defining characteristic of these trends dissolves, amongst many other things, the certainties of understanding management–employee relations in terms of the distinctive and relatively unambiguous class interests of capital and labour. In its place it leaves flexible technology and flexible specialisation which present both threats and opportunities to the shifting and multilayered and levelled interests which now characterise organisational relationships.

Badham and Mathews (1989) provide what is frequently identified as the most subtle formulation of the indeterminacy of the shift to post-Fordist organisational forms. These authors provide an alternative model of new production systems which incorporates key elements of the flexible specialisation and lean production argument, but which also allows for a far more varied and indeterminate set of outcomes. The model (see Figure 3.1) seeks to represent basic alternatives in three-dimensional space. The model distinguishes between the degrees of product innovation, process variability, and labour responsibility that are manifested in:

- an organisation's *production process* (i.e. its 'operating point along each of the dimensions');
- its *production strategy* (i.e. 'its preferred operating point along each production dimension'); and
- *production paradigms* (i.e. the 'idealised exemplary models or visions of efficient production' which inform strategy.

(Badham and Mathews 1989: 206–8)

An organisation may be *operating* at the medium point on each of the three dimensions of product, process and labour variability. This defines a unique point within the three-dimensional space of the production system model (shown as 'B' in Figure 3.1). However, the organisation may have a *strategy* where the desired outcome is a high point on each of the dimensions (shown as 'C' Figure 3.1). The strategic objective therefore is to shift the organisation's production system from point B to point C. Both the nature of the production process and the strategies pursued are informed by *production paradigms* which come to be defined in practice by firms clustering in particular spaces on the production system model. The model shows three such production paradigms; *Fordist*, *neo-Fordist* and *post-Fordist* (of which flexible specialisation may be regarded as a variant). Unlike some post-Fordists, Badham and Mathews suggest different paradigms will coexist and compete within national economies and indeed with the same industry. The dominance of one paradigm is not dependent upon the extinction of the others but rather is negotiated and mediated through social, economic, industrial and political institutions in nation-specific circumstances (1989: 211).

The process by which these paradigms are socially produced is important to understand (Badham and Mathews 1989: 209–11). They involve 'symbolic generalisations, over-arching beliefs and values, concretely embodied in exemplary models or puzzle/solutions'. The production strategies of individual organisations are conditioned by the availability of these 'models' and their success in practice. New paradigms are formed through the interaction of a variety of experts and opinion formers (for example academics, consultants, journalists, equipment vendors, government, training agencies) and the actual experiences of management, employees and unions in practice. As such, production paradigms, unlike the techno-economic variants discussed in Chapter 2, reflect not just the imperatives of product markets and technology but the interpretative schemes and political values of their authors.

Underlying Badham and Mathews considerable refinement of post-Fordist analysis, therefore, is a conception of change within organisations which identifies not just the behaviour but the interpretative schemes of organisational actors as key to shaping its outcomes. This idea provides the core of the next chapter which considers how the outcomes of technological change are mediated by choices, made and

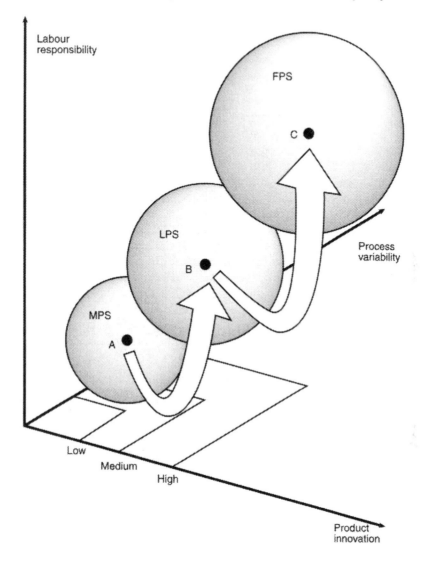

Figure 3.1: New production concepts

Source: Mathews 1994: 49.

Notes:
MPS   Mass production system
LPS   Lean production system
FPS   Flexible production system
As market conditions become more turbulent a firm will attempts to shift its production from
point A in the MPS region, through point B to point C in the FPS region.

negotiated, within the political and cultural systems of particular organisational settings.

Virtual organisation: the archetypal post-modern organisation?

In Chapter 1 we presented a largely positive and determinist image of the implications of contemporary advances in ICTs for 'virtual' forms of work and organisation. However, as Jackson (1996) points out, the notion that organisations are in essence information processing systems or brains can fuse the technical and social in a manner which conceals the social and economic basis of new organisational forms. At the same time the more negative aspects of work within them and its broader social and economic effects can be concealed (Jackson 1996: 27). Indeed, the creation of global electronic networks is not purely a technological phenomenon but one that is intimately related to broader developments in the world economy which are also a strong influence on organisational restructuring. 'Globalisation' refers to a number of such interrelated developments. These include the internationalisation of production and services to secure competitive advantage, the emergence of 'global' corporations able to operate across national boundaries, the growth and integration of world trade, and the internationalisation of the division of labour and financial markets (Thompson and McHugh 1995: 97–8). If we are to pursue the metaphors of organisations as 'information systems' or 'brains' or 'virtual realities' it is clear that we need to do so in a way which avoids technological imagery alone and deterministic accounts of the relationship between technology and organisation (Castells, 1996: 5).

However, for many commentators, organisational survival in the context of the commercial imperatives generated by globalisation and new technological possibilities unavoidably requires a move away from conventional 'modern' hierarchical bureaucracies to 'networked' forms of organisation (Davidow and Malone 1992; Grenier and Mates 1995; Handy 1995; Barnatt 1995b). In this sense, Brigham and Corbett (1996) see virtual organisation as an archetypal post-modern form of organisation which they suggest (quoting Reed 1992: 229) 'celebrates, even luxuriates in, the dissolution and demise of normative regimes and disciplinary practises associated with rational bureaucracy'.

Barnatt (1995b) in appropriate celebratory style suggests virtual organisations have three defining characteristics:

- a reliance on cyberspace in order to function and survive;
- no identifiable physical form; and
- employer–employee relationships which are transient and whose boundaries are defined and limited by the availability of virtual technology rather than bureaucratic rules or contracts.

According to Davidow and Malone (1992), to the outsider virtual organisations will 'appear almost edgeless, with permeable and continuously changing interfaces between company, supplier and customers'. To the insider they will appear 'no less amorphous, with traditional offices, departments and operating divisions constantly reforming according to need'. By the same token the content of jobs will 'regularly shift', whilst 'even the very definition of an employee will change, as some customers and suppliers begin to spend more time in the company than will some of the firm's own workers' (Davidow and Malone 1992: 5–6).

Campbell (1996) usefully provides a typology of 'virtual organisation' and in so doing starts to draw out a more contingent and variable empirical model of virtual organisational forms. He distinguishes between (see Figure 3.2):

- *internal virtual organisations*: where relatively autonomous 'enterprise' or 'business' units are formed within a large conventional bureaucracy to provide operational synergies and tailor responses to specific customer demands;

- *stable virtual organisations*: where conventional bureaucratic organisations outsource non-core activities to a small network of key suppliers whose activities become highly interdependent and integrated with those of the mother firm (for example as in the 'lean production' model);

- *dynamic virtual organisations*: where organisations concentrate on core competencies but introduce external partners in cooperative ventures throughout their operations;

- *agile virtual organisations*: a new type of organisational form, constituted as temporary networks rapidly formed 'to exploit new market opportunities through the mutual exchange of skills and resources' (Campbell 1996: 83).

Unlike the other types, 'agile networks' are not a variation on existing bureaucratic organisational forms. Rather they represent virtual organisation in its 'purest form'. They are manifested not as spatially and temporally fixed sets of systems and structures, but rather as a spatially dispersed and temporally flexible cultural community, the reproduction of which is dependent upon the learning and innovation of its constituents. Here, as Handy (1995) observes, management must seek to 'manage what they cannot see' through building relationships of trust with other network members.

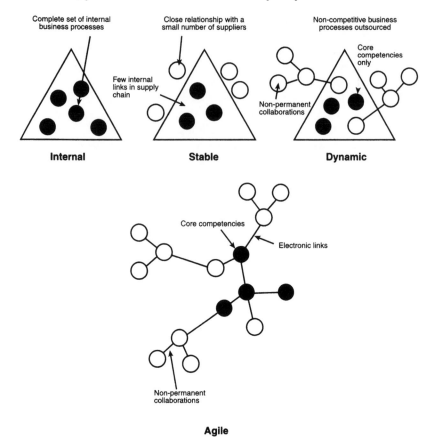

Figure 3.2: Types of virtual organisation

Source: Adapted from Campbell 1996.

The electronic panopticon

Whilst new production concepts and notions of virtual organisation may represent an anti-bureaucratic discourse which, instead of routinisation and alienation, promises a new world of high trust and empowered work relationships, some have drawn attention to the darker side and implications of such ideas. In particular, the capacities of such organisational forms to use electronic technology to 'generate subordination through uncertainty' (Lyon 1994: 65). The origin of this particular idea pre-dates much of the first, let alone any subsequent industrial revolutions. It can be traced to plans for a new type of prison made by Jeremy Bentham and published in 1791. This novel architectural design deployed a circular layout and other structural devices to render warders invisible to inmates. This allowed control to be maintained by the uncertainty on the part of the prisoner that they might be being observed. This design was termed by Bentham the 'panopticon' or 'all seeing place' (Lyon 1994: 63). The idea of organisations as a means of exercising panoptic power has been given more recent attention by the work of Michel Foucault (1977) and also received an earlier expression in George Orwell's dystopian vision in the novel *Nineteen Eighty Four* (1954). For Foucault, what is significant about the notion of the panopticon is not, as Orwell had portrayed it, the enforcement through fear and 'brain washing' of the centralised totalitarian power of the state but rather, the way in which it allows power to function in a dispersed fashion by virtue of the inmate's (read organisational member's) presumption that they are always being observed. In fact Bentham's organisational design permitted the effect of power being exercised to occur without power having to be exercised by power-holders and with the complicity of those over whom the effect of power was being felt.

For Foucault such disciplinary power has become a feature of all modern organisations as the panoptic principle diffused to inform the design of factories, hospitals, schools and so on. However, Lyon observes that Foucault himself did not seem to realise how advances in ICTs were enlarging and enhancing the possibilities for panoptic discipline through electronic surveillance (1994: 67), an apparent error which has not gone uncorrected by students of organisation in recent times (Burrell 1996). Lyon himself adapts an earlier typology of Rule (1973) to show how ICTs have increased the possibilities for surveillance through their quantitatively and qualitatively increased capacity for:

- storing information electronically, more discriminantly, and in smaller spaces, which permits the workplace to be 'watched' far more effectively than through direct supervision or bureaucratic monitoring and surveillance systems;
- enabling surveillance to occur through networked systems at dispersed locations but to be monitored centrally allowing new management styles which simultaneously devolve control to work teams but at the same time intensify the central surveillance of these operations;
- allowing information to be transmitted rapidly to allow more immediate organisational responses to changed situations, not through the 'organised' means of centralised bureaucratic control but via 'disorganised surveillance' of day-to-day activities of employees;
- permitting citizens as employees and in their other social identities, to 'identify' themselves electronically as they go about their every day work. They thus become 'transparent workers' whose actions are watched by 'invisible watchers', 'managers, workmates and, in a sense, by themselves'.

(Lyon 1994: 51–2; 131–3)

One highly influential analysis, also cited by Lyon, that has sought to explore the effects of electronic surveillance in an organisational setting is provided by Soshanna Zuboff (1988) in her classic book *In the Age of the Smart Machine*. She begins by making a key distinction between the 'automating' and 'informating' characteristics and capabilities of ICTs but stresses that the realisation of either of these possibilities is a matter of organisational choice concerning the deployment and use of these systems. The 'automating' effects of ICTs follows the logic of industrial automation since the nineteenth century, that is it seeks to replace the human body with a technology that enables the same processes to be performed with more continuity and control. Unlike other automation technologies, however, ICTs have a transformative potential. Alongside their automating effects ICTs simultaneously generate new information about the productive and administrative processes which constitute organisational activity. This capacity is the 'informating' effect of ICTs and this gives organisational activities transparency which hitherto they have not had. In Zuboff's words, 'activities, events, and objects are translated into and made visible by information when a technology informates as well as automates'. 'In this way' claims Zuboff, 'information technology supersedes the traditional logic of automation' (Zuboff 1988: 9–10).

The transformative potential of ICTs can only be realised in practice if fundamental changes amounting to a 'reinvention' of organisation occur, namely a 'dismantling' of functional hierarchy and its associated 'moral vision, social system, entrenched interests, and vertical focus'. In its place must be put arrangements which allow more organisational members to have both the knowledge, authority and technique to make the decisions which will allow value to be added, 'along the dimensions which their customers deem important' (Zuboff 1996: 16). This means designing organisations so that complexity is managed at the point of entry (e.g. customer interface, point of production, or act of service delivery) rather than 'being removed from lower level jobs and passed up to the management ranks' (ibid.). However, to achieve this:

> means opening up the information base of the organization to members at every level, assuring that each level has the knowledge and skills to productively engage with that information, and endowing all members with the authority to express and ultimately act on what they can know. It implies a new social contract that redefines who people are at work, what they can know, and what they can do.
>
> (Zuboff 1996: 16)

The problem, according to Zuboff is that this transformative opportunity is being lost by the persistence of prevalent but increasingly outmoded world views of managers for whom the allure of the panoptic power of ICTs are the principal attraction. First, the prospect of control being exercised remotely and without effort appears to resolve one of management's fundamental problems, 'how to get others to do what the organisation requires of them'. Second, authority relationships require the continual nurturing of the reciprocities which permit the manager and managed to benefit from their mutual dependency. This psychologically demanding effort and the uncertainty of its outcomes appear to be eliminated by ICTs which 'provide certain information about subordinates'' behaviour while eliminating the 'necessity of face-to-face engagement' (Zuboff 1988: 323). In the absence of any overall strategic intent to exploit the informating capabilities of ICTs such perspectives support the use of ICTs to automate and re-enforce managerial hegemony at the expense of subordinates who are prevented both from having equal access to information and from acquiring the skills necessary for them to do so (Zuboff 1988: 356). Moreover, employees collude in their own subordination through 'anticipatory conformity' by seeking to avoid errors on their part but also to identify and point out the errors of their peers. For Zuboff, like Foucault, the disciplinary power of the panopticon is an undesirable outcome of modernity. However, unlike him, she sees such a trend as avoidable. Indeed, such avoidance is a precondition of the emergence of a, post-modern, relationship between technology and organisation.

Assessment: control, flexibility or panoptic power through technology?

Many of the views outlined in this chapter provide an essential corrective to the technological determinism of perspectives which view the relationship between technology and organisation as one which is apolitical and involves understanding the 'effects' or 'impacts' of neutral, unavoidable, even 'natural' technological imperatives. The focus, as Kumar notes, in discussion of post-Fordism is on the relations of production not the forces of production (1996: 37). Thus, technological innovations are not seen to arise in a more or less neutral way out of the activities of inventors or professional research and development laboratories. Rather, the direction of technological development is viewed as a product of the direct influence of social, economic and political factors. Similarly, rather than technological development being portrayed as an inevitable vehicle for common progress, such innovation is seen as an arena in which divergent interests may be involved, or at least one where cooperation is conditional rather than given. As a result there is an analytical ambivalence about the 'effects' of technological change within and beyond organisations. This is captured in the tension between the apparent capacity for increased control and surveillance on one hand and the transformative possibilities promised by greater flexibility, 'leanness' and autonomy on the other.

For labour process theorists in particular, technology is designed and used to serve particular interests and organisations are seen as arenas of conflict rather than consensus. It follows that disagreement and dispute over particular technological configurations or changes is an inevitable and legitimate feature of organisational life, and certainly not the aberrant consequence of bad communications, poor management, 'Luddite' unions or inherent features of the technology itself (see Chapter 1). Moreover, how this 'contest for control' is resolved is a major factor in shaping the actual organisational outcomes of technological change. Braverman's contribution to this line of reasoning, incorrectly by the admission of most followers, was to suggest that the capitalist imperative that led management to control the labour process through technology inevitably meant, and inevitably has resulted in, a deskilling and degradation of work in ever increasing areas of organisational activity. Other labour process writers, as we have noted, have questioned the inevitability of deskilling as a control strategy and the inevitability of any management attempt in this respect having the desired or intended outcome. The idea of management being driven by the interest of capitalist imperatives, however, is not challenged to any significant extent.

It follows that there is little that is 'new' about the deployment and use of ICTs in contemporary organisations. They are a further stage in the long term trend towards the deepening of the exploitation of labour. This is not to say that the effects of these technologies are inevitably negative from an employee viewpoint. Braverman as we have noted, for instance, points to potential beneficial effects. The problem is that securing such positive consequences would be dependent upon the overthrow of capitalism itself.

This viewpoint contrasts strongly with that of the post-Fordist paradigm which suggests that positive outcomes from technological change are a possible, indeed are a necessary, outcome for organisational survival in a changing capitalist global economy. The flexible specialisation thesis, for example, argues that radical transformations are taking place without the kind of class-based political revolution that Braverman may have had in mind. ICTs, from this perspective are new in their effects precisely because they enable the economic production of goods in small batches for segmented markets, and the rapid change in products to meet shifting and new market needs. This 'flexible technology' gives rise to new production concepts such as 'flexible specialisation' and 'lean production' which, at least in the eyes of their proponents, are the key to organisations securing productive efficiency and developing and sustaining competitive advantage. At the same time, flexibility generates requirements for skilled workers and empowered team-based forms of work organisation. Employees, as a result, enjoy greater involvement in and satisfaction from their work (Kumar 1995: 44, 47).

Rather than being secure in their future as labour process theory seems to suggest, Fordism and mass production are shown in the post-Fordist model to be outmoded as, indeed, are the critiques of it. Indeed, flexible specialisation, and the broader current of 'post-Fordist' thought of which it is a core element represent, as Kumar observes, an attempt 'to save Marxist analysis' in a period when accepted categories of capital and labour are increasingly differentiated if not effectively dissolved (1995: 163).

Post-Fordist debates over new production concepts, therefore, point to a capacity (not always realised – see below) of critical analysis to present a more serviceable model of the dynamics underpinning the major continuities and discontinuities in the technology and organisation relationship. Further, echoing Max Weber, Morgan (1997: 340–41) notes that, such an analysis questions the rationality of technological innovation and associated organisation developments. Indeed, to fail to do this is to permit the pursuit of rationality itself to become a form of domination. The notion of the panoptic power of technology and its capability to enhance organisational capacities for surveillance and self-control presents an excellent example of how critical metaphors can expose the 'darker side' and more negative consequences of technological development.

Braverman and his followers are no doubt correct in their criticism of technological determinism, especially where it leads to conclusions that the introduction of automated technology will inevitably raise the general level of skill and autonomy of the workforce. However, the argument that the effects of technological change can be explained largely, if not wholly, in terms of the management strategies to deskill work is equally flawed. Even if allowance is made for the modification of management strategy by employees during its implementation, the model still assumes that labour control must be a requirement if capital is to effectively exploit labour. In other words, for most labour process writers, the deskilling effects of new technology are, at least in the long term, as inevitable as the 'upskilling' effects associated with the views of writers such as Woodward (see Thompson 1989: 118). Thus, in seeking to explain the changing relationship between technology and organisation, one kind of determinism is, in effect, replaced by another. As Kumar (1995: 33) notes, ideas such as 'Taylorism' and 'deskilling' are made to do 'a lot of work' in labour process analysis to establish the 'ideological' basis of claims concerning the positive effects of technology on organisational variables. However, this is to 'begin' and 'not end the analysis' (ibid.).

The post-Fordist thesis offers the beginnings of such a new analysis. However, it too runs the risk of replacing technological determinism by socio-economic determinism and, as with the labour process thesis, may be based on some questionable assumptions (see Rose 1988; Badham and Mathews 1989; Wood 1989; Smith 1989; Pollert 1991; Hyman 1991; Coriat 1991; Tomaney 1994; Amin 1994; Kumar 1995). For example, it has been argued that the dichotomous distinction between craft and mass production fails to recognise the more variable nature of production systems in industrial capitalist societies (for which see Woodward's typology discussed in Chapter 1) and the more complex nature of product markets. An important point here is that the flexible specialisation paradigm is based on alleged changes in manufacturing, a shrinking sector in most advanced nations, and ignores the expanding service sector. Moreover, product markets have not changed in the manner, or at least to anything like the extent, specified. Mass consumption of products such as automobiles and consumer electronics has not, it is argued by critics, peaked in saturated markets as claimed. Moreover, the core concepts of Fordism and flexible specialisation are too imprecise, in particular in terms of the criterion by which dominance is assessed, making it difficult to specify the extent of any move away from one mode of industrial organisation to another.

Second, the capabilities and characteristics of new computing and information technology are seen as assisting in a move towards more flexible production systems. Apart from a tendency towards technological determinism, this argument does not recognise that the new technologies have also been used in ways that tend to reinforce existing trends to substitute technology for human labour. Finally, the extent to which more flexible forms of work organisation actually upskill the content of jobs in any significant way has been questioned, as has the notion that this is a common outcome across different organisations when they adopt ICTs. Moreover, the upskilling of some jobs may be associated with the deskilling of others leading to a polarisation between a skilled 'core' of workers and an unskilled 'periphery'. Japanese lean production methods, for example, may result in a more flexible production system, but still involve tightly controlled jobs of relatively low skill. Finally, some of the major trends in the world economy since the 1980s and early-1990s, rising redundancies and unemployment, reductions in the power of trade unions and the significance of the collective regulation of employment relations, seem to represent a more pervasive and less optimistic vision of the future of work than any move towards flexible specialisation. Moves towards flexible forms of work organisation may in fact be no more than a manifestation of a free market ideology which will further deregulate labour markets and undermine working conditions.

These, and many other points of criticism, suggest that the distinction between 'mass production' and 'flexible specialisation', compelling though it may be, is difficult to sustain both theoretically and empirically. At best, the notion of post-Fordist production concepts provides a useful heuristic through which to map and assess contemporary organisational and other developments. To argue, however, that they present new models of 'best practice' which will inevitably result in the new capabilities of ICTs being used to secure organisational flexibility is fatally flawed.

Given that the positive images of the transformation of technology and organisation associated with metaphors of flexibility leanness and autonomy appear fraught with problems, it is perhaps hardly surprising that more recent discussion has shifted back to the more pessimistic imagery associated with metaphors of control and domination. The current obsession with the notion of the electronic panopticon and the exercise of disciplinary power through surveillance, however, raises concerns over whether this line of argument has itself been overdone. According to Lyon the origins of 'surveillance theory' in dystopian visions of an undesirable but also unavoidable future means that judgements about the phenomenon draw attention to the 'negative, constraining and unjust aspects' without offering ways of understanding and exploring more positive facets (Lyon 1994: 204). It is thus to be readily assumed in Foucaultian analysis that those who 'see' through electronic surveillance inevitably 'know' as a consequence and that those who are 'watched' are inevitably controlled by their speech. However, this is to stress the constraining elements of surveillance and ignore the enabling. The panoptic metaphor (like the control metaphor of labour process theory) 'generates only bad news and unremitting dystopia' (1994: 211). To move beyond 'post-modern paranoia' we need to recognise that 'surveillance is paradoxical and ambiguous' (1994: 219). For example, surveillance 'enables and empowers as well as constrains' and permits employees to ask more plausibly than ever before 'why have managers'?

Conclusion

In this chapter we have explored post-modern or post-Fordist concepts of the relationship between technology and organisation. We began with the criticism of 'Fordism' itself, or rather its ideological manifestation in ideas such as the 'post-industrial' and 'information society'. We then considered the argument that post-Fordist production concepts were replacing Fordism and effectively making such critiques redundant. Finally, we considered both positive and negative images of the virtual organisation. Ultimately we can suggest that it is not a question of whether the relationship between technology and organisation is best construed by metaphors of control (labour process theory), flexibility, leanness and autonomy (new production concepts/virtual organisation) or the panopticon (surveillance theory). These metaphors all represent possible organisational outcomes from the same set of technological circumstances.

Lyon provides an effective criticism of the post-Fordist debate as a whole, and the notion of panoptic power in particular, which captures the point. First, it is one thing to say that one of the effects of new ICTs is increased surveillance of workplaces but quite another to say that they are caused by the technology alone. Second, even if one accepts that technology is not the causal factor, this in itself does not mean that the new effects are caused by past patterns of social and economic relationships such as the conflict between capital and labour. Indeed, the new 'disorganised' patterns of post-Fordism may well mean that these technologies are applied by management in a range of different ways. The key variable here is 'choice' and:

> exposing such choices, how they are made and by whom, analysing the social and personal realities consequent upon them – including the possibility that new kinds of power may be involved here – is a vital task for contemporary social analysis.
>
> (Lyon 1994: 135)

It is to a consideration of choice that our next chapter turns.

4   Organisational choice, politics and technological change

Introduction

As we noted in the previous chapter, a common feature of Fordist and post-Fordist models of technological and technology-related organisational change is that, despite protestations to the contrary, they retain a strong flavour of change *within* organisations as an essentially adaptive activity determined by broader economic and technological imperatives. In this chapter an approach intended as a corrective to such views will be outlined which places far more stress on the role of organisation-specific processes of choice and politics concerning implementation and use of technology. The essence of this view is that, whilst factors such as product markets, technological environment and the like are important, they do not themselves shape the organisational outcomes of technological change. Rather, they act as 'reference points' for the choices, decisions and negotiating activity of key actors and groups within organisations. It is their actions which shape outcomes and the capacity to act is seen as derived from the dominant position of these actors within an organisation's power system. This 'strategic choice/organisational politics' perspective has given rise to a model of technology-related change, and organisational change more generally, which stresses its processual nature. Such models have particular implications for the activity of change management and the role of change managers and others seeking to intervene in, and direct, organisational outcomes. They also raise questions over the influence of technology itself: if it is not a determining variable, what if anything does it do?

The political/cultural metaphor

The image of organisations as political systems rests on the view that organisation is only made possible by the bringing together of 'divergent interests'. Organising therefore involves ongoing processes of 'wheeling and dealing', negotiation, coalition building and the exercise of mutual influence as efforts to resolve conflict arising from the pursuit of different interests are made (Morgan 1997: 160). Such efforts typically require the mobilisation of power resources through political activity. This in turn frequently requires the formation of coalitions as the loose networks of actors which comprise organisations seek to 'co-operate in relation to specific issues, events, or decisions or to advance specific values and ideologies' (Morgan 1997: 166).

In such a perspective conflict is an endemic feature of organising since organisations require both collaboration in the pursuit of common goals but also competition over the scarce resources required to achieve these goals (Morgan 1997: 167–8). Power, in this approach, can be understood as the 'medium through which conflicts of interest are ultimately resolved' (Morgan 1997: 170). Thinking of organisations in this way also draws attention to them as entities which are manifested in cultural terms, in particular in the sense that organising requires and produces degrees of 'shared meaning' amongst organisation members and the sub-groups to which they belong. Culture thus provides the bounded means through which organisational actors 'make sense' of their experiences in selective and distinctive ways (Morgan 1997: 138). There are, as we will see, clear links to the political process within organisation that become apparent when the manipulation of culture is seen as a means through which power can be exercised.

Walsham (1993) has sought to develop the political and cultural metaphors as a basis for analysing the relationship between ICTs and organisational change. Key elements of his framework are given in Table 4.1. This framework draws attention to:

- organisation as constituted in 'patterns of symbolic discourse and action' and as a loose network of groups or coalitions with 'divergent interests'
- the role of organisational members in enacting organisational reality through the sense they make of their experiences and the role of power and political processes in defining and legitimating particular versions of this 'reality'
- the importance of sub-cultures within organisations in maintaining competing views of organisational reality and in raising questions of a moral or ethical nature over the way power is used
- the role of management in influencing the evolution of cultures and as being able to manage multiple perspectives in the search for an appropriate balance in organisational outcomes between autonomy and control at different levels.

Such conceptions place considerable stress on the capacity of management and other organisation actors to shape the organisational outcomes of technological change. This leads to a more detailed consideration of the capacity of management to make choices, the factors which enable and constrain the choice-making, and the manner in which this can be

Table 4.1 Some key elements of political and cultural metaphors

	Cultural	*Political*
View of organisations	Organisations as patterns of symbolic discourse and action	Organisations as loose networks of people with divergent interests
Some key ideas	Culture is an active, living phenomenon through which people create the world in which they live Subcultures maintain distinctive character and ascribe different meanings to same events	Power is intrinsic to all human activity. Exercise of power is continuous, with subtle local properties Morality is involved in exercise of power. Can include domination, but this is never total
Management	Cannot control culture, but can influence its evolution. Need to manage for multiple perspectives	Need to actively manage the precarious balance between autonomy and control at multiple levels

Source: Walsham 1993: 47.

subjected to negotiation within organisations by other interest groups who may have divergent views.

Strategic choice and organisational politics

The concept of *strategic choice* was originally developed by Child (1972; see also 1997) as a corrective to the then dominant contingency view of organisations which patently ignored the role of power in organisations and instead stressed the determining influence of situational or environmental contingencies (see Chapter 1). The aim of the concept of strategic choice was to highlight the key role played by organisational politics and divergent stakeholder interests in shaping organisations where external factors are regarded not as determining, but rather as contextual *referents* for decision-makers when designing organisations and establishing their purpose (e.g. shape of management hierarchy, design of jobs, type of technology used, what kind of products to make and where to market them), defining salient features and even shaping elements of the environment (e.g. the price of products and pay rates) and by selecting and interpreting the criteria through which organisational performance is assessed. Thus, contrary to the focus on situational factors made in contingency theory, Child argued that it was 'strategic choices' on the part of decision-makers which were the critical variable in the theory of organisations (Child 1972: 15).

Given this scope for strategic choice, attention is drawn to the questions of who makes the key decisions in organisations, why particular choices are made and not others, and who benefits from the outcomes of such processes and who does not. According to Child, 'strategic choices' are made by 'dominant coalitions' of power-holders (typically senior managers) within the organisation and it follows that, in order to explain the structure of organisations, it is necessary to understand the subjective meanings given to their action by these power-holding groups e.g. their goals, values and assumptions through which they assign and give meaning to their action. However, strategic choices are subject to modification within organisations through interaction with other organisation members (e.g. managers outside the dominant coalition, trade unions, employees). The social action and interaction of these groups also needs to be taken into account in explaining organisation structure and behaviour. Taken together, all of this suggests that organisation can be seen as a form of 'negotiated order' (Strauss *et al.* 1973) – the outcome of a process of social choice and political negotiation by organisation members.

Although not intended in Child's original formulation (Child 1997), the strategic choice concept has been taken to suggest a dichotomous distinction between structural explanations on the one hand and those which stress the unhindered capacity of human agents to shape both organisations and even their environments on the other (see e.g. Donaldson's recent critique, 1996). This is frequently reflected in studies of technology and organisation by counterposing as competing explanatory models those which stress 'determinism' against those which emphasis 'choice' (see e.g. Scarbrough and Corbett 1992).

Whittington (1988) has argued that the problem with dichotomising agency and structure is that the preconditions for exercising agency tend to be overlooked and this gives the impression that actors exercise choice simply because of the absence of external constraint. On the contrary, suggests Whittington, agency is always constrained by the interpretative frameworks through which decisions are made which can serve to limit the range of available choices perceived and considered. A more realistic distinction, therefore, is that between 'environmental determinism' and 'action determinism'.

Child has recently endorsed this view as an 'enrichment' of the strategic choice perspective since, 'by drawing attention to the prior factors which shape the mind-sets of key actors' it complements the notion of internal politics shaping choice through a process of a 'coalescence of diverse initial action preferences into an agreed policy' (Child 1997: 51–2). In addition, suggests Child, it is also necessary to take account of deficiencies in the information used to inform choice. Such information may, for instance, be limited or ambiguous in character. Taken together, Child suggests, action determinism, intra-organisational political processes and informational imperfections, 'highlight the constraints upon' strategic choice over and above those 'imposed by an organisation's environment' (1997: 52). It is also important to understand that the 'imposition' of the environment is a function of 'enactment' by organisational members in the sense that such actions 'bring certain environments into relevance' which then 'assume objective properties' (ibid. 1997: 53).

The process and politics of technological change

The political metaphor and the strategic choice approach has influenced a broad range of contemporary research on the social implications of ICTs. This work has sought to show how the organisational outcomes of technological change are not a rational organisational adaptation to product, of environmental or situational contingencies in general and the technical characteristics and capabilities of technology in particular. Rather they have been shown to be a product of the strategic choices made by dominant coalitions within adopting organisations which are subsequently modified and altered through negotiation during the process of change with other organisational actors.

For example, in an important initial contribution, Wilkinson (1983) argued that organisations should be treated as 'emergent entities dependent upon the conscious political decisions of actors and groups of actors' (1983: 9). As such, the introduction of new technology in organisations is best conceived as a *process* with indeterminant outcomes. Within this process a number of analytically distinct stages can be identified, each of which provide 'critical junctures' or opportunities for power-holders to make and modify 'strategic choices' in relation to particular issues highlighted by change. It is the nature of these choices, and the way these are contested by formal and informal negotiation by other organisational actors – in particular at workplace level – that have the decisive influence on actual organisational outcomes of technological change. Outcomes are thus seen as the result of more or less unique organisational processes 'of change within particular organisations and the manner in which management, unions and workforce are able to influence substantive outcomes' (Wilkinson 1983: 21), rather than a consequence of uniform external forces 'impacting' on organisations and causing managers and other organisational members to adapt to change in particular ways (see also for other relevant UK based work Pettigrew 1973, 1987; Buchanan and Boddy 1983; Clark *et al.* 1988; Batstone *et al.* 1988; Baldry 1988; Burnes 1989; Walsham 1993; Dawson 1994; Clark 1995; Preece 1995; Willcocks *et al.* 1996; Hill *et al.* 1997).[1]

This focus on change as a process has resulted in a number of attempts to identify the key stages of change and the type of issues highlighted at these points which provide opportunities for choice, negotiation and so on. Clark *et al.* identify five analytically distinct stages (see Clark *et al.* 1988: 31) of initiation, decision to adopt, system selection, implementation, and routine operation. Similarly Wilkinson suggests that introducing new technology can be broken down into a number of stages, including those concerning the choice, implementation and debugging of technology (Wilkinson 1983; 21).

However, what is important here is not the precise specification of stages but rather the notion that critical points, or 'junctures', arise at which choices are made by dominant coalitions, which may then be contested by formal and informal negotiation by other organisational actors. According to Clark *et al.* (1988) these *critical junctures* can be defined as the points at which the *temporal stages* of change intersect with particular organisational *issues* raised by the introduction of a particular technology. They offer opportunities where organisational actors can seek to intervene in order to influence particular outcomes of change (Clark *et al.* 1988: 32).

Stage models seek to capture the temporal element of technological change. However, it should be born in mind that, although sequential in analytical terms, in practice organisations may 'regress' to earlier stages or inhabit two or more stages simultaneously (Dawson 1994). Moreover, the notion of 'stages' of change is open to and shaped by the interpretations of organisational actors:

> Although pertaining to a period of time, the history of past change projects may be rewritten to service present objectives and in many companies, post-hoc rationalisations of change are not uncommon. In this sense, past reconstructions and future expectations are important to understand current contextual conditions under which change unfolds. Within organisations, there are often a number of competing histories....These oral and sometimes documented histories, may also act to shape, constrain and promote the direction and content of future change programmes. In short,...the process of change is continuously influenced by the interplay and conflict between historical reconstructions, current contextual conditions and future expectations.
>
> (Dawson 1996: 26)

At the same time the nature of the issues which are highlighted during a change process, the manner in which choices are made (or not made) and these decisions negotiated or contested (or not as the case may be), will reflect organisational specific characteristics of the content of change itself and the organisational context and wider context in which change takes place.

The importance of viewing change in organisations as a process which occur in particular contextual and historical conditions has been emphasised by Andrew Pettigrew in a series of studies of mainly organisational development and strategic change programmes. He has developed a model which seeks to capture the dynamic and multilayered image of strategic change that such considerations evoke. This involves the following principles (see Pettigrew 1985, 1990; Pettigrew *et al.* 1988, 1992):

> First, the importance of embeddedness, implying the need to locate change in the context of interconnected levels of analysis. Secondly, the importance of temporal interconnectedness – the need to locate change in past, present and future time – should be stressed. Thirdly, the need to explore context and action (how context is a product of action and vice versa) is crucial. Finally, the central assumption about causation in this kind of holistic analysis is that causation of change is neither linear or singular – the search for a simple and singular grand theory of change is unlikely to bear fruit. For the analyst interested in the theory and practice of changing, the task is to identify the variety and mixture of causes of change and to explore through time some of the conditions and contexts under which these mixtures occur.
>
> (Pettigrew *et al.* 1992: 269)

These ideas have been applied more specifically to the analysis of technology-related organisational change by Dawson (1994; 1996) who adopts similar terminology to Pettigrew in distinguishing between the following as the 'determinants of change' (see Figure 4.1):

- The substance of change: the core elements of which are seen as the scale and scope of the change; the meaning and content of change itself; the time-frame of change which itself may be emergent; and the perceived centrality of the change to organisational survival.
- *The context of change*: the changing internal and external conditions which inform the organisation's historical setting, current operations and future expectations. Internal context includes contingent features such as human resource systems; the nature of the core product or service; existing technology; administrative structures; history and culture of the organisation.
- *The politics of change*: conflict and resistance, decision and non-decision making, negotiation and consultation, individual and group exertions of influence, 'power-plays', rationalisations, justifications and reconstructions of events.

Significantly Dawson notes how the substance of change is contextually specific and likely to be the subject of political activity that seeks to establish, shift or redefine aspects of its meaning as the process of change unfolds. As such, 'there is a continual interplay between these three groups of determinants during the process of organisational change' (1996: 29).

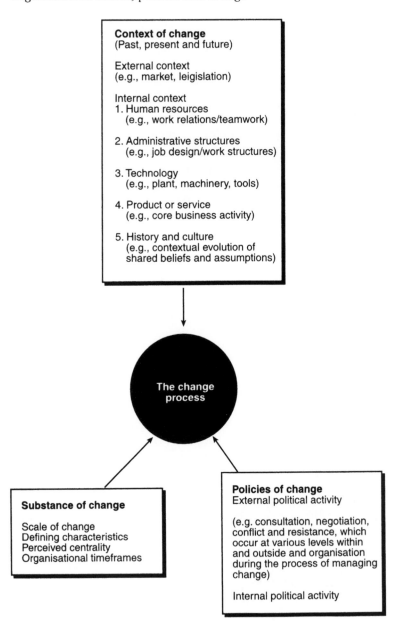

Figure 4.1: Determinants of organisational change

Change management and the micro-politics of change

The strategic choice/organisational politics approach rejects the notion implicit in contingency models that managers and other organisational actors are passive 'messengers' who react to the requirements of the economic and technological environment. Rather, it is suggested that managers are 'creative mediators' between the environment and the organisation. Their political action is a key element in the shaping of organisation, both in terms of structures and systems, and critically in terms of the cultural and meaning systems through which organisational actors make sense of their experiences.

By this token processual models of change claim a number of advantages over more conventional understandings when it comes to change management. Dawson (1994), for example, argues that the change management literature has in the past been dominated by 'one best way' organisational development models. Many of these draw on the work of Lewin (1951) who saw change as an 'event' and its management as essentially an activity of 'unfreezing' the existing attitudes and behaviour which restrain change, executing the desired change programme, and then 'refreezing' by positively reinforcing desired outcomes and encouraging the internalisation of appropriate attitudes and behaviour.

Whilst fitting quite neatly with ideas about the need for managers to adapt their organisations to prevailing commercial and technological imperatives, such prescriptions are less helpful in circumstances – such as those prevailing in network organisations under conditions of post-Fordism as discussed in the previous chapter – where market and technological change may be in perpetual transition. Here attempts to 'freeze' desired outcomes into a fixed form of organisation are rendered pointless by the very dynamics which underpin network modes of organising. Moreover, merely modifying the approach to suit different types of contingent circumstance still runs the risk of maintaining an overly rational model of change management (Dawson 1994: 13–22).

Process models aim to contextualise such concerns by seeking to reveal and explain the political nature of change and the actions of change agents, the manner in which the history of such decisions is socially constructed by the change agents who took them, and by seeking to deconstruct the 'rationalisations presented to justify them' (Dawson 1994: 25). As a result, they are capable of being used to 'formulate data generated guidelines for practitioners of organisational change' (1996: 29). A similar line is take by Pettigrew who suggests that having 'correct' policies for change is a necessary but not sufficient basis of action by managerial change agents. It is also necessary for the organisation in this broader contextual and historical sense to possess the 'capacity to change' (Pettigrew *et al.* 1992: 6). This draws attention to the way in which change agents secure through political action legitimacy for change.

The gaining of legitimacy requires intervention in the political and cultural systems of organisations in order to engage in the 'management of meaning':

> The management of meaning refers to a process of symbol construction and value-use designed to create legitimacy for one's own ideas, actions and demands and to delegitimate the demands of one's opponents. If one sees major change processes at least partially as a contest about ideas and rationalities between individuals and groups, then the mechanisms used to legitimate and delegitimate particular ideas or broader ideologies are crucial. Equally, the resolution of such contests about ideas needs to be sensitive to questions of power and control in organisations.
>
> (Pettigrew *et al.* 1992: 9)

According to Pettigrew effective engagement in political and cultural systems requires mobilising aspects of the internal (e.g. possibilities for exploiting new technologies in product or process innovation) and external context (e.g. an understanding of the implications of changing product market or technological conditions) of an organisation in order to create legitimacy for change. Moreover, these engagements are by definition interpretative processes whereby change agents and other actors construct their own versions of internal and external contexts (Pettigrew *et al.* 1992: 9).

Faced with this model, what are the features of organisations which enable them to manage change effectively? According to Pettigrew and Whip (1991) the following characteristics appear important:

- engagement in *environmental assessment* in a way that allows strategy to emerge from 'the way in which the organisation, at various levels, acquired, interpreted and processed information about its environment',
- leading change by creating a 'climate for change' which, rather than being the result of the action of one 'change champion', involves a broad range of actors at different levels engaged in fragmentary and incremental tasks and activities sensitive to the context of the organisation,
- a capacity to manage change *coherently* requiring 'coherence of purpose and belief amongst the senior management team' and 'an ability to manage a series of interrelated and emergent changes' which often take place in parallel (Pettigrew *et al.* 1992: 20).

However in the face of such claims Buchanan (1994) argues that, whilst process models may improve our understanding of organisational change, they still remain weak when it comes to informing its management. The very complexity of process models, it seems, mitigates against the detailed prescriptions which might improve managerial or other agents' capacity to intervene in shaping its outcomes (Buchanan 1994). Even where these are attempted, as for example by Dawson (1994: 172–80), they can appear remarkably similar to the 'listology' (Buchanan and Storey 1997) and 'mechanical manipulation' (Walsham 1993) of which the proponents of the strategic choice/organisational politics approach criticise contingency and other less theoretically well informed approaches .

Buchanan and Boddy (1992) have sought to begin to address this problem by identifying the expertise required by change agents in intervening and seeking to shape the outcomes of technology-related and other organisational change. They refer to the content, control and process agendas of change which refer respectively to technical or socio-technical issues, project management issues, and the human, political and cultural issues. The precise ordering of the agenda for change agents varies according to whether a programme is central or peripheral to the core task of an organisation, and whether the change is perceived in terms of its scale and pace as radical or incremental. The contention is that the more a change affects the core task and is perceived as radical the more vulnerable both it, and the change agent, are to problems during implementation and the possibility of failure or outcomes which fall far short of planned objectives. The source of such problems is likely to be related to organisational politics rather than technical or project management problems.

All this has implications for the skills and expertise of change agents since high vulnerability implies a set of skills capable of dealing first and foremost with the process agenda of change whilst also being able to attend to matters of project management and the technical/socio-technical content of change. Buchanan and Boddy suggest change agents in these circumstances need to develop a broader repertoire or 'extended tool kit' of capabilities:

> the change agent has to support the 'public performance' of rationally considered and logically phased and visibly participative change with 'backstage activity' in the recruitment and maintenance of support and in seeking and blocking resistance....'Backstaging' is concerned with the exercise of 'power skills', with 'intervening in political and cultural systems'...with influencing, negotiating and selling, and with 'managing meaning'. This is achieved in a *creative way*, through appropriate symbolic actions in attempts to legitimise change by suggesting different and new interpretations of events inside and outside the organisation.
>
> (Buchanan and Boddy 1992: 27)

In a subsequent development of these ideas it is suggested that the implications of this viewpoint need to be developed to provide a more adequate model of 'agency' in organisational change. This requires a shift of focus from a single change agent to one that involves a plurality of change agents; a recognition that change agents take and switch roles in a 'creative manner' to progress change; and an exploration of the political processes through which these roles are mobilised, advantage gained, and coalitions and alliances formed (Buchanan and Storey 1997: 129). In this sense, evoking a musical metaphor, change agency can be understood as the 'orchestration or interplay between' different actors. Change is thus construed as 'a creatively orchestrated performance, rather than as a carefully planned and managed process' (Buchanan and Storey 1997: 130).

Orlikowski and Hofman (1997) follow a similar line of argument but focus more specifically on ICTs and related organisational change which frequently provide, as we noted in Chapter 2, examples of technology which are 'open-ended and customisable' during adoption and implementation. Indeed, these types of change make Lewinian stage models a particularly poor basis for guiding change agents. They evoke another musical genre, although they prefer jazz and the notion of collective improvisation around a theme, as the most appropriate metaphor. Thinking in this way, they argue, allows us more readily to recognise that the introduction of ICTs and related organisational change is not an event which, once completed will return the organisation to an already known state. Rather, the full extent and likely outcomes of technological and organisational change of this type cannot be *anticipated* a priori.

In fact, three types of change are likely to occur:

- anticipated – changes that are planned for initially and occur as intended,
- *emergent* – changes that arise 'spontaneously from local innovation' and were not planned or intended, and
- *opportunity-based* – changes which intentionally occur during change in response to problems or opportunities that arise during the process.

Rather like a jazz performance such change involves 'enacting an ongoing series of local innovations that embellish the original structure, respond to spontaneous departures and unexpected opportunities, and iterate and build on each other over time' (Orlikowski and Hofman 1997: 13). These authors conclude that improvisational change management, applied in appropriate circumstances, is likely to yield more innovative results than conventional Lewinian models. Implicit in such views is that change, in particular technologically related organisational change, is increasingly highlighting the political nature of such processes. This is a theme we will return to in our concluding chapter.

The independent influence of technology

The strategic choice/organisational politics perspective suggests strongly that the resultant form of technology and work organisation should be viewed, not primarily as a reflection of the technical capabilities and characteristics of technology but, 'as an outcome which has been chosen and negotiated' within adopting organisations (Wilkinson 1983: 20). As a result, as we have seen, the search for an explanation of the effects of technological change moves rapidly from the nature of the technology to an attempt to understand the full content, context and process of change and the manner in which these are shaped by intra-organisational political processes. Indeed, in the light of this, it has been suggested that, 'to consider the impact of a particular technology is to consider the wrong question, or at best to consider only part of the issue' (Huczynski and Buchanan 1991: 276).

A rejection of the argument that the characteristics and capabilities of the technology determine organisational outcomes – or at least are the 'most significant contingency' shaping such changes – still leaves the puzzle of what role, if any, technology has to play. This issue was initially not given any serious analytical consideration by studies of technological change influenced by the strategic choice perspective. However, a close reading of research findings of many of these studies, even though rejecting technological determinism, seems nonetheless to point empirically to technology having an influence. For example, in his classic study of British and French oil refineries, Duncan Gallie (1978) argued that the forms of work organisation in the four settings that he studied reflected features of the cultural and institutional framework of the two societies rather than, as Woodward might have argued (see Chapter 1) the technical capacities of continuous process production technology. Having said this, he also referred to particular observed influences that the technology *did have* at workplace level, such as being 'more conducive' to the adoption of semi-autonomous team working (Gallie 1978: 221).

Clark *et al.* (1988), in adopting a processual approach informed by the strategic choice perspective, questioned whether technology should be left out of the analytical equation in this way if such influences were being observed empirically at the micro-level of the workplace. Indeed, following Winner (1977), they suggested that it was a contradiction in terms to assume that technology itself was of little significance in shaping the outcomes of technological change since 'if [technology] were not determining, it would be of no use and certainly of little interest' (Winner 1977: 75). One problem with the strategic choice approach, they argued, was that in the effort to avoid the technological determinism perceived in contingency theory, it ran the risk of the technology 'baby' being jettisoned with the determinist 'bathwater'. In other words, although not the single most important determinant, Clark and colleagues (1988) put forward the proposition that technology may still have influence over organisational outcomes, in particular those closest to workplace level such as task and skill requirements, job content and work organisation. At the very least technology appeared to enable and constrain choice and negotiation in relation to these issues. The problem was to find an analytical framework which would allow a better understanding of how.

The question of what such an analytical framework might be, raises again the question of how 'technology' should be defined, how its technical influences can be identified, and in what ways these factors should be incorporated as a variable in a broader processual 'strategic choice/organisational politics' model. Clark *et al.* suggested answers to these questions as follows. First, a restrictive definition of the scope of technology was proposed which saw technology as constituted by artefacts and as technical systems (hardware and software). The term 'engineering systems' was evoked and it was suggested that these were comprised of an 'architecture' (system principles and overall system configuration) which was manifested in an implementation (physical realisation in a given technology) (Clark *et al.* 1988: 13). Second, it was suggested that the actual workplace effects of an engineering system were significantly influenced by the way a system was dimensioned or configured to suit a particular installation (e.g. in terms of physical layout of the hardware or customisation of software) and that the experience of working with the system was shaped by its 'appearance', that is its visual and audible features, ergonomics and aesthetics. Third, the role played by technology so defined could be regarded as *one* factor shaping organisational outcomes. The technical capabilities and characteristics of engineering systems were thus viewed as 'soft determinants' in that they could enable and constrain the scope for choice or room for manœuvre available to various organisational actors during the process of change.

The need for a detailed conceptualisation of the material dimensions of technology has also been highlighted by Kling (1991a). As he puts it 'convenient fictions' such as 'the computer system' mask different technical features, as well as the social organisation, of particular implementations of such systems. It is precisely these differentiations which may have enabling and constraining effects on important social variables such as skill levels and the possibilities for work redesign (1991a: 356). Orlikowski (1992) has also attempted to rehabilitate technology as an explanatory variable but at the same time confront the distinction between the two approaches to technology outlined in the Introduction (between those which see technology as in some way having a distinct material existence in parallel with human and social systems, and those which see technology mainly, if not entirely, as a social construct). Orlikowski's suggestion, drawing on Gidden's 'structuration theory' (1979, 1984), is that such a dichotomy is inappropriate. Rather, technology can be seen as both a material entity and a social construct. Since we have yet to consider the idea of the social construction of technology in detail we will return to this particular line of argument later.

Assessment: process, politics, power and technology

The strategic choice/organisational politics perspective seems to provide, as it claims, an essential corrective to technological and socio-economic determinism. In particular, the 'political metaphor' opens the 'black box' of organisation in a way that 'machine', 'organismic', 'information system' and 'evolutionary' ways of thinking about the technology–organisational relationship do not do. In particular it exposes change as being far from a rational and linear event and seeks rather to capture it as 'non-linear, spiralling process of technological development' (Dawson 1996: 53). The perspective therefore exposes the dynamic and unfolding processes that occur within organisations at the micro-level which critically shape outcomes in particular circumstances. It also highlights the role of power in enabling dominant groups to be the principal authors of these outcomes but, at the same time shows how, within organisations' political and cultural systems, other stakeholder groups can advance and protect their interests in relation to change. Although not outlined above, this approach is also particularly sensitive to cross-national variations in the way institutional frameworks and historically embedded norms, values and beliefs at the societal level provide the basis for shared-interpretative frames at the organisational level (see e.g. Lane 1989).

Work within this perspective has also drawn attention to sector specific influences which also have a similar patterning effect on the nature of strategic choice and its outcomes by showing, for example, how the mind sets of dominant coalitions might be shared and reinforced by those of actors of other organisations in the sector as the result of a process of historical institutionalisation (Child and Smith 1987). Finally, in one of its most recent applications, the approach has drawn attention to the complexity of inter-linkages between strategic choices in relation to product innovation, process innovation, managerial organisation and the organisation of work, in a way which suggests strongly that post-Fordist models of new production paradigms make erroneous assumptions about the causal consequences of changes in product and technological environments (Hill *et al.* 1997).

The strategic choice/organisational politics approach also promises, although has yet to adequately deliver (although see Buchanan and Badham 1999), the possibility of providing more effective analytical and practical guidance to change agents, be they practising managers and other organisational actors, or external parties seeking to intervene within organisations. We shall argue later that this is a key aspect of creative technological change and that the kinds of models which currently seek to guide change agents are seriously deficient in the guidance they provide.

This is particularly the case for a growing category of innovation involving ICTs and related organisational change which – when conceived as a form of socio-technical change – takes on a peculiar 'vulnerability' in its confrontation with the divergent stakeholder interests and multiple perspectives of organisational sub-groups that mediate the relationship between technology and organisation. In short, this approach is not only a way of showing that different organisational outcomes are possible, it potentially provides a basis for guidance on how to actively engage in the shaping and reshaping process through interventions in political and cultural systems, in order to mobilise support for, and legitimate, alternative organisational outcomes and methods for their implementation. This is requirement which may well be heightened by organisational attempts to shift from Fordist to post-Fordist production concepts (see Chapter 8).

Against such insights, however, can be put a number of criticisms. First, one consequence of conceptualising change as a process in this way is that it makes little sense to seek to find or predict uniform effects or outcomes a priori of an analysis of change processes. Moreover, there is doubt as to whether it is useful to see such intra-organisational political and cultural processes as critical mediating factors in the face of the generalised structural tendencies and globalised trends presented in generic models such as 'flexible specialisation' and 'lean production'. The price, as critics have not been slow to argue, is that a preoccupation with process can unhealthily separate technical-organisational change issues from the broader 'structural' contexts which give rise to them in the first place and ultimately limit the range of possible outcomes. The consequence is that the organisational outcomes of technological change tend only to be explained in terms of highly localised and 'idiosyncratic' factors where the 'subjectivity' of organisational actors seems to dominate (Reed 1985; Whittington 1988; Elger 1990; Donaldson 1996).

On this reading the notion of environmental determinism – of long term historical trends, patterns or trajectories, in shaping the relationship between technology and organisation – appears to be anathema to the strategic choice/organisational politics approach. For critics, the apparent eschewal of contingent circumstance appears to suggest that technological innovation and its strategic management is purely a product of 'political infighting' amongst factional groups (Pavitt 1990) whilst, from another viewpoint, an unwillingness to accept at least some notion of a predetermined historical trajectory appears to be an 'empiricist sell out'. However, this is not a necessary outcome, and the view that it is lies in the misleading interpretation of the strategic choice/organisational politics perspective as a 'voluntaristic' one. As we noted above, the strategic choice approach does not view agency as capable in any circumstances of acting independent of other interpretation context or of environment. This is a point we will return to in our concluding chapter; suffice it to say that Child's recent reassessment points to ways in which a recognition of the mutual interaction between choice and constraint in the strategic choice concept, suggests strong resonance with evolutionary models of technological development.

Second, the concept of power deployed in the strategic choice/organisational politics model is, perhaps surprisingly given its insistence on it being central to understanding organisation and organisational change, rarely articulated or discussed at length. In fact the strategic choice/politics perspective tends to see power in terms of the 'face one' and 'face two' as defined by Lukes (1974). That is, the exercise of power through observable behaviour where by virtue of the formal organisational authority invested in them, A is able to engage in actions which force B to do something they would otherwise not do, and B's compliance is based on a recognition of the legitimacy of the power being exercise by A ('face one'); and 'face two' where powerful groups are able, through informal non-observable behaviour (e.g. 'behind the scenes networking and alliance building to win support and fix debates and decisions), to prevent some options or choices from getting into the decision-making process (i.e. through agenda setting). Notions such as change agency as the 'management of meaning' also allude to elements of the 'third face' identified by Lukes. That is, the exercise of power through ideological or symbolic means where the material position of powerful groups is legitimated and enforced by ideologies which uphold their position as decision-makers and prevent those under power from realising their real opposed interests to this situation. An appropriate extension (and probably improvement, see Clegg 1989) of this particular concept of power is to see powerful groups as seeking to define organisational 'reality' for their subordinates by drawing upon language, symbols and ideological resources in order resolve or even induce conflict. Seen in this way, the 'management of meaning' becomes a key device for legitimating the use of power (Pettigrew 1977).

However, critics of this view have suggested that perspective on organisations is hampered by taking as its basis such conceptions of the nature of power in organisations. In particular, each of the 'three faces' views power as 'something which is possessed' by some groups/individuals and not others. In addition 'politics' tends to be viewed as temporary and 'deviant activity which disrupts organisational operations' and the otherwise rational pursuance of organisational goals and objectives (note e.g. Buchanan and Boddy's distinction between apolitical 'public performance' and the highly politicised character of 'backstaging') (e.g. Knights and Murray 1994; Koch 1997b).

Knights and Murray (1994) draw upon an alternative perspective – inspired in large part by Michel Foucault – and view power as a relational concept. That is, rather than being possessed by actors it emerges out of relationships and interactions engaged in by actors (Clegg 1989: 207). Thus, the fact that A, or B, possess, or do not possess, power is not a fixed characteristic of them as agents (e.g. managers or employees) but rather a specific consequence of how the players have 'positioned and fixed' themselves through particular interactions between them, the rules that govern such interactions and the nature of the 'game' that the interactions constitute (Clegg 1989: 208–9). As such 'politics' lies at the core of all organisational relationships and is not just an episodic feature manifested when power is observed to be used by one party over another in some way.

In construing power in these terms Knights and Murray, rather ironically given the focus of their concern with the organisational politics of information technology, evoke the metaphor of a rather aged electromechanical gaming device – the pinball machine. Their suggestion is that organisations are rather like these machines where 'political process stands in the middle' and is 'bombarded by the steel balls that are energised in different parts of the organisation'. This bombardment creates a dynamic whereby 'the motor of political process' shoots the balls back against 'other conditions of the organisation, such as those of subjectivity, structure, socio-political and economic context and technology possibilities'.

> At the centre of this process is a knot of individuals scrambling to achieve a degree of emotional, symbolic and material security. The heavy metal balls of the organisation crash and wallop into them, reconstructing their sense of themselves and the reality around them thus, transforming subjectivities, identities and power relations as they go.
>
> (Knights and Murray 1994: 49)

In a study of the introduction of information systems in a variety of organisational settings, Knights and Murray suggest that the political process can also be seen as a strange kind of dance where developers and users of systems 'constantly re-position themselves as they change their interpretations of the project and its chances of success' motivated by self-interested, masculine, careerist concerns and a desire to be a 'proud parent' of a system's success and 'miles away' from anything that looks like being defined as 'failure' (Knights and Murray 1994: 247). As such the development of information systems is a political process in the sense that 'the meaning of particular technological opportunities or developments' is established in such a way as to 'become an undeniable reality, the social construction of which is lost or forgotten' (Knights and Murray 1994: 250).

These ideas draw strongly on, although having clear points of difference with, actor-network theories and other elements of social constructivism which we consider in Chapters 5 and 6. One of the insights that Knights and Murray seek to exploit is that by construing power in relational terms, not only the organisational outcomes of change, but the interpretative representation of technology itself can be seen as a product of the political machinations that characterise organisational life. However, doubts have been expressed over the accuracy of Knights and Murray's characterisation of the role of power in the strategic choice perspective as some kind of peripheral and unwanted engagement. Neither is it the case that the novelty of their approach comes from the focus on the politics of techno-logical change *per se*, which is hardly uncharted water (Dawson 1996: 52–3). Nevertheless, what is of interest is the notion that the technology–organisation relationship is a continuously changing whole – rather than organisational outcomes alone, are all seen as the upshot of some kind of political process. This is an idea which we shall explore further in subsequent chapters.

This leads us to the final point of criticism, the question of technology itself. As we have noted 'technology' does appear to slip from the analytical gaze of the strategic choice/organisational politics perspective. In most instances it appears marginalised as one of a complex range of contextual referents or is submerged, even sunk without trace, in a gumbo soup of the 'substance of change'. We shall argue in the concluding chapter that this is not a necessary consequence of adopting a strategic choice/organisational politics perspective. However, for the moment we must note that the efforts such as those of Clark *et al.* to attempt some kind of analytical rescue in the name of 'saving the baby' from the 'determinist bathwater' remain one of the only attempts to seriously address this issue to date. However, critics have suggested that any such attempt ends up 'falling back into the deter-minist bathwater' where technology itself is given fixed, independent, characteristics and capabilities, *even if* their effects are seen as realised in organisations as a consequence of social choice (Parayil 1990).

In other words, the problem with the 'soft determinist' position is that it appears to fail to realise that technological capabilities and characteristics, not just their organisational effects, are socially shaped. One retort might be that whilst this is the case during design (which is often temporally and physically remote from most adoption contexts), and even post-adoption during the implementation, there comes a point when what a technology is and what it can do become more or less fixed. At this point one can talk, in a strictly limited sense, of 'impacts', 'enabling and constraining' effects and, as we saw in the previous chapter, of the potential for ICTs – because of their informing as well as automating capabilities – to enable a transfor-mation of organisations along 'post-Fordist' lines. However even this position, it has been argued, retains a strong flavour of technological deter-minism because it implies that such 'effects' are 'transparent' features of the technology and therefore independent of the mediation of human interpre-tation. The point is that 'what is technical' is in fact always and continuously 'a social construct' (Grint and Woolgar 1997: 129).

Conclusion

In this chapter we have considered ways in which the interaction between technology and organisation can be understood in terms of political and cultural metaphors. The strategic choice/organisation politics approach seeks to explain the organisational outcomes of technological change as a product of intra-organisational processes of choice and negotiation. Outcomes therefore reflect the capacity of power-holding groups to persuade, negotiate or impose their particular interpretations and desired solutions on other stakeholder groups within the organisation. Their capacity to do this is not a statement of the primacy of agency over structure but rather of the mutual interdependence between the action of organisational members and the contextual constraints within which they operate. Originally, this approach was developed as a corrective to determinism in organisational analysis, hence its attractiveness to those seeking to counter technologically determinist accounts of the relations between technology and organisation. John Child has recently observed that the strategic choice concept is more likely some twenty-five years later to be useful as a corrective to approaches which 'would deconstruct organisational life down to the untrammelled actions of sense-making individuals' (1997: 72). To see how this new corrective orientation might be deployed in the analysis of technology and organisation we first need to concern ourselves with perspectives which have sought to show how technology is socially shaped, indeed, even socially constructed entirely by the interpretative schemes of organisational and other actors.

Notes

1 The strategic choice/organisational politics perspective, or something like it, has also influenced research outside of the UK. For example, in the USA see Kling's resume and reflections on several of his own research studies over a twenty year period on the implementation of ICTs, which stress the politics of the 'consumption' as the principal factor shaping the degree to which organisational transformation follows from the adoption of these technologies (Kling 1991a). Similarly, Useem and Kochan (1992) drawing on a wide range of research studies from the USA and beyond stress the political dimension as one of the key pathways of contemporary technology-related organisational transformation. In Denmark and Germany the concept of the 'company specific social constitution' (Hildebrandt and Seltz 1989) has been used to explore both the influence of internal organisational politics on shaping organisational outcomes (Clausen 1997) but also the broader context of the politics of relationships with the suppliers, developers, consultants and other actors involved in the introduction of new technologies and systems into adopting organisations (see e.g. Koch 1997a, 1997b). Finally, in Australia the processual perspective has been used to analyse workplace reform (Dawson 1994; Badham 1995).

5 Inside the black box:

Social constructivism and technology

Introduction

In the previous two chapters we have seen how a range of theorists have been critical of the view that technology is 'neutral' in character, follows 'natural' trajectories and has inevitable determining 'impacts' or 'effects' on organisations. The criticism of 'technological determinism' has also been pursued by a broad school of thought which has been concerned to show how technology is 'socially shaped'. In this and the following chapter we will focus mainly on such approaches which start from technology and 'work outwards' to show the *social content* of a particular technological development. Chapter 7 will consider approaches which, in contrast, start from social context and 'work inwards' to show how this *shapes* technology and the direction of technological development (Edge 1995: 16).

The 'work outwards' approaches adopt a 'social constructivist' position in relation to the definition of technology. That is, as we noted in the Introduction, what technology is and what it can do are seen entirely as a product of human interpretation. In this sense technology is viewed as a 'cultural' product. In order to understand 'technology' we have to 'open the black box' and 'get inside' to follow actors as they engage in the making of 'technology' (Latour 1987: 13). The social constructivist perspective is meant, therefore, as a strong antidote to technological determinism, one that is claimed to be a far more effective analytical 'cure all' than has been applied by the perspectives considered in earlier chapters. However, as we will see in this and the following chapter, the effectiveness of constructivism in ridding analysis of technology of determinist tendencies is a matter of considerable internal debate amongst the various strands which constitute this approach. Some constructivist 'cure-alls', it turns out, claim greater efficacy than others.

The social construction of science and technology

The origins of the constructivist approach to technology lie significantly, although not exclusively, in developments in the 1970s and 1980s in the sociology of scientific knowledge (SSK). These developments sought to move beyond previous empirical approaches to the study of science, which focused on institutional arrangements and the norms, careers and rewards of professional scientists (see e.g. Cotgrove and Box 1970), to focus on scientific knowledge itself (Pinch and Bijker 1987: 18). A particular objective here was to show how such knowledge, rather than being a superior version of 'truth' and a better 'way of knowing', was in fact, in epistemological terms, no different to other knowledge systems. In other words it could be understood and explained as a social construct, 'that is, explanations for the genesis, acceptance, and rejection of knowledge claims are sought in the domain of the social world rather than the natural world' (Pinch and Bijker 1987: 18).

This approach was referred to by its proponents as the 'strong programme' in that it took as its starting point the view that the investigator or analyst should adopt an impartial position with regard to the truth or falsity of the beliefs embodied in any knowledge system. In other words such beliefs should be 'explained symmetrically' (Pinch and Bijker 1987, citing Bloor 1973). Studies that adopted this approach typically involved detailed 'anthropological' and ethnographic research of scientific activity. This revealed how the process of scientific development could be seen as comprising key points at which ambiguities are present in the development of a scientific knowledge base – for example, when a controversy exists between competing theories seeking to explain an empirically observed phenomenon (see e.g. Collins and Pinch 1982). The resolution of these ambiguities has a significant impact on the future development of the area of scientific knowledge concerned and much broader implications in terms of the understanding of science by decision-makers and the public at large (Collins and Pinch 1995). Explaining why one interpretation wins out over others through the establishing of its plausibility by its proponents within the scientific community, and ultimately beyond it, is a key objective of SSK.

Since the early 1980s attention has been turned by some of the SSK community to the social construction of technological knowledge embodied in individual artefacts and systems (Edge 1995). The defining characteristics of this 'turn to technology' (Woolgar 1991a) have been described by three of its principal early exponents as a:

- move from considering the individual inventor as the key explanatory concept in technological innovation
- rejection of 'technological determinism' (in particular linear/rationalistic models of the process of technological development), and
- regarding the social and the technical as a 'seamless web' where no clear distinctions between the technical, social, economic and political elements of technological development are made (Bijker *et al.* 1987: 3).

For the social constructivist, the idea that it is the essential capacity 'within' a technology which, in the end, accounts for the way we organise ourselves, our work and other life experiences is the defining characteristic of technological determinist thought (Grint and Woolgar 1997: 2). In contrast, from the constructivist or 'anti-essentialist' position the capacities embodied in technological artefacts are seen as the product of social antecedents involved in their production. As such, technology can be regarded as 'congealed social relations' or 'society made durable' (Latour: 1991). It follows that, seen as a social and cultural product, technology and technical systems are open to social analysis, 'not just in their usage but especially with respect to their design and "technical" content' (Bijker *et al.* 1987: 4).

The key questions from a social constructivist position therefore are not to do with the social effects (for example on work or organisation) of the 'machine-like' characteristics and capabilities of a particular technology, technological paradigm or trajectory of technological development. Rather the burden of explanation shifts to questions such as: 'how do technologies "firm up", "congeal" and become "durable entities"?'; 'why is it that they take the form they do, rather than some other configuration?'; 'how do these processes develop and become resolved?' (Bijker and Law 1992: 8).

What marks constructivist approaches out from those considered so far, therefore, is their recasting of the relationship between technology and the social 'as a network rather than as parallel but separate systems' (Grint and Woolgar 1997: 10) or as Bijker and Law put it, 'technologies are not purely technological...they are heterogeneous' and as such, 'embody trade-offs and compromises' in the form of 'social, political, psychological, economic, and professional commitments, skills, prejudices, possibilities, and constraints' (Bijker and Law 1992: 10). Where and when the line between the technical and the social is drawn, therefore, is contingent.

The two principal approaches normally identified in the literature as constituting the main examples of this 'turn to technology' within SSK are: the social construction of technology or 'SCOT' approach and actor-network theory (ANT). These will now be considered in turn.[1]

The social construction of technology

Pinch and Bijker (1987, also Bijker 1995a, 1995b) have applied the principles of SSK to the development of what they term the social construction of technology (SCOT) approach. In this they argue that technological development is not a linear process with only one possible outcome but rather a 'closure' process during which the form of an artefact or system becomes 'stabilised' as consensus emerges among key social groups with a stake in the design. As such the development of technology can be regarded a multidirectional process where a range of alternative design options exist and are gradually eliminated as a consensus is established by relevant social groups over what the 'technology' is, what it can and cannot do and so forth. It is only through 'retrospective distortion that a quasi-linear development emerges' (Pinch and Bijker 1987: 28).

The analytical starting point for SCOT is the concept of *interpretative flexibility* carried over from SSK. Just as different truth claims in science exist during scientific development, differing perspectives on what a technology is and can and cannot do also exist during the process of technological development. Thus, 'relevant social groups' will articulate different definitions, identifications, etc. of a technology, their meanings in effect giving rise to quite different artefacts or systems in the sense that there is no 'one best way' to design an artefact (Pinch and Bijker 1987: 40). Further, just as in SSK, different definitions of technology, what constitutes a successful or unsuccessful design and so on, have to be treated by the analyst symmetrically. That is, competing claims by relevant social groups regarding a technology are to be regarded as equally valid. The final form of a technology does not, therefore, reflect its technical superiority, but rather the social processes which establish consensus around the belief that it *is* superior. Or to put it another way, that a technology 'works' is the result of the establishment of consensus on what a properly 'working' technology is rather than a reflection of any inherent technical characteristics or capabilities of the final artefact or system.

Relevant social groups are comprised of those who share a particular set of understandings and meanings concerning the development of a given technology. These groups may include designers, employers, consumers, protesters and so on. Each group will be identifiable through the different views they have with regard to the most appropriate design of the artefact, or even whether it is a desirable technology at all. They will thus each perceive different problems and potential solutions to them.

The different goals, values and tools for action that groups possess are derived from their *technological frame*. That is, their shared assumptions, knowledge and expectations or underlying belief systems in relation to the technology. These enable 'thinking and action' but at the same time, by setting certain parameters as to what constitutes a design problem and an acceptable solution to it, also constrains action (Bijker 1995a: 190). As the frame develops such constraints become more pronounced. Thus, at the start of a process of technological development a variety of technical, social, legal and moral solutions are likely to be articulated as possible ways of resolving a range of perceived problems. This in turn gives rise to a range of views as to the most appropriate design of a technology. The thought and action of relevant social groups is thus more enabled than constrained by the emergent technological frame (ibid. 1995a: 192–3). However, over time more powerful and dominant social groups, or the more powerful members of particular groups, will be able to establish the legitimacy of their interpretations as to the most appropriate way to construct problems and derive solutions which inform the design of the artefact. Hence, as a technological frame becomes established it acts more to constrain thinking and action.

One question that arises from the SCOT perspective is how the relevant social groups can be identified. The answer to this highlights a key point, which is that 'relevance' is not something that can be imputed by the analyst on the basis of some perceived a priori interests ascribed in theoretical terms to social groups. For example the view of some radical theorists (see Chapter 3) that employers will be interested in the development of a technology because of their need to pursue profits and exploit workers, or that employees will resist innovation in defence of the common class interests, is roundly rejected. Rather, consistent with the principle of symmetry in any process of innovation, relevant groups are identified by the empirical device of asking the actors themselves, although in the first instance such groups might be sketched intuitively by the analyst. This method of 'following the actors' allows a picture of which groups are relevant in the eyes of those actually involved in the innovation process to be gradually built empirically in 'snowball' fashion. This picture can be supplemented by 'historical snowballing', that is, by examining the role of groups over time, through for instance documentary sources. This is not to say that what is 'relevant' is entirely defined by the actors themselves. Rather, as this process develops the analyst will order and refine groupings in a manner that gives analytical and explanatory purchase.

Once relevant social groups have been identified and the interpretative flexibility of a technology demonstrated, the next analytical task for the SCOT approach is to demonstrate how closure occurs. This can take place in two ways (Pinch and Bijker 1987: 44–5). First, through 'rhetorical closure' where competing designs are eliminated because one is seen by a relevant social group as a better solution to their perceived problem (for example consensus may be reached through acceptance by social groups of an argument concerning the superiority of a particular design). Second, through 'problem redefinition' where the utility of a design is demonstrated by redefining the problem itself (for example a design which is presented as a solution to one problem without a consensus emerging may be stabilised by the device of simply presenting it as a solution to another problem which generates acceptance amongst a broader constituency of social groups).

In sum, SCOT seeks to open the 'black box' of technology by showing how technological artefacts can be viewed as both culturally constructed and interpreted, not just in terms of how they are viewed by different groups, but more fundamentally in terms of the actual design of technology and technological systems. This is accomplished by revealing how 'technical decisions' are a matter of meaning, established throughout a social process of interpretation and negotiation (Pinch and Bijker 1987: 40).

Actor-network theory

Actor-network theory has its origins in the work of Michel Callon, Bruno Latour and John Law. It takes as its starting point the argument that the relationship between the technological and the social cannot be understood by reductionist arguments which view either the technological or the social as ultimately determining. Whether it is the technological, social factors or other material or natural factors which determine the relationship between the technical is a complex empirical question the answer to which will vary from context to context. No definitive line can therefore be drawn between that which is 'technological' and that which is 'social'.

In common with other constructivist approaches, therefore, ANT is concerned with the heterogeneous nature of the socio-technical world and in particular the manner in which new socio-technical configurations come to be built or assembled and, in some instances, disassembled. However, unlike other constructivist approaches it asks us to make the challenging counter-intuitive assumption that 'technology' and other material as well as natural phenomena, are capable of intentional action in the same way as human agents. The key to our understanding is thus, not just the role played by human actors, but also non-human actors as they create complex heterogeneous webs of juxtaposed technical, social and natural elements. The method here is similar then to SSK and SCOT in that what is proposed is a detailed anthropological and ethnographic approach to the empirical study of scientists, engineers and other 'actants' as they engage in the building of the 'actor-networks' which constitute the 'black box' of 'technology' (see Latour 1987).

For actor-network theory, innovation is understood as a process of changing networks of social and technical relations – identities, expectations, beliefs, values, machines, material resources, etc. In this perspective technology is a form of congealed social relations which 'just happens to take a material form' (Woolgar 1997). The formation of new socio-technical relationships involves the alignment of an initially diverse set of actors and interests into new relationships and networks. This process can be understood in terms of the following steps or elements the outcome of which comprises a stabilised set of relationships between both human (organisational, economic, political, legal, etc.) and non-human (technical, material, natural, etc.) elements.

- Translation: actor-networks are the consequence of an alignment of otherwise diverse interests. Alignment is dependent upon the enrolment of different actors into the network. This is accomplished through a process of translation where the interests of actors change to accord with those prescribed by key actors (individuals, groups, organisations, technology) that are seeking to bring about innovation.

- *Problematisation*: these key actors seek to construct scenarios which demonstrate to potential members of the network that their interests – for example the way they construct problems and define their solution – are best served by enrolment into the network.
- *Displacements*: once actors have been enrolled through the problematisation process a range of entities are mobilised to ensure stabilisation of the network.

Stabilisation is threatened by:

- *Juxtaposition*: actors are members of juxtaposed actor networks and membership of other networks may be a stronger influence in the definition interests and perceived 'problems' and 'solutions'.
- *Simplification*: enrolment in a network is thus dependent upon an actor's willingness to accept the simplification of their interests in the process of enrolment to new networks.

The activities of network builders or 'heterogeneous engineers' reflects the all pervasive nature of power. This is defined, not only in terms of the capacities of actors to exert power over other actors given the resources that they possess (see Chapter 4), but also in terms of the way power is constituted and reconstituted in the manner understood by Machiavelli. That is, through conscious strategies and the unintended consequences of alliance building, enrolment and re-enrolment of support engaged in by 'Princes' (see Clegg 1989: 202–7, for discussion). Production of the 'machine' therefore, in Latour's phrase, is a process defined by and inscribed with the 'machinations' of human and non-human actors (Latour 1987).

The role of 'machinations' is given particular emphasis by Latour (1987: 108–32; see also Callon 1986). He suggests we view innovation as a rhetorical controversy whereby the resolution of arguments occurs when the 'claims' of a 'contender' are accepted by other actors who as a result are enrolled into the network. This might be the result of:

- a successful attempt to cater for others' interests in developing the innovation (e.g. the need of a finance house to make a profit);
- the convincing of others that the innovation is a means they can use to achieve ends which they could not achieve by existing means (e.g. the innovation provides a means of improving real time data for management);
- the invention of a new group that needs the innovation (e.g. an untapped market of workers who would rather telecommute than commute);
- persuading the enrolled group that their interests are driving the innovation (e.g. suggesting to the customer that their needs define the

product 'everything we do is driven by you') such that the distinction between 'enroller' and 'enrolled' is blurred; and

- making sure that accounts of successful innovation attribute that success to the contender and not the enrolled groups (e.g. Microsoft's success is due to the entrepreneurial genius of its founder rather than the fortuitous acquisitions of technologies developed by other organisations).

If successful all these translations in combination lead to the indispensability of the contender and their innovation such that, in geometric terms, 'whatever you do, and wherever you go, you *have* to pass through the contenders' position and to help them further their interests,' and in a 'linguistic' sense, 'whatever you want' means that you 'want this as well'. In a very strong sense the position of Bill Gates, his Microsoft company and the Windows operating system that it has developed would seem to present an archetypal case of such indispensability.

This highlights a key aspect of the building of an actor-network: the control of enrolled actors to ensure that their behaviour remains consistent with that required to sustain the network. Intriguingly, and unfortunately most difficult to grasp, 'keeping interested groups in line', as Latour puts it, frequently involves the enrolment into the network of a non-human element. This is needed to address weaknesses in the existing network which are a source of dissent – for example a design problem which threatens support by some actors for a project might be resolved by the adoption of a new technology, system or component. In so doing this enrols new and non-human actors into the network. Of course these non-human actors may pose new problems as they interact with other actors in the network, new components may not work well with existing ones and so on. This underlines the shifting, unpredictable nature of alliances between human and non-human actors and network builders have to decide which actors they need to keep within the network and which they can jettison in order to achieve their goals – themselves shifting as the web of alliances and enrolments of other shifting interests takes place.

The element which ultimately ties the network together and allows it to stabilise is the building of a 'machine', the product as already stated of the 'machinations' which gave rise to it, but which, on being built, assumes an autonomy closer to our common sense understanding of what an artefact is. Again, to put it simply, a 'black box' with its lid firmly closed. In this sense the machine becomes an 'obligatory passage point' which holds the human and non-human elements of a network together. If successful, the machine 'concentrates in itself the largest number of hardest associations...that is why we call such black boxes "hard facts", or "highly sophisticated machines"' (Latour 1987: 139).

Turning briefly to discussion of networks in earlier chapters, it is worth emphasising that ANT draws our attention to the manner in which networks are built or formed, rather than taking this process as 'given' as in the evolutionary approach (see Chapter 2). Thus, the manner in which common goals and agreements are established and the way competing motives and values are aligned to permit this become the focus of analysis (Coombs *et al.* 1996: 5). Similarly, the concept of actor-network is different to that in the portrayal of the virtual organisation as embodied in electronic networks (Chapter 1), or post-Fordist organisational forms constituted by non-market and non-hierarchical social and economic relationships (Chapter 3).

Having said this, its proponents argue that the ANT approach is frequently misused and misrepresented precisely because of misunderstandings over the meaning and use of the terms 'actor' and 'network'. In particular by focusing on networks as either technical or social phenomena these entities are erroneously reduced to distinctive and pre-given social and technological categories (Latour 1996; also Callon 1991).

The social construction of 'ICTs'

The constructivist perspective was initially developed through empirical studies which, although broad and diverse to say the least in their technological focus, in the main were not concerned with contemporary developments in information and computing technology. However, in recent years there have been numerous individual studies of ICTs and several major research programmes which have sought to apply and develop a constructivist perspective (see e.g. Sætnan 1991; Woolgar 1992; Bloomfield *et al.* 1992; Brigham and Corbett 1997; Orlikowski and Cash 1994). How then might this sometimes challenging approach be applied to enhance our understanding of the relationship between contemporary technological developments in ICTs and organisation? Can, for instance, allowing computers, software, optical fibres, digital switching mechanisms, cyberspace and all of the other non-human entities which are captured by the 'fiction' of the generic acronym ICT really cast new light, as proponents of ANT would claim, on the interaction of 'technology' so construed and organisation?

One immediate issue is the continuing relevance of talking of the effects of social construction of artefacts such as computer hardware and software, telecommunications systems and so on *per se*. Rather, the 'seamless web' metaphor invites us to discontinue drawing such a priori distinctions between the 'technical' and the 'social'. Bijker has recently suggested the use of the term 'socio-technical ensemble' to reflect the basic constructivist premise that 'the technical is socially constructed and the social is technically constructed' (Bijker 1995b: 273). It follows, therefore, that when we talk of 'ICTs' from a constructivist perspective we are really referring to a complex heterogeneous web or network of socio-technical relationships or as Misa puts it, 'Properly understood, "technology" is a shorthand term for the elaborate socio-technical networks that span society' (Misa 1994: 141). In short, we are no longer talking simply about technical artefacts or systems as if they were outside of or immune to the social.

With this refocusing in mind, Jackson and Van der Weilen (1998) provide one example of an attempt to provide a constructivist perspective on the evidently socio-technical phenomenon of teleworking and virtual organisation. They suggest that much literature on this topic has treated these ideas as an 'objective phenomenon' which is 'out there' in the 'real world'. At the same time, the field is hampered by problems of defining precisely what telework and virtual organisation actually are, and there's also a tendency to collapse these ideas into a purely technological representation. The lack of conceptual clarity that flows from the inevitably variable, and sometimes clearly deterministic, answers which are given to such questions means problems of gauging the extent of and predicting trends in teleworking are legion (a common observation is that there are actually more people researching this problem than there are actual teleworkers!).[2]

A constructivist position, on the other hand, points to the need to 'open the black box' of 'telework' and related ideas (Jackson and Van der Weilen 1998: 9–12). First, these concepts are at a stage in development where there is much 'interpretative flexibility' over their meaning and a range of actors (technology designers and suppliers, potential users and customers, policy-makers, managers, trade unionists, human factors engineers, economists, etc.) have begun interacting in attempting to define, conceptualise and understand the implications of these phenomena. Second, the successful development of these innovations is dependent upon 'network builders' (e.g. the suppliers of technology and associated work systems) developing images of the technology and the possibilities for organisational redesign and the transformation of work which are attractive, for instance, to key organisational decision makers. They will need to draw on rhetorical devices, such as those outlined above, that persuade such actors that the problems they have can be solved by their proposed solutions.[3] Third, if through such devices these and other actors can be enrolled into the network through a translation of their interests, then a stabilisation of the network will begin, enforced by effectively implemented and operational organisational forms which are dispersed in time and space.

What such an outcome might look like remains unknowable and whether it will be achieved is highly problematic. Failure may well arise due to an inability of system-builders to enrol key actors such as employees and their representatives who might resist the idea that working from home constitutes an improvement in their working and domestic lives. Equally, suppliers may find it difficult to develop an adequate understanding of user needs and requirements and instead fall back on 'technological fixes' to resolve problems which further exacerbate the difficulties human elements of the network might have aligning their interests with that of the technical components. ANT, argue Jackson and Van der Weilen, provides a framework within which such a complex web of relationships, interactions and agendas might be better understood. At the same time, they suggest, it points to a way in which a creative rethinking of concepts of dispersed and networked organisations might be more effectively pursued. For example, seeking new metaphors to guide the thinking and action of actors seeking to build such networks.

Brigham and Corbett use ANT to develop a similar analysis of the emergence and development of electronic mail (e-mail) in an organisational setting. Rather than frame this issue in terms of a study of the 'effects' of e-mail on organisational structures, processes or inter- and intra-communications, the adoption of an ANT perspective draws attention to the 'dynamic dimensions of organisational and individual power' through which 'attempts to constitute, renegotiate and/or extend a view about what is technological and what is social' take place (Brigham and Corbett 1997: 25). There is, in other words, little point in talking about the 'impacts' of a technology when what the technology is, what it can do, and so forth are themselves matters of social choice and negotiation. It follows, that the conclusions reached about the consequences of the use of e-mail reflect, not fixed and inherent technical features of such systems, but rather 'an emergent property of the interaction between e-mail and its organisational context' (Brigham and Corbett 1997: 26). Thus, Brigham and Corbett suggest the nature of this interaction can be understood in terms of how individual and collective actors engage in micro-political activities to 'articulate conceptions of the natural and social worlds' and then 'impose these on others', the success of which 'generates ordering effects 'such as' devices, agents and organisations' (Brigham and Corbett 1997: 27).

Thus, in their particular study the e-mail system emerged as having contradictory implications for power relations, offering a means of decentralisation on the one hand, but a means of centralisation on the other. At the same time it became an 'obligatory passage point' making the organisation 'visible' and indispensable to the actions of organisational members if they were to be effective. This required new forms of self-discipline and self-control. Organisation members had to be prepared to change their beliefs and learn new behaviours (e.g. remembering to regularly check their e-mail in case there were important messages!) and to be prepared to substitute electronic for face-to-face communication. Thus, rather than being viewed as a 'given' technology with particular effects mediated by organisational political processes (see Chapter 4), the deployment of an ANT perspective reframes e-mail as an agent of 'organisational power' able to provide a basis 'against which the behaviour of other actors is judged, ... enfram[ing] not only people's communications and perceptions, but also shap[ing] their values and conceptions of social reality' (Brigham and Corbett 1997: 33).

A preliminary assessment of constructivist approaches to technology

We will leave a full assessment of the constructivist perspective until the end of the following chapter. However, for the moment we can note a number of points of contrast and comparison with respect to the two perspectives so far considered. First, they both draw on a variety of metaphors – 'black box' 'seamless webs', 'networks' – to help us think about the way in which technology is socially constructed and that the relationship between the 'technical' and the 'social' is a contingent one. As such, the constructivist perspective can provide a means by which the multiple actors, agendas, interactions and complicated web of relationships involved in 'making technology' might be more adequately understood. In this respect SCOT and ANT share much common since they are both concerned with the way in which what we take to be 'technology' comes to be stabilised (see Westrum 1987; Law 1987: 112–13).

In Latour's terms the 'Janus-faced' nature of technology is recognised (Latour 1987: 4). That is, on the one hand, discourse around technology provides a language which describes 'ready made' and autonomous machines with definitive capabilities and characteristics inherent in the artefact or system itself and which promotes a linear view of innovation as a process where 'science invents and technology applies'. On the other there is the language, normally hidden and inaccessible to non-technologists, of 'technology in the making'. Here discourse is laced with controversy and dispute over what the machine is, what it can do, what it is for and so on which reveals a far more iterative, indeterminate and contingent relationship between science and technology which questions the possibility of any a priori distinction between the two. The final form of the artefact resolves these questions but masks the social process by which they were resolved by viewing technology 'as fixed by nature'. However, SCOT and ANT show that seeking to 'follow the actors' in the places and over the time where the construction of artefacts actually occurs, the social basis of technology can be exposed.

However, the two perspectives diverge to varying degrees on exactly how the social construction of technology can be understood and explained. For SCOT it is the networks of 'interested parties' or sponsors that are the concern and the manner in which differing meanings given to the technology in terms of the solutions it offers to the problems of the 'relevant social groups' are resolved through argument. It is this resolution which brings with it diminishing 'interpretative flexibility', 'closure' and 'stabilisation' around a 'one best' design and the embodiment of these and other enabling and constraining elements in a dominant 'technological frame'. Unlike ANT, the SCOT approach is less concerned with conflict. Instead emphasis is placed on the building of consensus between 'relevant social groups' through negotiation within networks. Finally, networks are seen as constituted by human beings in the sense that social factors are assumed to lie 'behind' and direct the development and stabilisation of technology.

In contrast, for ANT the focus is on entrepreneurial political activity in enrolling human and non-human actors into actor-networks. The key process is one of changing meaning through discourse where rhetorical devices are deployed to effect translations of interest which ultimately yield a set of meanings that we take in common sense terms as 'the machine'. The creation of meaning is not just a technical debate but a process of conflict between contending entrepreneurs where social, political and economic arguments are unavoidably bound up with the technical. ANT is thus keen to expose the political machinations that lie at the core of the formation of actor-networks. It is in this sense that network building can be understood as 'heterogeneous engineering' involving the political actions of human and non-human actants in promoting, enrolling, alliance-building, negotiating and stabilising an actor-network (Koch 1997b: 130). Finally, the actor-network concept – by focusing on actors rather than institutions and viewing technology as a social construct rather than an exogenous variable – breaths necessary life into the concept of 'networks' as deployed, for example, in the models of technological collaboration which have been an increasing focus of attention of the evolutionary perspective (see Chapter 2).

Networks, for ANT as we have already noted, are not then to be seen as exclusively social phenomena, or for that matter as exclusively technical (Latour 1996). It follows that whether social factors exercise the key influence over the formation of a network is contingent and can only be established by empirical means. Thus:

> Other factors – natural, economic, or technical – may be more obdurate than the social and may resist the best efforts of the system builder to reshape them. Other factors may, therefore, explain better the shape of artefacts in question and, indeed, the social structure that results...*the stability and form of artefacts should be seen as a function of the interaction of heterogeneous elements as these are shaped and assimilated into a network.*
>
> (Law 1987: 113, original emphasis)

Hence, ANT sees networks as being built through a struggle with hostile or indifferent elements which encompass social, economic, technological and natural elements. The resultant associations, though relatively stable and durable, can be dissociated by superior forces, for example natural phenomena.[4]

What is in fact being proposed here is an extension of the principle of symmetry outlined above as one of the key elements of the 'strong programme' of SSK. In the SCOT approach this principle is operated by suggesting that natural forces or technological objects always have the status of an *explanandum* – what is to be explained – and that the social *explanans* (how things are explained) that are offered should each be treated with equal validity by the analyst in empirical enquiry. The central issue, to state it once more, is not to arbitrate between competing accounts of what a technology can and cannot do, but rather to understand and explain how these social constructions are articulated and how one accounts over time, 'wins out' over others in order to allow an artefact or system to stabilise through the closure of debate. However, ANT proposes a principal of 'generalised symmetry where technology and other non-human elements of networks are in principle treated as *explanans* as well as *explanandums*' and 'have a voice of their own in the explanation' such that 'the same type of analysis' is made 'for all components in a system whether these components are human or not' (Law 1987: 132). Having said this, there are signs of significant convergence between SCOT and ANT in some key respects. Bijker for example, has recently outlined an approach which accepts the principal of generalised symmetry; refers to the stabilised entities which result from closure as 'socio-technical ensembles' rather than purely technical artefacts or systems; and emphasises the importance of enrolment and 'power games' as a means of including actors within a 'technological frame' and bringing about stabilisation (Bijker 1995b: 273–6).

At this point we need to note a major criticism of both SCOT and ANT from within the constructivist perspective. Both approaches make use of the 'black box' metaphor. Whilst the notion that the 'box' can be opened and what is inside subject to social analysis is a useful antidote to the tendency to take technology as a 'given' in the approaches considered in earlier chapters, it also carries with it other connotations which some critics within the constructivist perspective see as far less helpful. For example, Grint and Woolgar (1997) admit that notions of 'closure', 'network-building' and 'translation of interests' associated with the metaphor are fruitful ways of showing that there is 'no one best way' to design a technological artefact or system, 'let alone a way determined by the technology itself'. However they also convey the idea that once 'technology is designed, its capacities and effects become embedded in material form' – a black box . The point is that once constituted the technological black box appears *then* to be capable of having 'effects' insofar as it 'offers considerably more resistance to human attempts to use it for purposes other than those prefigured by the designer' (Grint and Woolgar 1997: 20).

[A]s we have asserted, there is the implication that at the close of an (often protracted) contingent process of 'negotiations', the artefact stabilises: at this point, the technology becomes what it is generally accepted to be. The difficulty is that constructivism is thereby made to seem only (or most) applicable to those periods of time when there is overt disagreement between (or uncertainty on the part of) significant actors.

(Grint and Woolgar 1997: 20)

It is thus the argument of these critics that a more 'thoroughgoing' application of constructivism is needed. This they suggest would take the view that neither attitudes towards, nor control structures over, nor the form, effects or use of technologies are determined: they are all elements in a negotiated order (Grint and Woolgar 1997: 20). In the next chapter we shall, amongst other things, see where this constructivist critique of constructivism takes us.

Conclusion

In this chapter we have seen how social constructivists have attacked the idea that the form of technologies is necessarily fixed and derived from an immutable technical logic. They invite us to 'open' the hitherto closed lid of the 'technology black box' in a far more fundamental way than that proposed by the other perspectives so far considered. Just as organisational sociologists stress the role of choices in, and the negotiated nature of, the organisational outcomes of technological change, the social constructivist perspective uses the 'black box' metaphor to point to the socially contingent form of technology itself. Critically, this analysis extends not just to the context of the design and development of technology but to its 'technical' *content*. We have also noted, however, that doubts have been expressed over the extent to which SCOT and ANT as primary examples of this approach do in fact avoid technological determinism. To explore this critique further we need to examine another metaphor which seeks to help us understand the interaction of technology and organisation – 'technology as text'.

Notes

1 Historians of technology have also contributed to the development of the social constructivist approach. For example, Thomas P. Hughes (1983, 1987) has developed the 'technological systems theory' to explain the growth and expansion of large-scale technological systems. The late-nineteenth century provides a number of examples of such systems, for instance electric light and power transmission systems, whilst notable early-twentieth century systems might include the system of mass production in industrial assembly. Developments in the Internet and global systems of computer-based telecommunications would

constitute a contemporary example. As with other constructivists Hughes is adamant that no a priori distinction can be drawn between the 'technical' and the 'social' elements of such systems. He similarly evokes the metaphor of the 'seamless web' and suggests we view such 'technological systems' as comprising both physical artefacts and a range of social, political, organisational and legal elements and even the natural resources upon which such systems might draw to function. Moreover, 'technological systems' can be seen as highly malleable in the sense that they are both socially shaped and are themselves 'socially shaping' (Hughes 1987: 51). Hughes draws attention to both 'patterns of evolution' and the role of a range of entrepreneurial actors or 'system builders' in shaping their form.

2 I am grateful to the DMS lunch time crew for yet another intellectual insight; may the discussions continue to range far and wide in my absence.

3 For example, at the time of writing in late-1997/early-1998, BT in the UK is running a corporate marketing campaign in the national media under the slogan 'why not change the way we work' which is an effort to represent new 'virtual' products and services as solutions to corporate problems of communicating and competing in a globalised market place; a means of resolving the dysfunctional corporate, social and environmental costs of employee commuting; and as a way of achieving increased workforce flexibility – see http://www.business.bt.com/main.htm

4 Law himself shows how the durable and robust association of network elements that enabled exploration of the African coast by Portuguese explorers could on occasion be readily disassociated by the superior forces of nature (1987: 117–18) whilst on others, following the enrolment of new allies in the form of superior ship design, in navigation and weaponry, prove a superior form of 'heterogeneous engineering' able to disassociate the hostile natural and social forces encountered in extending trade into the Indian Ocean (1987: 127–9).

6 Transforming the organisation?
Technology as 'text'

Introduction

This chapter explores further the possibilities of developing our under-standing of the interaction between technology and organisation through constructivist analysis. Here we will be concerned with three different approaches which have chosen to use the metaphor of 'technology as text' – two of these can be viewed as examples of 'restricted constructivism' as identified in the previous chapter and one, as 'thoroughgoing constructivism'. The treatment of technology as 'text' can be seen as a further attempt to break out of the deterministic traps that constructivists see as inherent in attempts to grasp the social and cultural character of technical artefacts which refuse to see technology itself as a cultural product. As we will see, the metaphor has proved particularly resonant in seeking new ways to represent the nature of human–computer interaction and, in particular, the nature and organisational consequences of increased electronic mediation of social relations. The metaphor has also proved the focus for a heated debate between constructivists which strikes at a core problem of the role of technology in contemporary organisational analysis – to what extent do advances in ICTs create the possibility for organisational transformation?

Technology, text and culture

A useful starting point for the use of the 'technology as text' metaphor is provided by Stephen Hill in his book *The Tragedy of Technology* (1988). Hill is concerned with the potential for liberation and domination in technological development. For Hill the development of technology and its impacts are 'produced in *cultural* interactions' (1988: 36, original emphasis). The cultural context in which technology is developed and used provides an essential 'text' through which meaning is attached to technological artefacts and systems:

> Unless we know what machines are for, and how to use them, they remain as rusting and inconvenient pieces of matter that we must negotiate our way around in everyday life.
>
> (Hill 1988: 42)

The opacity of the technology text to the human agent has a key influence on people's capacity to use the artefact or system. It is the ability to read the technology text which brings technology 'to life'. For those ignorant of how to use the technology the text is totally opaque. For those who know how to use the technology but who are ignorant of its inner workings and logic the text is 'relatively opaque' (Hill notes that the problem of technology transfer to the Third World is frequently one of having been provided with knowledge of how to use machines but not with the knowledge of how to make them work). For those knowledgeable of both the use and inner working of technology the text is 'transparent'. Moreover, this transparency is associated with an ability not only to read the technology text but to write (i.e. design) it.

The level of opacity/transparency is determined by the degree of alignment, 'between the stock of knowledge that we have access to within our life-world experience, and the stock of knowledge hidden in the artefact' (Hill 1988: 43). Whilst this knowledge appears as 'technical knowledge' it also embodies knowledge of how the artefact relates to the broader technological systems of which it is a part, and knowledge of the social and moral context of its use (for example, the knowledge required to drive a car embodies not only ability to use the controls, but also knowledge of the road transport system as whole, and of the social purpose and moral frameworks governing the use of transport technology). In this way:

> The physical artefact stands before us as a cultural symbol that is imbued with acquired meanings that are salient within the overall cultural grammar of our society....Furthermore, the text of the artefact stands in a wider *con*-text, against which the textual meaning makes sense. A machine-system only makes sense as a machine when it is located in a physical and cultural context that indicates its machine-usefulness.
>
> (Hill 1988: 43)

The technology text has many of the characteristics of a written rather than oral culture. In the latter cultural traditions are continuously sustained through the spoken word of the present. In this way cultural traditions can readily be brought into realignment with present experience to create consistency between the past and present. Meaning, therefore, is dependent upon and embedded in immediate life experience which 'embodies all history, interpreted and re-fashioned to make sense of present events, social practices and relationships' (Hill 1988: 60). In contrast, in written cultures the past is recorded in the written word which permits its recall beyond the limits of living human memory. This gives written and technology texts an autonomy and objectivity, whilst how the text is read and understood is not directly related to the intentionality of the author. Hill also notes the peculiar authority that is acquired by the technology text in advanced industrial societies. This is due to the objectification of historically sedimented cultural meanings within 'solid' artefacts and systems which are closed to scrutiny thus making immediate negotiation and reinterpretation out of the question. As a cultural text, technology in industrial societies appears as a 'closed book' (Hill 1988: 58).

Zuboff's highly influential work *In the Age of the Smart Machine* (1988), which has already been referred to in earlier chapters, also utilises the distinction between oral and written culture. She does this to portray the transformation of knowledge, skills and the process of their acquisition, that occurs with the introduction of computer-based electronic information and communication technologies. It is this which opens up the broader possibilities for organisational transformation which have already been discussed (see Chapter 3).

The computer mediation of work, Zuboff suggests, radically extends the process of codification begun when written cultures first encroached upon the oral culture of the workplace. Know-how in oral work cultures is encapsulated in terms of what can be recalled. Repetition is the key to the preservation of knowledge and experienced workers are highly valued as 'vessels' of such knowledge. Such cultures are generated and sustained through the practice of action-centred skills. These are characteristic of work which has not been subject to high levels of automation. Here the performance of work tasks is based upon sentient information derived from physical cues from the work environment. The work involves the physical performance of tasks. The skills used are context dependent and highly personalised. That is, they only have meaning within the context in which the associated physical activities can occur and through the act of physically performing the tasks. Action-centred skill is therefore intimately bound up with the physical performance of work tasks – 'acting on' or 'acting with' raw materials, work pieces or technical artefacts, etc. Or as Zuboff puts it, 'I see, I touch, I smell, I hear; therefore I know' (Zuboff 1988: 62–3). Automation, in this context, is focused on tasks which involve 'acting-on' and 'acting-with', thereby making this kind of human labour redundant (Zuboff 1988: 181).

In the past, the power-resources available to the possessors of such skill have been a key factor in their ability to resist the codification in written form of the discrete activities or procedures which constitute their know-how. However, when computer mediation of their work occurs, the informating (as distinct from the automating) capacity of the technology creates an 'electronic text through which organisational events, objects, transactions, functions, activities, and know-how' can be 'enacted or observed' (Zuboff 1988: 179).

This electronic text differs from paper-based systems in that: it provides a sophisticated, comprehensive and systemic electronic 'window' on production and organisational processes (*visibility*); the programmability of computers allows managerial and operator knowledge to be codified and built into the text (*depth*); access to the text is not limited by location or time since, although the knowledge base is highly centralised, access to it is extremely decentralised and 'in principle can be constituted at any time from any place' (*temporality and spatiality*); and, the text does not have one author, rather it is produced by multiple individuals or through impersonal and autonomous automatic processes (electronic sensors, scanners, etc.), and as such appears distanced from human authorship, more definitive and less easy to criticise ('the computer can't be wrong') (*impersonality and obscurity of authorship*) (Zuboff 1988: 179–81).

The electronic mediation of work and organisational transformation

The creation of electronic texts fundamentally changes the nature, not only of the skills required by employees, but also of the work task and the employee experience of that task. Thus, access to electronic texts is provided through work tasks which are now mediated by an electronic 'data interface'. This is the means by which information is provided to the employee by computing and information systems and through which information can be input to the system by the employee. Work with a 'data interface' requires new and more abstract 'intellective skills' as opposed to the 'action-centred' skills associated with the physical performance of work tasks. These new skills involve a qualitatively new experience for the employee since they require mental rather than concrete physical activity. Instead of cues from the immediate physical environment the employee's responses must be based on abstract cues provided by the data interface. These responses involve thought processes in which options for action are considered, and choices made which are then translated into terms that can be understood by the 'data interface' (Zuboff 1988: 71).

Emphasis is therefore placed on the performance of mental tasks, or 'procedural reasoning'. This enables employees to understand the procedures according to which abstract cues can be manipulated to bring about in the desired effects. This requires an understanding of the internal structure of the information system and its functional capabilities; an ability to make a correspondence between abstract cues and actual processes and their systemic relations; an understanding of what actions at the data interface lead to appropriate outcomes; and an ability to interpret new data as feedback on the results of responses. The performance of work tasks is experienced in an entirely different way. According to Zuboff, thought is removed from the action context, 'absorption, immediacy, and organic responsiveness are superseded by distance, coolness and remoteness' (Zuboff 1988: 75).

One consequence of textualisation is that it can both destroy and create meaning in relation to work. On the one hand action-centred skills and oral cultures can be rendered 'obsolete' or 'thinned'. On the other, the new distance from experience created by computer-mediated work can become the basis for a more complete and defined understanding which is experienced by individuals as 'a source of instruction and empowerment' enabled by the capacity to de-couple their knowledge and action from temporal and physical constraints.

> When meaning is uncoupled from its action context and carried away in symbols, a new playfulness becomes possible. Events and the relationships among events can be illuminated and combined in new ways. As surrounding events and processes become the objects of a disengaged awareness, they become susceptible to examination, comparison and innovation.
>
> (Zuboff 1988: 180–1)

The consequence is that organisation members can use computers to experiment and test scenarios or simulate conditions in work operations, thus arriving at innovative and creative solutions to problems that it was not possible to achieve before. Ultimately, the full acquisition of intellective skill and the capacity this gives to manipulate the electronic text provides the basis, in Zuboff's view, for a creative transformation of the nature of work and organisation.

Nohria and Eccles (1992) put further flesh on these points when they argue that electronically mediated exchange cannot entirely replace face-to-face interaction. Moreover, it is ironically in networked rather than conventional bureaucratic organisations (see Chapter 1), where tasks are likely to be characterised by high levels of uncertainty, ambiguity and risk, that electronically mediated forms of interaction are likely to be least effective. Seeking to create 'post-Fordist' organisations through the 'automation of automation' and the 'immersion' of employees in 'virtual worlds' (see Chapter 1), is thus fundamentally flawed.

The basis of this argument is the view that electronic communication is an information lean rather than information rich medium when compared to face-to-face interaction (Daft and Lengel 1986). For example, electronically mediated interaction requires, almost by definition, no co-presence of the participants. Such encounters are stripped of the multiplicity of social clues that contextualise face-to-face interaction, and they involve none of the physical and psycho-emotional dimensions of such interaction (the impressions 'given off' as well as those 'given' are lost); furthermore, the sequential nature of electronically mediated interaction means that the capacity in conventional encounters for interruption, repair, feedback and learning are lost.

The result is that electronically mediated exchange offers only limited impressions upon which to construct meaningful identities, for example in the context of team formation, places limits on the capacity of actors to resolve uncertainties and ambiguities. It also makes it more difficult for collective action to be mobilised in order to seize new opportunities or deflect threats, and is likely to constitute a set of relationships which are less than robust in contexts where strength and adaptability are at a premium (see Nohria and Eccles 1992: 293–9). The paradox is that 'in order to derive the benefits of the increasing capability of electronically mediated exchange, the amount of face-to-face interaction will actually have to increase' (Nohria and Eccles 1992: 300), with the implication that, *'network organisations are not the same as electronic networks, nor can they be built entirely on them'* (Nohria and Eccles 1992: 289, original emphasis). As with Zuboff, therefore, these authors see a stress on using electronic communication technology to 'automate' human interaction as fundamentally mistaken. The organisational transformation enabled by such technologies can only occur if choices on its use stress its 'informating' capacity (see Chapter 3).

Restrictive and thoroughgoing constructivist views of technology as text

In the previous chapter we noted the distinction drawn by Grint and Woolgar (1997) between essentialist and anti-essentialist positions concerning the social shaping of technology. That is, on the one hand is the notion that the internal characteristics of technology are fixed and immutable and on the other the constructivist view that such properties are a product of interpretations made in the social context in which technologies are developed and used.

However, Grint and Woolgar suggest that, despite their apparent 'anti-essentialist' credentials Hill and Zuboff are both guilty of 'residual essentialism'. In this sense their constructivism, as is that ultimately of the SCOT and ANT approaches discussed in the previous chapter, is 'restrictive'. In turn, this questions the viability of arguments that suggest it is advances in ICTs which have created possibilities, albeit not as yet realised, for transformation and the emergence of post-Fordist organisational forms.

For example, Hill's notion of a 'transparent' understanding of the capacities of technology assumes consensus is possible on what these capacities actually are, independent of interpretative context (Grint and Woolgar 1997: 31–2). Similarly, Zuboff's distinction between the 'automating' and 'informating' effects of technology (see Chapter 3) – that underpins her view of the nature of electronic texts – whilst recognising that such effects are a product of the way technologies are used, still views the 'informating' capacities of information and computing technologies as an 'intrinsic' feature of these systems. That is, organisations are free to choose to use computing and information technologies in ways which automate rather than informate, but they are unable to challenge the informating capacities of the technology itself, thus 'the impression given is that there can be no dispute over the potential capacity of the technology, just whether or not this (actual) potential has been realised' (ibid. 1997: 134). Such restrictive constructivism, as we have already noted in the case of SCOT and ANT, gives the strong impression that, once socially constructed, technology has characteristics and capabilities which can have effects. In the case of ICTs these effects are frequently viewed as transformative both at the level of the organisation and in facilitating and supporting the development of new production paradigms and trajectories.

To fully exploit the text metaphor, Woolgar and Grint argue that a 'post-essentialist' or 'thoroughgoing constructivist' position needs to be developed. That is, one which views the 'technical capacities' of machines and systems as never fixed but 'essentially indeterminate' and open to 'interpretative flexibility' (Woolgar 1991a, 1991b; Woolgar and Grint 1991, 1992). In this view, what a technology can and cannot do is a product of *continual* representation and re-representation in the interpretative contexts in which it is being produced and consumed:

> what a computer is for, what it can do and achieve, is…regarded as an interpretative issue on any occasion that it is described, planned, talked about, marketed, sold, used, reviewed, dismantled and so on…in other words, technological artefacts can be construed as texts that are *essentially* embedded in (and, at the same time, constituted by) their interpretative contexts.
>
> (Grint and Woolgar 1992: 370)

For the 'post-essentialist', it is wholly mistaken to take the view that, at some point, artefacts can ever have a 'definitive character or effect'[1].

The metaphor of technology as text provides 'a vivid way of stressing the "interpretatively flexible" nature and capacity of a machine or system'.

> In this view, machines [systems] do not have inherent capacities; rather their capacity and capability is the upshot of users' interaction with the system. In the post-modern adage, it is the reader who writes the text. Relatedly, the notion of machine/system as text encourages us to view processes of design, construction and use of systems as analogous to processes of producers writing and consumers reading text.
>
> (Woolgar 1994: 205)

Whilst encouraging us to see the nature of technologies as in their reading this does not mean, though, that any reading is possible. Rather, in practice only a limited number of readings can be offered, the number of which is delimited by 'the organisation of the text' which suggests certain readings and denies others.

Configuring the user: transforming the organisation?

What are the implications of a post-essentialist position for questions concerning the relationship between technological change and organisational transformation? One set of possibilities is explored by Grint and Woolgar (1997) with reference to 'the problem of the user' in computer system design. The user problem is particularly significant for the development of ICTs. As Friedman and Cornford (1989) have shown, the history of the development of these technologies was initially characterised in the 1950s and 1960s by a need to improve the reliability, reduce the costs, and improve the processing capabilities of system hardware. Subsequently, in the 1960s and 1970s, the focus shifted to developing improved software to increase the range of applications, utility and connectivity of systems. Since the 1980s consideration has turned to the problem of matching technological capabilities with the needs of the user.

Conventionally this problem is viewed as one of devising appropriate methods by which system designers can 'capture' the requirements of the user and thereby design a system to meet them. However, Grint and Woolgar note that, in practice, 'capturing' users' requirements has proven highly problematic. Users 'do not know what they want', 'they know them but cannot articulate them', 'they keep changing their minds', 'say different things to different people', etc. As a result, implementations of ICTs fail to achieve their planned targets or are simply abandoned. The inability of system designers and users to understand each other is therefore seen as major constraint on technological possibilities being realised in practice. One response to this by system designers and developers has been to try and develop more sophisticated methods of requirements analysis which, in particular, recognise the social not just technical dimensions of the problem. The 'user problem' therefore is perceived as one that is not fully understood because of deficiencies in existing methodologies and techniques for identifying user requirements and so forth. Interest in how insights from ergonomics, psychology and sociology can be used to improve these methodologies has therefore been a rapidly growing area in systems development which is increasingly seen as an activity that is, or at least one that ought to be, multidisciplinary (see Woolgar 1992).

However, the post-essentialist perspective suggests that the problem is more fundamental than being one of method and a willingness to focus on socio-technical rather than just technical dimensions of system design. Rather it suggests that the apparent inability of users to say unambiguously what they require is not a result of the shortcomings of users or the methods of designers. Rather it is an outcome of the different ways in which a computer system can and cannot be represented by designers and other groups – hardware engineers, product engineers, project managers, salespersons, technical support, purchasing, finance and control, legal personnel, etc. – who are likely to interact with users in the process of developing, implementing and operating a complex ICT system. Users cannot say what they want because there is no fixed and immutable account available from the groups as to what the technology is and what it can do.

Thus the textuality of the technology confronts both readers and its authors with problems of definition and interpretation. Designers 'author' the system 'text', and in 'writing' the text contribute to a definition of the 'reader' (user) and the parameters of their actions. However, because system design embraces a broad range of individuals and groups there is a multiplicity of perspectives as to 'how' the 'text should read and be read' by users. Indeed, in essence, claim Grint and Woolgar, the process of technological development from inception, design, manufacture, marketing, launch and sales, 'can be construed as a struggle to configure (that is, to define, enable and constrain) the user' (Grint and Woolgar 1997: 73–4).

However, configuring the user is problematic because the knowledge about 'what the user is like' held by system 'authors' differs from group to group and varies over time. In an ethnographic study of a project to produce a new range of microcomputers, several dimensions of this struggle were encountered by Woolgar (1991b). For example: there were disagreements over whether company personnel could see the world from 'the user's' point of view; claims and counter claims concerning the motivation and capacity of technical and non-technical functions to understand 'the user'; tales and stories of encounters with 'the user' in the field were a key source of knowledge, there was an unwillingness to view 'the user' in the plural and as a possibly highly differentiated entity; and a view that users did not know what they wanted and technical experts did, in particular in relation to future technological developments.

Many of these issues were manifest during usability trials on the new product. Of particular symbolic importance was the computer's outer case. Typically, computers do not have one of these whilst under technical development. However, those responsible for the trials felt this was an essential component if the user's experience of the machine was to be properly assessed. The importance of the case was that it defined the boundary of the system and, indeed the boundary between the organisation and outside of the organisation. The inside of the company, and the innards of the machine, were not for consumption by the user. Rather the case and accompanying literature prescribed for the user appropriate methods, provided information, sources of assistance, and sometimes dire warnings of the consequences of inappropriate actions. These were intended to enable the user to operate (read) the system (text) in the 'correct' fashion. The computer casing, or rather its symbolic aspects, made the technology a 'black box', but one which never had a final definitive meaning.

One of the implications of this perspective on the nature of the relationship between system design and users is that any 'organisational transformation' that might arise from the adoption of a technology is highly consequent of the effectiveness of 'user configuration'. Put another way, configured users are 'disciplined' users who will adopt behaviours and attitudes towards the technology text consistent with those intended – after due struggle and deliberation – by its authors. Poorly configured or unconfigured users will, on the other hand, be 'undisciplined' in their reactions to and use of the technology. They will read the technology text in ways unintended by its authors. They will not use its capabilities and capacities effectively, they will resist using it, and may not even use it at all and criticise those who do or protest about and campaign against its use entirely. In this perspective 'organisational transformation' and the part played by 'technology' within it remains a continually contestable, negotiable and open-ended condition.

Assessing the constructivist approach to technology

We can now attempt a full assessment of the constructivist approach to technology. Clearly notwithstanding the convergence noted in the previous chapter, there are still considerable differences of emphasis between subvariants, most notably that between 'thoroughgoing' constructivists such as Grint and Woolgar, and the more 'restrictive' constructivism of SCOT and ANT considered in the previous chapter and that of the likes of Hill and Zuboff considered above. These differences will need to be born in mind during the assessment that follows.

The overriding strength of the constructivist approach is that it asks how 'technology' comes to be 'technology'. In so doing it reveals that the distinction between the 'technical' and the 'social' is not given but socially contingent and constructed. This 'analytical scepticism' concerning what a technology is and what it can do offers a considerable methodological advantage and encourages the analyst to continually challenge and question what might otherwise be seen as the inalienable knowledge of technical experts.

This analytical scepticism extends to linear models of technological and related concepts of technological paradigms and trajectories (see Chapter 2). As we noted, these assume a rational progression through successive stages of invention, design and first adoption. Moreover, explanations for the success or failure of an innovation largely ignore the technology itself whose characteristics and capabilities are essentially 'given', even 'natural'. In the constructivist perspective the lid of the 'black box' is 'lifted' to show the way social factors explain why some variants of a design 'die' and others 'survive'. Thus, rather than being unilinear, technological innovation can be regarded as 'multidirectional' and, only in hindsight, can it be made to look to have followed a rational sequential progression through distinct stages, to have a 'natural' 'trajectory' (Bijker and Law 1992: 17) or to be seen as having 'impacts' on a separately constituted society (Latour 1987: 132–6), or as having actual 'effects' on users independent of relations with users (Grint and Woolgar 1997: 93), or as possessing its own 'momentum' (Hughes 1987).

Such a perspective, therefore, shifts attention away from an emphasis on the supposed forces and trends inherent in technological development and the apparently fixed characteristics and capabilities of a technology. It also questions the idea that such development or capability has distinctive 'social' effects. Rather, attention has to be concentrated on the strategies and choices inherent in shaping technology from the start. According to Callon, for example, whilst conventional innovation studies might admit the heterogeneity and complexity of the outcomes of technological development, the problems that are to be solved during the process are still regarded as essentially technical. In contrast, the constructivist perspective takes the view that right from the beginning innovation is a technical, scientific, social, economic and political process (Callon 1987: 83–4). Or as Westrum puts it: 'the focus is now on the way that decision-making about technologies takes place; with different decisions we get different directions for society' (1987: 76).

The constructivist approach therefore allows 'non-experts' to 'follow' technologists and others involved in the social construction of technology – both in its production and consumption – further than they might otherwise do. It permits a questioning and critical insight which, at the same time, is agnostic to the claims and counter claims of 'experts' as they attempt to negotiate the final form – at least as they see it – of 'socio-technical ensembles', 'actor-networks', 'configured users' and so on. Thus, just as the organisational politics/process approach stresses the role of choices in, and the negotiated nature of, the organisational outcomes of technological change (see Chapter 4), the constructivist perspective points to the socially contingent form of technology itself and the way in which technology is socially constructed in both its production and consumption.

The result is a replacement of the notion of technology as not only having a determining capability but also a determinant character. Indeed, for some, it is the particular indeterminacy of the character of ICTs which makes them so distinctive and potentially transformative. For example, following Weick (1990), Fulk draws attention to the 'equivocal' nature of these technologies, which she suggests

> provide unusual problems in sense making because their processes are
> often poorly understood and because they are continuously redesigned

and reinterpreted in the process of implementation and accommodation to specific social and organisational contexts. Communication technologies in particular link disparate entities in a seamless web that engages joint sense making in the process of mediated interaction.

(Fulk 1993: 922)

Second, and following from this, constructivism can be seen as peculiarly capable of supporting and even generating alternative images of the relationship between technology and organisation. In particular by challenging the determinism of the 'machine' and 'organism' metaphors which have dominated both academic and especially practitioner discourse new possibilities for organisational design can be envisaged. In this regard Zuboff's notion of the electronic text and its related dimensions such as 'visibility' and the 'impersonality' of 'authorship' of the text (take for example the growing use of electronic mail and its effects on organisational relationships cited above) is a much more subtle and vivid metaphor through which to regard and come to terms with the idea of organisations dispersed in time and space. Similarly, as Woolgar's exploration of the designer/supplier–user relationship illustrates, the text metaphor exposes both the weaknesses of conventional conceptions of 'the user' and their 'requirements' and, potentially at least, offers up new kinds of possibilities for rethinking user involvement in technological development. In principal, therefore, the constructivist approach – be it through the 'black box/embodiment' or 'text' metaphors – appears to be capable of illuminating new ways of thinking and acting in relation to both the design of artefacts and systems and the redirection of programmes of technological development (Bijker 1995a).

Against these undoubted insights, however, the constructivist approach also has some significant weaknesses. For some the relativist underpinnings of constructivism of whatever variety make it an untenable approach. Metaphors such as 'actor-network' and 'technology as text' have a degree of counter-intuitiveness which may well lead in many eyes to their failing a key test of their utility: that is, their ability to cross the boundary between source and target domains. As a result the metaphor is regarded as too 'weak', rather like a joke that turns out not to be funny (Black 1993), or 'anomalous' in the sense that source and target domains have few relationships or attributes in common – for example 'technology is like text' might be equated with a similar apparent absurdity 'a computer is like coffee' (Tsoukas 1993).

Winner refers to the application of constructivist ideas to the study of technology as an 'intellectual tragedy' whose basic assumptions mean an agnostic stance in relation to different lines of technological development and an intellectual inability to intervene in public debates over their appropriateness. The relativist position is also highly controversial for some practising scientists and technologists who regard it, incorrectly in the view of constructivists (see e.g. Collins and Pinch 1995), as an attempt to undermine the basis of their expertise, as no more than a crude 'conspiracy' and as 'flying in the face' of nature and the *real* accomplishments of modern science and technology (see e.g. Atkins 1994). As one such critic has observed, whilst the theory of aerodynamics might be described as a social construct it does not explain why constructivists prefer to 'entrust their air-travel plans to a Boeing rather than magic carpet'. From this point of view it follows that a 'relativist at 30,000 feet' is a 'hypocrite' (Dawkins 1994).

Other non-constructivists, or at least those whose position is not fully subsumed by such notions, prefer to point in more sober fashion to a number of more subtle but no less objectionable difficulties. In particular, they are concerned that the approach appears to downplay, ignore and even deny the influence of broader societal, structural and systemic factors that provide the context in which processes such as closure, network-building, and the reading and writing of 'texts' take place.

Williams and Russell (1987: 4–8), for example, raise a number of objections in relation to the relevance of the SSK approach for examining the social shaping of technology. First, it places too much stress on closure being achieved through consensus, as though the achievement of stabilisation in the rather different social and commercially driven settings within which much technological development occurs would take place as in scientific communities. In the former settings particular solutions are as likely to be imposed by employing organisations on the various groups involved without a consensus rather than worked out in the more consensual and collegiate environment of the scientific research laboratory. Second, the focus is on the social construction of 'technological knowledge' rather than 'technology' in its material manifestation, context and effects. Insofar as technological development is strongly orientated towards economic and political goals (in a way that scientific development is not) its significance lies not so much in its inception during design and development but in the consequences which follow from its realisation during implementation and use (see also Mackay 1995). Third, this raises problems of identifying appropriate 'relevant social groups' and constituents of 'actor-networks' since the range of groups involved in the realisation of a technology goes way beyond the narrower 'technological communities' which may be at the core of its inception. The focus in constructivist analysis on early stages of development of radically new products, in particular although not exclusively in historical settings, reflects these difficulties and gives only a partial view of technological development, i.e. only that which takes place where institutional structure and practices resemble those found more typically in scientific communities.

This is important since it is in work organisations, rather than scientific laboratories, where much technology is developed, implemented and used. Too much emphasis placed on the social constructed nature of the behaviour of members of work organisations can lead to a focus on the way actors define their power position *vis-à-vis* their adversaries, rather than the material basis of such power itself. As Rose (1988) argues, to deny the material basis of power and instead focus purely on its symbolic aspects, places too much stress on the actor's ability to construct interpretations of the situation and not enough on the features of the situation which enable and constrain the actor's interpretative capacity (see also Russell 1991).

Indeed the denial of the material basis of power, in preference for its semiotic expression, can render constructivist metaphors open to the charge that they are no more than a further layer in the ideological mystification of technology. Thus, it is frequently claimed that, by refusing to recognise the need to answer the questions of why a technology is developed, in whose interests it is designed and used in a way which shows the linkages between such capacities and broader structural, systemic and institutional frameworks of inequality of material and other resources, critical – if not central – issues concerning the role of technology in organisations are ignored by constructivists. Even Zuboff's counter posing of the 'informating' and 'automating' effects of computing and information technologies, which does show sensitivity to issues of power and domination in organisations in these senses, has been accused of missing the essential point that these are in essence *both* means of management control in capitalist society (Knights and Murray 1994; Wilmott 1995).

Many of these points are also echoed in feminist criticisms of constructivism (see e.g. Gill 1994; Cockburn 1993; Cockburn and Ormrod 1993; Webster 1996). For example, according to Gill,

> [if] it is the way we read or interpret a piece of technology that is crucial, then we need to ask why it is that particular readings hold such sway, and others disappear without trace. The answer lies not in some formal property of the interpretation which makes it 'better', but in the capacity of actors to make interpretations stick...[T]hat capacity is not evenly distributed; we do not live in a semiotic democracy.
>
> (Gill 1994)

Indeed, feminist critics have drawn attention to the failure of constructivists to explain 'missing' social groups and actors in their accounts of technological development. Why is it that women, ethnic minorities, shop floor workers and so on are not amongst the 'relevant social groups', 'entities' in an actor-network, or amongst the suppliers seeking to 'configure the user'? This is not to deny, argue Cockburn and Ormrod, that 'local action and individual agency' are important, indeed they can be shown to be an essential means through which both gender identities and technology as cultural product are socially shaped. However, it is critical to recognise that such interactions are embedded in 'longer-lived and more widely spread social structures' (Cockburn and Ormrod 1993: 10).

In respect of many of these observations, the arguments of thoroughgoing constructivism seem to 'push the metaphor too far' by seemingly suggesting that 'interpretative flexibility' of technology has no limits – or at least only limits that are socially contingent and constituted. We have already noted in Chapter 4, Orlikowski's argument that technology can be seen as both an 'objective reality and as a socially constructed product' and as such the interpretative flexibility of any given technology is partly constrained by 'the material characteristics of that technology' (Orlikowski 1992: 405, 423). In fact, this issue has proved the focus for an illuminating debate between Woolgar and Grint and Robert King concerning whether guns have a superior capacity to kill and maim than roses and the extent to which the weaponry preferences of Los Angeles street gangs have anything to do with the material characteristics and capabilities of the artefacts in question! (see McLoughlin 1997 for discussion).[2]

The crux of this problem of whether or not there are material limits to 'interpretative flexibility' is seen by Collins (1994; also Collins and Yearley 1992a, 1992b) in terms of a distinction between methodological (or epistemological) relativism on the one hand and ontological relativism on the other. They suggest that debates in the sociology of scientific knowledge, and by inference more recent developments in the sociology of technology, have been engaged in a 'game of chicken' where some parties – thoroughgoing constructivists to name the guilty – have sought to turn the principle of symmetry, first applied to accounts of what constituted a scientific 'truth', on to the social study of science and technology itself. If what a technology can and cannot do is subject to interpretative flexibility, the argument goes, then it must also be the case that accounts of what a technology can and cannot do, are themselves subject to interpretative flexibility, as indeed are all accounts, even the one you are currently reading. All this is very well, suggest Collins and Yearley, but the outcome of such 'generalised symmetry' – such as ascribing agency to 'things' as actor-network theorists wish to do, 'gets us nowhere' (Collins and Yearley 1992a: 305).

Following Collins and Yearley's line of argument, interpretative flexibility – over what a technology can and cannot do – might be best regarded as an important methodological principle because it provides the basis upon which the 'expert' answers to these questions can be understood in their own terms without a priori privileging one account over another. By adopting this method it is possible to understand how the 'technology' came to be 'the technology' as rival and competing accounts gave way to one definitive design solution through some process of social negotiation. Such epistemological relativism allows us to look inside the black box without seeing the 'box' as the (technological) determinant of accepted accounts of what it is.

To question whether the 'box' can, after its socially constructed character has been explicated, still have 'independent effects' involves 'ontological relativism' (Collins 1994). This again requires treating accounts of what 'the effect' of the technology is as inevitable and definitive in a symmetrical manner. Again, this is a methodological device which, if one accepts the insights of the text metaphor offered earlier, may well help us look further into how the consumption as opposed to the production of technology is socially shaped. However, that it supports a view that roses and guns are equally effective means of taking human life is more of philosophical interest rather than practical relevance. It is at this point perhaps that, for practical analytical purposes, Orlikowski's notion of the material limits to interpretative flexibility should, it might be suggested, be left to prevail.

MacKenzie makes a similar point when he argues that there is little analytical 'added value' in questioning the material efficacy of technological artefacts *once* disputes over this question amongst relevant groups have been settled. In this respect ANT usefully points to the importance of the 'unverbalised reality' of the 'non-human' material world as an independent causal factor in shaping – but of course not determining – beliefs and verbal accounts of it (MacKenzie 1996: 15–16). Or to put it slightly differently, the reasons why roses make good gifts, bad weapons, and are lousy methods of conveying voice and non-voice data, do not lie exclusively in the persuasiveness of texts and their reading (McLoughlin 1997: 219).

Conclusion

In this chapter we have explored how construing technology in terms of the metaphor of text can open up new ways of thinking and perhaps acting in relation to the interaction between ICTs and organisation. In particular, interesting insights have been revealed concerning the 'equivocal' meaning of this technology, the nature of the electronic mediation of work tasks, and the relationship between the suppliers/designers of technology and its users. More generally, the constructivist perspective offers a way of opening the technology black box that reveals the social and political dimensions of the way in which technologies are produced and also provides new purchase on questions of why espoused technological possibilities for organisational transformation are rarely realised. However, the discussion of the strengths and weaknesses of the constructivist position would suggest a marked tension between the capacity of the metaphor to generate alternative images of the technology–organisation relationship and the plausibility of such alternative concepts being translated in organisational practice. If the technology has no definitive effect, why bother introducing it? What is the relationship between different perceptions and the material world which they seek to represent?

More generally, the metaphor illustrates tensions within the constructivist position concerning the limits or otherwise to interpretative flexibility and, at the same time, points to a general problem faced by constructivists in relation to the broader structures, material relations and power systems in which interpretation takes place. Indeed, some constructivists have started to realise the weaknesses of a position which, according to its critics, seems to involve 'opening the black box, getting inside and closing the lid behind you' (Williams and Russell 1987: 6–7). Bijker for instance has recently argued that 'there is life beyond contructivism' and that 'studies have become absorbed in the internal intricacies of development' and have lost sight of 'the objective of demonstrating connections to wider interests' (Bijker 1993: 115–17). It is now time, it seems, to look once again outside of the 'black box'.

Notes

1 The difficulties associated with Grint and Woolgar's approach are fully recognised when they observe that we are 'prisoners of the conventions of language and representation' and that the avoidance of technological determinism ultimately requires 'nothing short of a re-working of the categories and conventions of language use'. However, whilst 'it is better to say that technologies are constituted rather than shaped or constructed; that antecedent circumstances are inscribed in, rather than merely informing design; that users are configured, rather than just enrolled' they ask 'do we end up putting "scare quotes" around everything' or instead 'explore new forms of writing and reflexivity, to invent new monsters and marginal beings which might displace standard units of analysis and transcend conventional categories and distinction?' (1997: 114–15). Not for nothing do Grint and Woolgar exclaim 'all this post-essentialism is hard-work'! (1997: 114).

2 Woolgar and Grint take issue with Kling because he sees technical influences as one possible factor shaping how a technology is designed and used. The debate is crystallised in a discussion of the relative merits of guns as opposed to roses as effective means of terminating human life (see Woolgar 1991b; Woolgar and Grint 1991; Grint and Woolgar 1992, 1997; and Kling 1991a, 1991b, 1992a, 1992b).

Kling:

1 Firearms have the unique technical capacity to wound, maim and kill human beings – 'it is much harder to kill a platoon of soldiers with a dozen roses than with well-placed high speed bullets' (Kling 1992a: 362).

2 This does not mean that the sale of every gun results in a violent act on a human being. How the technology is consumed or used depends on social factors. Guns, for example, might be acquired as 'trophies' which act as symbols of manhood to their possessors. However, guns give certain social groups – street gangs in Los Angeles for example – a superior technical capacity to ply their trade.

3 A social analysis might, therefore, reasonably attribute some independent influence on the social phenomenon of high murder rates in Los Angeles to the unique technical capacities of guns.

Grint/Woolgar:

1 Being shot is an essentially social phenomenon that can only be understood in the specific context of a killer being united with a gun. The human element (killer) and non-human element (gun) from a network

and it is during the fusion of this network that the event 'being shot' is socially constructed.

2 'Being shot' can be viewed as comprising a number of onion like layers. Restrictive constructivists assume that the onion has a technical core – the capacity of a gun once designed to maim and kill. Thoroughgoing constructivists argue that this is illusory since the seriousness of the wound, the perception of the amount of pain, the definition of if and when the recipient is 'dead', represent a series of social (re)constructions which are contingent upon social, cultural and historical context.

3 The fact that the recipient has a bullet hole in their head is dependent upon this socially constructed knowledge of how it got there in the first place. That the hole was caused by the bullet is not a reflection of the technical capacity of the gun but is a testament to the persuasiveness of one interpretative account over all others. The 'effect' of a bullet in the head is no more transparent than the 'effect' of technology on society, 'even the most self-evident case of determinism is, to capture the metaphor, shot full of holes' (Grint and Woolgar 1997: 164).

7 Outside the black box

The socio-economic shaping of technology

Introduction

In this chapter we are concerned with those examples of the social shaping approach which start from social context and 'work inwards' to show how socio-economic factors *shape* the origins and development of technology. We begin by reviewing some of the basic premises of this approach and then illustrate its application in two classic areas of study – the political shaping of the production of technology by class and other interests and the gendering of technology in the context of patriarchal social relations. We then review some more contemporary developments in the social shaping perspective, in particular the notion of innofusion, which refers to the post-adoption shaping of technology during its consumption. The focus on both production and consumption is particularly relevant to understanding the social shaping of ICTs. An understanding of how these and other technologies are shaped leads to the proposition that they can be reshaped. This possibility is explored through a review of contemporary models which, taken together, offer the prospect of a 'new' socio-technical theory and an alternative paradigm, even trajectory, of technology, work and organisational design. Much of this variant of the social shaping perspective rests on an 'embodiment' metaphor, that is the notion that interests, values and assumptions of social groups are 'built into' and manifested in the effects of technology. The final section of the chapter explores the strengths and weaknesses of thinking and acting in relation to technology in these terms.

The socio-economic shaping of technology

The socio-economic shaping perspective is represented in a variety of studies and research programmes that have sought to identify factors which influence the origins and evolution of technology (see e.g. MacKenzie and Wajcman 1985; Edge 1995; Williams 1997a). As with the other social shaping perspectives reviewed in the previous two chapters, notions of 'technology' as having 'impacts' and 'natural trajectories' are firmly rejected:

In this [deterministic] view, human and social factors merely mediate, and can perhaps control the timing of, developments that are essentially inevitable. The emphasis of research and policy therefore shifts to attempts to understand and predict the likely *consequences* of evolving technologies, so that the more negative effects might be ameliorated.

(Edge 1995: 14)

Instead, what is proposed is a perspective which reveals the social and economic factors which 'mould and form the content of technology itself' and thus permit the identification of 'the factors that shape the evolutionary paths of technologies' (Edge 1995: 15).

Having said this, for the socio-economic shaping perspective, technology itself is still seen as capable of having independent effects. That is, whilst the idea that technology has 'causal effects' on society is rejected, the idea of technological influences on the shaping of technology itself is not. A precondition of much technological innovation is in fact seen to be existing technology. Indeed, it is the development and gradual evolution of existing technological know-how, rather than 'flashes of inspiration' amongst inventors, which is responsible for much new technology (MacKenzie and Wajcman 1985). Similarly, insofar as new technologies are increasingly required to operate within or in the context of broader technological systems, there are constraints on how they can be designed. The point here is similar to that made by Hughes (1987) when he argues that much innovative effort can be seen as driven by the 'reverse salients' within large-scale technological systems. That is, the need to innovate arises in response to deficiencies or malfunctions identified in the operation of existing technology.

Obviously, the social shaping perspective does not see technological factors alone as shaping technology. Indeed economic factors such as cost are inextricably bound up with the technological lines of reasoning which identify problems such as 'reverse salients'. More generally, questions of profit and loss play a crucial role in decisions over both which and where technological innovation takes place. However, as MacKenzie and Wajcman (1985: 15–18) argue, the economic calculations which guide technological innovation are themselves socially shaped and, to a highly significant extent, social factors can override economic calculation in determining particular lines of development.

For example, whilst all societies have to come to a view over the costs and benefits of a particular technological design or choice, the form that this judgement takes is highly variable, differing, for example, between advanced Western capitalist economies, the former state socialist societies and developing societies. What is 'economically rational' with respect to technology is informed in each of these settings by the nature of the social context in which decisions are made. Even within a particular social setting, economic calculation is not straightforward and is open to challenge. For example, proponents of an innovation will present calculations which show the benefits of change in a positive light, opponents will present calculations which highlight damaging costs, and the basis upon which they do this will reflect values, goals and norms which lay behind the particular social interest they are seeking to advance or defend.

Finally, whilst the capacity of firms to escape profit and loss criteria is circumscribed, the state can play a particularly important role in promoting, underwriting or supporting, lines of technological development which private enterprise calculates to be economically unworthwhile. Here explicitly social factors can have an enormous influence on technology and innovation. For example, the most important source of state influence is through its sponsoring of military technology. As MacKenzie and Wajcman note, war and the threat of war, have 'coerced' the shape of technology. In so doing otherwise insuperable economic barriers to technological development have often been overridden by the military interest, ultimately permitting civilian technologies to develop – in areas such as nuclear power, air transport and electronics – which otherwise might have remained dormant or unrealised (1985: 18–20).

For the socio-economic shaping perspective the relationship between technology and social factors is seen as complex where 'causes' and 'effects' stand in indeterminant relationships and where the relative weight of the influence of the 'technical' and the 'social' varies over time. This can be illustrated by considering successively complex models of the innovation process which lead in turn to more complex models of the social shaping process itself (see Figure 7.1).

Model 1 is a conventional 'product cycle' representation of the innovation process (see Chapter 2). It assumes a broadly chronological and linear movement from the generation of new technological knowledge, its development into new product and process designs, adoption, diffusion and effects on organisational, institutional and other social variables. This determinist model is of course the one rejected by the social shaping perspective. It ignores the broader socio-economic, political and cultural context, assumes a technological logic drives innovation and ignores the complex interactions between, for instance, design and the experience of using technologies once adopted. Nevertheless, the model is an advance on technological impact perspectives which take the process of innovation as 'given' and are concerned only with the effect of 'technology' on social variables (Model 2), or additionally with the factors which promote or act as a barrier to adoption and diffusion (Model 3), and in some cases recognise feedback loops between different phases (Models 4, 5 and 6). These are essentially the perspectives of much of the literature reviewed in Chapters 1 and 2.

The social shaping perspective introduces a further model (Model 7). This involves two things. First, a full recognition of the role of 'feedback' loops between the various stages in the innovation process. These show,

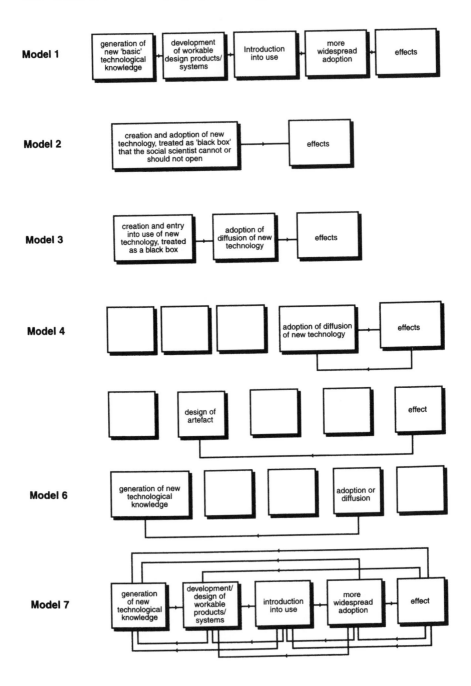

Figure 7.1 Models of technological innovation and social shaping
Source: Edge 1995.

for example, how subsequent designs might be influenced by the experience of the actual effects, intended and unintended, of a technology in use. Second, a recognition that the complexities that such processes introduce render any simplistic model of the innovation process untenable and point to the recursive nature of the interaction between technical and social variables. According to Williams and Edge (1992a) such a perspective 'problematises' the innovation process. This occurs, first, through the questioning of the notion that technologies have fixed and determinant characteristics and, second, through the suggestion that innovation is more than a 'rational-technical' process of finding solutions to problems. Thus, instead of being 'black boxed' at the point of invention, the characteristics and capabilities of a technology are seen as being constantly shaped and reshaped by feedback and interaction that occurs during their 'upstream' deployment. The content and form of technology thus remain malleable throughout the process of innovation and, as we will see below, during its implementation and use. In effect, rather than viewing technology as socially shaped, it ultimately makes more sense to view the relationship between technology and social variables, including organisational ones, as one of mutual shaping.

Interests in the production of technology: class, politics and gender

A central assumption for the social shaping perspective is that the content of technology and the direction of technological development can be explained in terms of the social, political and economic interests which give rise to and direct its invention, design, implementation and use. Early social shaping studies focused on the way in which social interests could be seen to be embodied in technological artefacts and systems during their invention and design. Thus, Noble (1979) in his classic study of the origins and development of computer numerical machine tools in the USA shows how the automation of lathes, milling machines and the like was strongly influenced by the interests of a constituency comprising the military, General Electric, university researchers and manufacturers. They rejected alternative possibilities for automating these tools, which would have enhanced the skill and autonomy of operators, in favour of one which offered the prospect of increasing management control at the expense of the skilled craft workers who operated conventional machines.

Similarly Winner argues in more general terms that 'artefacts have politics'. This can occur in two ways. First where there are a range of alternative design options or configurations of an artefact this flexibility can 'provide convenient means of establishing patterns of power and authority in a given setting' by dominant social groups. Second, where no such flexibility exists and once lines of technological development have been established there is little scope for reversing them – for example the development of the nuclear industry – then initial adoption decisions become key and are likely to be strongly influenced by prevailing patterns of institutionalised power and authority (Winner 1980: 36).

The range of actors, institutions and other agencies focused upon in these early studies was relatively small and the relations between elements, therefore, more or less straightforward. However, subsequent social shaping research has developed a far more complex and differentiated understanding of the web of relationships involved and has developed a more sophisticated notion of the role of interests in shaping technology. In particular attention has been given to the political actions required in order to build alliances amongst key interest groups. Such 'socio-technical constituencies', as they have been termed (Molina 1994), are the product of successful attempts to enrol a range of interest groups – for example, suppliers, experts and users – and deploy the resources and expertise that they have to define and solve innovation problems. The dynamics of the process of building socio-technical constituencies thus render attempts to 'read off' particular social shaping outcomes from the assumed interests of groups according to variables such as class position or ethnic origin as overly simplistic.

Increasingly the social shaping perspective has pointed, not only to the way in which class and political interests shape technology, but to the way in which gender relations also play a crucial role. That is, rather than just its use and effects being seen as a function of the patriarchal relationships (see Chapter 3), the content of technology itself is considered to be gendered. An illustration of what may be involved here is given in Figure 7.2. This shows mock-ups of two alternative designs for an iron produced by two industrial design students. Picture (b) is a design produced by a male, and (a) is a design by a female. The male's design is a variation on existing (male) designs of this type of artefact. The female design appears radically different and suggests a greater attention to functional require-ments and ergonomics. How might these differences be explained?

Feminist perspectives on the social shaping of technology take a variety of forms. Grint and Gill distinguish between three broad positions (see also Wajcman 1991). First, 'eco-feminism' where technology is seen as an example of male attempts to dominate and control both the natural world and females. Women, by virtue of their biological make-up, enjoy a much closer affinity with the natural world and possess values which both lead them to oppose, and mitigate against them wishing to develop, technolo-gies of control and domination (for a similar view see Cooley 1980a). Second, 'liberal-feminist' perspectives see the exclusion of women from technological development as a function of gender stereotyping which can go as far as shaping women's self-images of what are and what are not appropriate work and careers for them. Typically technological work and careers are seen as inappropriate in this way. Finally, there is the social shaping perspective which views technology as historically and culturally

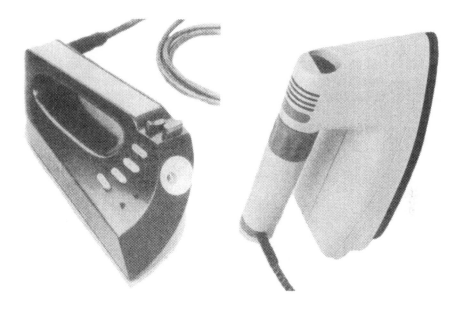

Figure 7.2 Irons designed by (a) female and (b) male industrial design students
Source: Open University T362 Course Team 1986b: 24.

shaped as masculine and thereby 'gendered'. In this perspective technology embodies the 'knowledge and practices' which are required in its use. This knowledge can be understood as a cultural product and the social relations embodied in technology as a reflection of male expressions and views of their relationships with machines (Wajcman 1991: 149).

How might these approaches account for the differences observed in Figure 7.2? First, the eco-feminist perspective might seek to use the apparently greater functionality and ergonomic nature of the female design to further justify arguments for the exclusion of men from the design process in general so that feminine values can be permitted to shape technologies for use by women. Second, for the 'liberal-feminist' what would be at issue here are the gender stereotypes which give rise to a rigid segregation of males and females in both the domestic and economic division of labours. The designs can be seen as a reflection of a domestic division of labour which distinguishes between the roles of male 'breadwinner' and female 'homemaker'. Whereas socialisation into the breadwinner role would have exposed the male student to knowledge about the iron – what it is for and what it can do, for example – it is likely that he would have had little practical and extended experience of day-to-day use of such an artefact, this activity being undertaken most probably by his mother (and subsequently by a spouse and/or mother-in-law). The female student, on the other hand, might be expected to have had first hand experience, perhaps unwillingly, in preparation for what her parents would possibly have seen as her eventual role as 'wife and mother'. This practical experience of using such artefacts, it might then be argued, has resulted in a design which more directly reflects the requirements of the predominantly female user.

The implication of both these perspectives however is that the technology itself is 'neutral'. For example, the eco-feminist perspective makes culturally and historically naïve assumptions concerning the nature of 'feminine values' which also bring with them overtones of biological determinism. The result is a tendency to promote 'separatism' in the search for 'feminist technologies' but without any questioning of the way technology itself is a social product (see Grint and Gill 1995: 5–6). Similarly, the liberal-feminist perspective suggests that the problem highlighted by the two different designs could be remedied if more females would and could be persuaded to take up technological careers (and by the same token more males to engage in household tasks). The implication is that women's exclusion from the design and development of technologies is somehow a result of their failure to adjust to its requirements (see Grint and Gill 1995: 7).

The social shaping perspective would argue that the differences in the two designs are a result of a process by which the content of technology became gendered. In fact it has frequently been argued that the development of domestic technology has been shaped by male values and interests and that this reflects a broader cultural association between technology and masculinity from which females are excluded (Faulkner and Arnold 1985). Alongside this, as Gill and Grint (1995) observe, there is also a paradoxical view that women have played a key role in generating innovations but that this has, in Rothschild's (1983) words, been 'hidden by history'. This suggests that the linkage between technology and masculinity may be more ideological than real and rest on a 'specific understanding of the technical and a set of exclusions which position women outside the technical realm' (Gill and Grint 1995: 4). The difference between the two designs is therefore a cultural product and these social relations are embodied in the artefacts which we observe.

How then does such a gendering of technologies come about? The answer to this question begins with the radical labour process analysis outlined in Chapter 3. However, the claim made by the social shaping perspective is that technology is shaped not only by the divergent interests arising from class divisions but also by those arising from gender divisions

(Wajcman 1991: 20). The emergence of industrial capitalism has had the consequence of deepening and extending these divisions with the effect that the division of labour within organisations systematically excludes females from the production of technology, both in the sense of their involvement in the process of invention, design and development, and in the sense that their needs and interests as potential 'users' are not considered other than through a male perspective (Wajcman 1991: 21–2).

Whilst the consequences of this process of segregation and exclusion are well documented (see Chapter 3) detailed understanding of the means by which technologies become gendered in this way is, relatively speaking, patchy (an exception is Cockburn and Ormrod 1993). In part this results from a 'gender blindness' in the social shaping perspective itself which has meant that 'there are few cases where feminists have really got inside the "black box" of technology' (Wajcman 1991: 22). However, the idea of technological innovation as a process of network building through the development of socio-technical constituencies, actor-networks or the seeking of consensus by relevant social groups, does offer a means by which the gendering of technology can be understood *provided that* 'the underlying structure of gender relations' is taken into account (Wajcman 1991: 24). That is, not only the members of networks and the like one should study, but also the groups who have been excluded from involvement in the social shaping of technological developments. According to Wajcman:

> Preferences for different technologies are shaped by a set of social arrangements that reflect men's power in wider society. The process of technological development is socially structured and culturally patterned by various social interests that lie outside the immediate context of technological innovation.
>
> (Wajcman 1991: 24)

In other words, it is not enough to show how technology is shaped by the resolution of competing views about its form and content or by the differential power capacities of key constituents, actors or groups. When, as a result, technology becomes 'stabilised' it does so in the context of a 'masculine culture' which has already excluded female interests from the argument.

Thus, Webster (1996: 66) suggests that technology can be seen as being gendered in the following ways. First, promoters, critics and potential users 'make sense of' and give meaning to a new technology, through gendered social and technical *visions* which underpin design and development. Second, designer's decisions may be based on gendered knowledge or assumptions about users, the context of use, and the way artefacts and systems are to be applied. Given the gendered division of labour this frequently means, in the case of ICTs for instance, male designers shaping technologies in accordance with knowledge and assumptions they have about female users, contexts and applications. Third, users may themselves respond in a gendered way to the technologies and systems designed for them. For instance, there are important historical examples – for example the development in use of the telephone – where the use and application of technology has been shaped by women in ways not envisaged by male designers.

In sum, the socio-economic shaping perspective reveals how technologies can be seen to embody the interests of particular social groups. By the same token, it also suggests how others are excluded from having a similar say over not just the deployment and use of technology, but its actual content. These arguments focus on the role of interests in social shaping during the production of technology, with some recognition of 'feedback' into this process from the context where technologies are subsequently used. More recently, however, the socio-economic perspective has become concerned with the way technologies are actively shaped whilst they are being 'consumed' or used in their adopting context.

Interests in the consumption of technology: suppliers and users

Socio-economic shaping studies now see the adopting context as a key arena in which the final form and content of technologies are defined. The basis of this focus is the realisation that the malleability of certain types of technology and the openness of their design to 'upstream' feedback means that innovation extends well beyond the conventional point of innovation conceived as the point of first successful adoption (see Chapter 2). Rather, innovation occurs during the implementation of systems within adopting organisations as they diffuse to a wider and wider range of users. This process has been termed 'innofusion' (Fleck 1987) and with it comes a much more explicit focus on the 'users' of technology as key actors in its socio-economic shaping, in particular through their interactions and relationships with suppliers.

Innofusion is particularly significant when innovation involves what Fleck (1993) terms 'configurational' as opposed to 'generic' technologies. This distinction can be illustrated by considering a simple artefact such as the bicycle. The bicycle can be regarded as a generic technology in the sense that it is a 'recognisable and more or less standard system for human-powered transport' where all possible user requirements and information about the circumstances of use, are largely anticipated in the design of the system prior to first adoption. Whilst individual users will fine-tune or customise their cycles to suit their particular requirements and purposes, these acts amount to 'adjusting the parameters' rather than fundamentally 'altering the essential character' of the system.

Configurational technologies, by contrast, do not possess generic qualities which allow them to be applied with only minor adjustments by other users. Rather, configurational technologies are largely shaped in each application by user requirements and the specifics of the circumstances in which they are to be used. Or, as Fleck puts it they 'essentially comprise more or less unique assemblies of components, some standardly available, others specially developed, built up to meet the particular requirements of user organisations' (Fleck 1993: 19).

Significantly, many microelectronics-based ICTs have turned out to have configurational rather than generic characteristics (see e.g. Fleck 1987; Tierney and Williams 1990; Webster 1990). Fleck points to the example of the industrial robot. Originally this was envisaged by its inventor as a generic technology which could be applied 'off the shelf' to replace human workers doing any physical manipulation task. In practice, more or less uniquely different types of robot models and configurations have emerged in user organisations specific to local requirements and circumstances. These configurations cannot be readily applied elsewhere by other users to do different tasks.

Williams (1997a) draws on the concept of innofusion to point to the significance of the user organisation as an arena in which social shaping occurs. Two factors are particularly important. First, local expertise and experience. This comprises tacit and broadly dispersed knowledge about the business and organisation itself that, in order to produce a functioning system, has to be combined with generic knowledge about ICTs. This knowledge tends to be formalised and concentrated in expert groups. Second, links between the supplier of ICT systems, normally the repository of generic knowledge, and the user organisation where tacit knowledge about the business is located. The task of producing a functioning system therefore requires collaboration in a joint development process between supplier and user (Williams 1997a: 173–4).

Moreover, such collaborative episodes are unlikely to be 'one-off' events but dynamic processes of development and implementation cycles both within single organisations but more broadly across several organisations as innofusion in one context emerges as an innovation which can be diffused, and further adapted, to other settings. This perspective permits the biography of technologies to be mapped as they develop over time (see Figure 7.3) and allows us to see how local innovations can become globalised as the process of innofusion repeats itself in different organisational settings (Williams 1997a).

A similar path is followed by Clark (1997) who, drawing on insights from evolutionary economics, suggests innovations such as CAPM can be understood as the evolution of dynamic configurations comprising combinations and consolidations of diverse technical and social elements. For the user the shape and uses of an innovation are problematic and will be perceived differently by different user groups, even within the same organisation. This is likely to result in contending struggles. In fact the actions of users are crucial

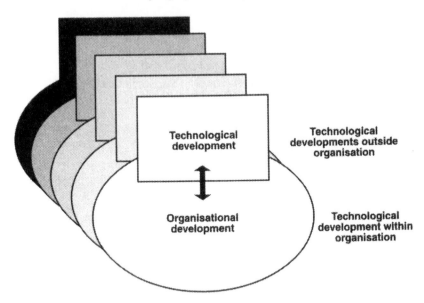

Figure 7.3 Schematic model of the development of technology and organisation
Source: Williams 1997a: 113.

to the context specific shaping of an innovation and its use. This may involve unbundling and reshaping an innovation as well as developing new uses. Users in effect have to uncover the 'contingent specificity' of an innovation and seek to embed it in the distinct socio-cultural context of the adopting setting. The success of these efforts within a given 'socio-economic selection environment' over time will determine the extent to which an innovation is effectively appropriated by an organisation. Such appropriation involves 'cumulative and progressive transformation of the innovation coupled with modifications to existing knowledge bases in the user organisation' (Clark 1997: 33) and involves interactions between supplier(s) and the user (or rather differing coalitions within the user organisation) in key 'decision episodes'. It is through these interactions and their embedding within the organisation that the shaping of an innovation occurs.

The complex dynamics alluded to in different but parallel ways by Williams and Clark underpin a development by which initially novel applications can become standardised over time but by the same token subsequently become differentiated into discrete applications as they are 'reinnovated'. Such a perspective means it makes little or no sense to see ICTs as an external variable transforming work and organisation. Rather, technology and work organisation develop in tandem. Pre-existing models of work organisation, with visions of how these might be transformed, become embedded in information and computing technology applications. Implementation problems for packaged solutions often reflect lack of fit between the social relations in the firms in which a system was initially developed, which become embedded in the software, and the actual circumstances of the user.

(Williams 1997a: 176–7)

Webster (1993: 58) further illustrates this point by suggesting that technologies emerge from, develop within and come to embody particular production concepts and cultures. In this way 'innofusion' and mutual shaping can be seen to extend to new production concepts and their constituent techniques. Further, paradigms and visions of production can be seen to subsequently evolve within, as they are adapted to, the local structures and cultures of adopting organisations. The result is a hybrid of the new paradigm blended with existing practices. In turn these processes are fed back into activities such as software development consultant products and academic research which leads to further conceptual and other innovations. Webster would also remind us at this point that showing how the innovation process is shaped by innofusion and the like is only part of the story. The social divisions which 'generate these processes' also need to be incorporated in the explanation (Webster 1996: 190).

Indeed, the focus of the socio-economic shaping perspective on the consumption of ICTs provides a further, although as yet rarely exploited, opportunity for bringing gender relations and women into the account. According to Webster, whilst 'women may be largely absent from the design and creation of IT systems in the early stages of their development' they are much more frequently, 'strongly involved in their consumption and use'. Therefore, 'women may actively intervene to configure and deploy the information technologies which they use at work and so leave the imprint of their gender identities at work upon them' (Webster 1996: 28). Thus, the socio-economic shaping perspective points not only to the gendered nature of the effects of the production of technology but also strongly suggests that it has a role in the shaping of technology during consumption through innofusion.

Reshaping technology and organisation: 'new wave' socio-technical systems

The dysfunctional 'machine' models of the technology–organisation relationship outlined in Chapter 1 have spawned a long tradition of socio-technical theory and research. The objective of this academic and practical activity has been to reshape the relationship between technology and organisation around more humanistic and human-centred ideals. Such objectives have been given added impetus since the late-1970s by the growing evidence that ICT-based technological and related organisational changes frequently fall short of planned objectives and sometimes fail completely precisely because the 'human' and 'organisational' dimensions of change are inadequately understood and handled (McLoughlin and Clark 1994; Storey 1994).

In the 1950s and 1960s socio-technical theorists and practitioners claimed to have found a way of optimising the requirements of technology with the needs of humans. The chief lesson of the research was that if management concentrated on maximising their economic gains by improving the technological system of the organisation *without* similar attention to the social system, then the economic benefits would be less. Hence a socio-technical systems approach was required which took both elements into account in the pursuit of economic efficiency. Socio-technical researchers subsequently developed principles of good work design which they argued should be followed in the design of jobs and work organisation if an appropriate fit between the technical and social elements of a socio-technical system was to be achieved (see e.g. Trist *et al.* 1963; Emery 1978).

However, whilst this 'traditional' socio-technical approach emphasised the central importance of focusing on both technology and organisation at one and the same time, in practice, it tended to concentrate on the reshaping of organisation rather than technology (Van Einjatten 1993; Badham and Naschold 1994). At the same time, concepts of organisation tended to draw on systems ideas which stressed equilibrium and stability as the norm and competing interests and conflict as dysfunctional. One consequence was that the socio-technical practitioner too often appeared to take the role of the servant of dominant organisational interests (Rose 1988). In addition, attempts at reshaping technology and organisation according to socio-technical principles were most commonly marked by their evident failure in practice (see e.g. Bailey 1983; Majchrzak 1988; Buchanan 1989).

It has been claimed that these issues have been more adequately addressed by a range of new socio-technical theorists and practitioners who have broadened the socio-technical constituency considerably since the 1960s. From its Anglo-Australian origins, socio-technical theory and research now also embraces work in Scandinavia and other Northern European countries and increasingly well beyond (see van Einjatten 1993). This new body of work – frequently based on action research projects and methods – has sought to develop alternative models of production systems and methods of system design and implementation that aim to avoid the 'technocractic' assumptions of more conventional approaches. These models cover a broad range and are known by a variety of names – for example, 'human-centred systems', 'anthropocentric', 'computer supported cooperative work', 'symbiotic', 'feminist system design', 'integrated organisational renewal' and most recently 'developmental work' (see e.g. Cooley 1980a; Rosenbrock 1985; Rauner *et al.* 1988; Brödner 1990; Winnograd and Adler 1992; Clausen and Langaa Jensen 1993; Green *et al.* 1993; McCarthy 1994; Salzmen and Rosenthal 1994; Benders *et al.* 1995; de Sitter *et al.* 1997; Clausen and Nielson 1997). Taken together these models can be seen as constituting a new, if eclectic, wave in socio-technical theory (Mathews 1997).

This new socio-technical theory seeks to address many of the weaknesses of more traditional work in the area which many see as contributing to the failure of reshaping initiatives in the past (see Van Einjatten 1993; Bødker and Greenbaum 1993; Benders *et al.* 1995; Badham and Naschold 1994; Blackler 1994; Clegg *et al.* 1994; Webster 1996; Majchrzak 1997; Mathews 1997). Thus, unlike the earlier socio-technical approaches, these models – albeit to varying degrees:

- seek to replace 'hard systems' and 'positivistic' models and methods which privilege the expert and their abstract knowledge with 'soft systems' and more interpretative alternatives which value the local knowledge of the user; and give far more attention to specifying and incorporating human-centred design principles into *both* technical *and* organisational systems;
- more readily recognise that the application of alternative socio-technical principles are not appropriate in all national circumstances – for example those lacking a higher skill-base or established trade union structure – and increasingly realise that there are substantial constraints on the full development of a socio-technical paradigm or trajectory, such as the resistance of existing Taylorist/Fordist forms of organisation, the resilience of 'technocractic' design principles and methods, and the unintended threats to jobs, working life and individual well being posed by socio-technical solutions which can make union and worker support problematic;
- seek to address the 'gender blindness' of conventional system design, although few of the new socio-technical approaches are free from this problem;
- realise to a greater extent than ever before that the politics of organisations and change need to be more effectively addressed by design tools, methods and techniques if the promotion and implementation of socio-technical change is to be achieved more effectively;
- increasingly recognise that the context in which models of socio-technical systems – just as with other configurational technologies – are applied is the key arena in which 'working' socio-technical systems are made and this involves compromises and trade-offs in relation to overall socio-technical principles as well as an engagement with the business context of implementation.

In the most general terms some of the essential features (readers will, for instance, note the apparent gender blindness in this example) of this new 'socio-technical' paradigm are summarised in Table 7.1. First, the organisational context of socio-technical system design is recognised by incorporating products, processes and labour dimensions. Second, several essential antecendents are identified as necessary inputs if socio-technical requirements of human-centred design, customised products, flexible production, and autonomous teams are to be realised and sustained. These include an existing supply of skilled and knowledgeable labour, appropriate management strategies and support, high-trust employment relations and a shared objective of organisational democracy. Finally, desired outcomes embrace both 'human' and 'business' objectives to include not only intrinsically satisfying and extrinsically rewarding work in which employees enjoy considerable autonomy and discretion as part of an overall democratic goal, but also the business benefits from high quality, continuous improvement, innovation and commitment.

Table 7.1 The socio-technical production system

Organisational features
• Customised production (competitive advantage based on price, quality, responsiveness and innovation)   • Flexibility of process (quick change over; just-in-time)   • Functional flexibility of labour (multifunctional, semi-autonomous teams: production cells)   • Human-centred techno-organisational design
Outcomes
• High quality, medium cost, innovative products   • Flexible specialisation of labour   • Low inventories and low buffer stocks   • Functional flexibility, continuous improvement   • Informed worker commitment to production goals
Inputs
• High commitment, close customer and supplier relations   • High level of skills with intellectual content   • Team-based, overlapping coordination   • Management focus on strategic directions and facilitation of production   • High-trust industrial relations   • Organisational democracy as goal

Source: Mathews 1994: 44.

Assessing socio-economic shaping

The socio-economic shaping model points to the dynamic and interactive socio-economic context, form and content of technological development. Technological innovations, initially shaped in one organisational context, are turned into working technologies by local customisation within a broad range of other organisations where adoption takes place. In turn, if a line of technological development is to endure, this experience and knowledge needs to be embodied in future innovations by suppliers within their own organisations. In turn the consequent innovations are again subject to local adaptation in adopting contexts and so on.

At its simplest the social shaping approach suggests we make sense of the interaction of technology and organisation in terms of the metaphor of 'embodiment' whereby economic, social and political interests are 'built into' the design of the technology. However, the multiple feedback relationships that exist between a complex of designers and suppliers of technology on the one hand, and a complex of users on the other, suggest that technologies so construed are far from clear-cut and stable entities. The possibilities of post-adoption innovation by users and its reappropriation as reinnovation by suppliers suggests that 'embodiment' is better regarded as a 'crystallisation' of a highly malleable socio-technical phenomenon in particular and ever changing contingent circumstances (Fleck 1993). The socio-economic model of the shaping of technology has thus moved towards a conceptualisation of technology and organisation which maintains a notion of 'technology' as having independent effects in specific contingent circumstances but, at the same time, shows that these 'effects' are shaped by evolving constituencies and networks of socio-economic relationships and structures.

The concept of the 'mutual shaping' of technology provides a useful broadening out into a more panoramic perspective of the conventional interests of organisational studies which have tended to focus on and emphasis the 'impact' of technological change on the organisation and have failed to explore the 'socio-technical' constitution of the adopted technology. The resultant 'collision' has in the past only been partially understood. However, now it can be more fully explicated by situating the adopting context of the workplace within a broader network of socio-economic relationships and structures (Williams 1997b: 111). At the same time, the wide variations in actual organisational outcomes observed in workplace studies can be understood and explained in terms which go beyond the idiosyncrasies of the political systems and culture of the adopting organisation.

Moreover, by conceptualising technological development so conceived in terms of an evolving socio-technical constituency of stakeholders, interests and institutions, the idea of innovation as a process of network building – also highlighted in other variants of the social shaping perspective – is also incorporated. Further, the notion of innofusion directly maps across to evolutionary models of innovation since it seeks to capture the way in which organisations develop new characteristics in response to environmental change by reconfiguring socio-technical arrangements that are subsequently transmitted to succeeding generations of technology

(Fleck 1993: 28). Ultimately, such models provide the prospect of being able to specify the generic effects of technological change in terms which see such paths and trajectories as shaped by the evolution over time of complex socio-technical interactions.

What is interesting about contemporary developments in ICTs in these respects is, following Fleck (1993), precisely that the 'uncertain process of experimentation and discovery' which gives rise to indeterminate outcomes has yet to, indeed may never, become embodied in stable generic systems of knowledge, or 'technological regimes' or 'paradigms'. Rather, it is the case that, 'local contingencies continue to resist stabilisation or crystallisation' and that, 'development is a matter of a sequence of highly individual configurations' that may not always be progressive or intended (Fleck 1993: 29).

On the face of it then, the socio-economic shaping perspective provides a seemingly robust and potentially integrative model of the shaping of technology and organisation and reflects many of the convergences in theoretical development identified within its own ranks (e.g. MacKenzie 1996; Clausen and Williams 1997) and by proponents of other variants of social shaping (see e.g. Bijker and Law 1992) and observers from within other perspectives (see e.g. Badham 1993; Fulk 1993; Coombs *et al.* 1996; McLoughlin and Harris 1997). However, the socio-economic variant also has its critics and their principal objections will now be outlined.

One set of problems revolves around the precise nature of the socio-economic factors that shape technology. As noted above the socio-economic perspective 'works inwards' in its analysis of the shaping of technology. One consequence is that it can appear to give explanatory primacy to structural factors in explaining the socio-economic shaping of artefacts and systems (Clausen and Williams 1997: 4). This can happen, for example: at the societal level by pointing to historical trends towards 'rationalisation', 'globalisation', 'feminisation of labour' and the like that cut across national boundaries; in terms of the environment of organisations by stressing the influence of nationally specific factors such as the operation of product and labour markets, industrial relations and innovation systems and so on; and within organisations, by stressing the role of characteristics such as organisation structure, size, and institutions and processes of management/labour relations. The upshot is that actors appear to be left by these arrangements with little scope themselves to actively shape either the production or consumption of technology, in particular in terms of the meanings and interpretations given to artefacts and systems (Mackay and Gillespie 1992).

As we have seen, this criticism is less well-founded, especially as the socio-economic perspective has shifted focus to the way in which technology is consumed. Indeed, actors (user organisations, suppliers, professional associations, research institutions, management, workers and their representatives and so forth) are placed at the centre of a model of shaping, which views technology as an outcome of 'social processes of negotiation through a complicated and heterogeneous network of diverse players with different commitments and positions on the structure', where the players 'are primarily characterised by their different interests, related to their societal position and function and access unequally distributed power and resources' (Clausen and Williams 1997: 6). It follows that the outcomes are far more indeterminant than an exclusively structural account would yield since no one actor is able in the long run to exercise decisive influence on the shaping of technology.

However, even this position is unsatisfying for variants of the social shaping perspective which stress entirely the role of action and actors and question, even deny, the possibility of structural influences which exist a priori of action. Law (1987), for example, takes issue with the socio-economic shaping perspective insofar as it represents the social interests which shape technology as relatively stable entities whose essence – class interest, gender interests, bureaucratic interests and so on – once recognised can be assumed to be fixed. Rather, he suggests that these aspects of the 'social', as well as the way in which they shape technology, need to be established empirically each time an episode of social shaping is examined. Taking inspiration from the work of Hughes (1983, 1987) he argues that the social interests shaping technology can only be as seen as they appear to 'system builders' (or as in Law's own formulation 'heterogeneous engineers'). It is only through their efforts, rather than the assumptions of the analyst, that the force of the social in shaping the technical is established. Inequalities between classes or genders are thus to be seen not as a priori features of social structure shaping technology but rather as 'an outcome of socio-technical struggles' (Law 1987: 422).

This argument is pursued further by Grint and Woolgar (1995) who accuse the social shaping of technology in general and the socio-economic and feminist variants in particular, of a 'failure of nerve'. They identify three problems with the conceptual premise of 'social shaping' (Grint and Woolgar 1995: 50–3). First, the idea that 'antecedent circumstances' such as the interests of particular social groups are 'built-in' or 'embodied' in technologies is ambivalent since it seems to suggest that technologies are neutral up to the point that a social and political 'veneer' is attached by a particular interest. Second, such 'antecedent circumstances', for example the interests and motives of the designers of technology, are themselves open to 'interpretative flexibility'. Third, it still seems to be the case that socially shaped technologies are assumed to have 'independent effects'. Thus the notion that it is the requirements, capabilities and characteristics of technology which have the 'effect', rather than the historically and culturally bound interpretations of what the 'effect' of a particular technology is, is retained. In effect what happens, argue Grint and Woolgar, is that the social shaping perspective seeks to replace technical determinism in explaining the content of technology with social and political determinants whose embodiment in the technology explain the 'effects' it has. Feminist accounts of social shaping are a specific example of this error.

For example, let us return to the images in Figure 7.2 and the possible explanations offered by feminist theory. All these positions according to Grint and Woolgar, including the socio-economic shaping perspective, view technology as either determining or neutral. Moreover, the definitions of gender and its consequences which underpin them are insufficiently problematised. Grint and Woolgar's suggestion would thus be that we need to question why we see the images in the figure as examples of gendered technologies in the first place. Such properties are not reflected by the artefacts themselves but a construction made from the interpretative context within which they are given meaning. Thus rejecting irons which reflect male rather than female values, or getting more females involved in the design of irons, misses the point completely. What needs changing, 'through the alliance of sufficiently powerful forces' is the cultural context in which irons – or technologies in general – come to be regarded as gendered (Grint and Woolgar 1995: 71). Grint and Woolgar's contention, therefore, is that the 'gender' of a technology 'does not lie encased in the fabric' of the machine or system. Rather, 'it is instead the temporary contingent upshot of on-going interpretation by designers, sellers and users' where the technology is not neutral but rather the product of 'social constructions not objective reflections' (Grint and Woolgar 1995: 70).

A final potential weakness with the socio-economic shaping approach resides with the possibilities for reshaping technology that the theoretical premise of the perspective exposes. As we have now seen, the insights offered by the social shaping approach as a whole, and the socio-economic shaping variant in particular, offer up the conceptual possibility of reshaping technology in ways which reflect the interests, beliefs and values of groups and institutions other than those which currently have the dominant say in how technology is produced and consumed. In particular, the social shaping model offers a thoroughgoing critique of prevailing models of policy-making and other interventions which see the design and development of new technologies as a matter largely for suppliers; downplay the human and organisational elements of system adoption; cast the suppliers and consultants as 'experts' selling 'best practice' models and as trying to influence the practice of relatively ignorant consumers and users; and ignore the role of gender in the production and consumption of technologies (Webster 1993, 1996; Clark and Newell 1993: 70). In contrast the 'user', as a complex human, gendered and organisational entity, is placed at the centre of analysis by the socio-economic approach. It follows that user involvement becomes a central factor in the mutual (re)shaping of technology and organisation and this in turn leads to a requirement to understand how effective collaborative relationships between suppliers, users and a range of third parties are built and sustained.

Despite this theoretical opportunity, however, social shaping research has had far less to say on the issue of reshaping technology and organisation than one might expect. Part of the reason lies in the fact, noted in the previous chapter, that the perspective as a whole has been pre-occupied with sometimes highly abstract theoretical and epistemological debates over the appropriateness of particular metaphors and so forth. As a result the socio-political consequences of the arguments have not been fully recognised, explored or developed (Bijker 1995b). Having said this, the socio-economic variant is more directly committed to such an engage-ment, in particular through its use of a metaphor which allows for broader structural, political, economic and gender interests being 'embodied' in technology and which can shape lines of technological development.

However, to date this commitment has been evident more in the construction of complex models of the mutual interaction of the tech-nology and organisation to reveal the manner in which such embodiment or crystallisation takes place. At the same time, others no doubt sympa-thetic to, if not sometimes consciously or unconsciously informed by insights from the social shaping perspective, have been engaged in a wide range of activity in defining new principles of system design, identifying tools and methodologies, and some significant action research and other experiments in seeking to either produce demonstration systems or actu-ally achieve implementation. At present, though, it seems that there is a gulf between the knowledge and practice of those who are seeking to inter-vene more creatively in technological change and the broader, more theoretical and research-based understandings gained through social shaping studies (Badham 1993). As we will see in the following and concluding chapter, there is now every reason for these communities to seek a more active engagement with each other.

Conclusion

In this chapter we have completed our discussion of the social shaping perspective. The material considered here has attempted to link concerns over the social shaping of the technical content of technology with the broader social and economic context in which this arises and takes place. To understand what goes on 'inside the black box', argues the socio-economic shaping perspective, we need to also understand what goes on outside it. Although we have considered many competing and conflicting views in the preceding chapters, the basic idea to emerge from the discus-sion here is that of the mutual shaping of technology and organisation during its production and consumption. This suggests the possibility of reconciling aspects of, at least some, of the competing perspectives considered. An exploration of this possibility is the focus of the concluding chapter. Indeed, it will be argued that a more creative approach to thinking and acting in relation to technology and organisation requires it.

8 Conclusion
Creative technological change

Introduction

The title of this volume has the potential, partly intentional, to mislead. The idea of 'creative technological change' might suggest to the reader – and organisational actor or manager or other change agent of some kind – that lessons concerning how to think and act more creatively when actually performing these roles will now (at last) be revealed by the author. Well, yes but mainly no. The perspective of this book has not been driven by the perceived needs of the actual or would-be organisational performer for such prescription. Rather, the assumed stance is that of the theatre or cinema critic, perhaps even any member of the audience, keen to sharpen their critical awareness and capacity in order to better understand and explain the action and its context as it is played out before them. That is not to say that the organisational performer can learn nothing from such critical observation. On the contrary, for those prepared to do so, the material presented and discussed in the preceding chapters provides a basis for reflection, contextualisation and learning in the manner of Schon's (1983) 'reflective practitioner'.

This stance is taken since it also offers the rather intriguing prospect of exploring what can be learnt when critics try their hands at being performers. The assumption here is that such 'amateur dramatics' may well do much to sharpen the faculties of the 'reflective observer' by providing them with insights that can only be gained through the experience of, or at least exceedingly close proximity to, performance rather than just its mere observation and critique. Appropriately, given this rather oblique beginning, we start by revisiting the notion of metaphor and its promise of opening up a more creative understanding of the interaction between technology and organisation.

Metaphors, technology and organisation

The various perspectives that have sought to illuminate our understanding of the interaction between technology and organisation are, it has been argued, themselves best made sense of in terms of the metaphors which underpin their conceptualisation and analysis (see Figure 8.1). The approach here is based on Morgan's (1986, 1997) seminal contribution and the observation that, for both observers of organisational performance and the performers themselves, thought and action are based on and informed by metaphorical constructs.

Thus, in Chapter 1 we saw how the metaphors of 'machine', 'organism' and 'information processing brains' have been evoked at different times and in different ways to provide a deterministic understanding of the relationship between technology, technological change and organisations. Such arguments have strengths in terms of the way they variously helped to make sense of the undoubted relationship between mechanistic organisational designs and productive efficiency, the need to take the 'human side' of change into account when organisations adapt to new technological and other contingencies, and in understanding the way advances in ICTs not only have effects on organisations, but may well require a rethinking of what an organisation, and the work conducted therein actually is. On the other hand, such perspectives have major limitations in so far as they can draw us into thinking of technology as both having an autonomous logic of its own and as being capable of having independent effects on organisation independent of human interpretation or choice.

In Chapter 2 the biological theme was developed further by looking at evolutionary approaches to understanding technological innovation. This

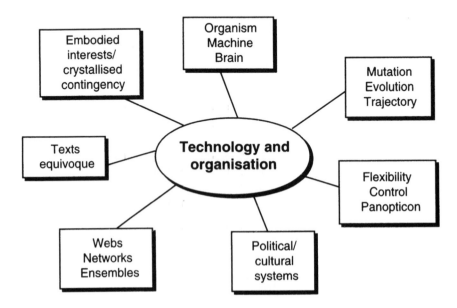

Figure 8.1 Metaphors, technology and organisations

literature, mainly from the periphery of orthodox economics, has shown increasing resonance with certain developments in organisational theory. This is most evident in relation to the notion of the learning organisation as a 'species' capable of generating the kind of innovations (mutations) necessary to bring about the economic (environmental) variety required to sustain organisational growth and survival. The strength of this approach is that it focuses attention on what organisations can do in terms of developing strategies for both producing and adopting innovations which can have a decisive effect on their innovative potential. By the same token, organisational learning is identified as a key capability that embodies the capacity of the organisation to influence its own fate in the broader process of technological development and economic progress. A major weakness, however, is the tendency to focus on the behaviour of organisations as objective entities. One consequence is that the pathways within which innovation in organisations develops, and the broader trajectories of which these are an element, can appear as 'natural' rather than 'social' in origin, direction and objective.

The post-Fordist debate on the relationship between technological change and organisational transformation was considered in Chapter 3. This is also concerned with the broader context of economic, technological and social development. However, the approach here is to usefully refocus our attention on the 'relations' rather than 'forces of production'. That is, technological development is seen not as autonomous but as embedded in broader economic, political and social changes. However, precisely what these changes are and how they should be interpreted and understood is a matter of considerable controversy. On the one hand it has been argued that they represent no more than refinement of existing Fordist production paradigms and concepts. On the other hand, other analysts endorse at least the possibilities of a shift to post-Fordist forms. They stress how the flexibility of new technology enables the increasing organisational flexibility required to compete in more differentiated and uncertain global product market conditions. Some also stress the possibilities for humanising work that new production concepts and post-modern organisational forms bring. A further line of argument focuses on the consequences of the panoptic characteristics of ICTs and their implications for the electronic surveillance of the behaviour of organisation members, for instance, through new forms of disciplinary power and self-control. However, although providing many insights, these lines of argument can still carry with them strong deterministic overtones, if not in relation to technology, then in terms of the way broader social and economic trends are deemed to impact on organisations.

Appropriately, Chapter 4 examined perspectives on technology and organisation which started with the metaphor of organisations as political and cultural systems shaped by, and shaping, the choices and decisions of organisational members. In this perspective, technological change and its outcomes were seen as the product of a process of choice and political negotiation, made in the context of, but certainly not determined by broader technological or economic imperatives. The strengths of looking at technology and organisations in this way are that it reveals a complex world of shifting coalitions, interpretative schemes, and power balances which are far more decisive in shaping the 'effects' of technology than the characteristics and capabilities of technology itself or broader economic imperatives. In particular, it highlights the political nature of the roles, behaviours and activities of those in organisations engaged in the process of innovation and change. The problem with this perspective is that it can, although key proponents deny that this is the intention, give too much stress to the causal role of actors and their subjective interpretation of situations, to the exclusion of the influence of structural features of the organisation's context and environment, including technology itself.

No such qualms constrained the perspectives considered in Chapters 5 and 6 which sought, from a broad social constructivist position, to show how the content of technology itself, not just its effects, are socially shaped through the interpretations and meanings given to it. A variety of metaphors were evoked to open the technology 'black box' in this way – 'seamless-web', 'actor-networks', 'socio-technical ensembles' and 'technology texts'. In their different ways these perspectives sought to show that technology is, in Weick's phrase 'equivocal'. That is, what a technology is, what it can do, what constitutes its effective working and so forth are all subject to 'interpretative flexibility' in the context of its production and consumption in organisational and other settings. Whilst there are disputes between constructivists and others concerning whether there are material limits to interpretation of this kind, the fundamental insight from this perspective is that the term 'technology' is a mere shorthand for a complex network of socio-technical relationships.

Chapter 7 addressed some of the weaknesses of the constructivist position by suggesting that it is more productive to seek to open the technology black box by 'looking' inwards to show how organisational and other socio-economic factors shape content, rather than just 'looking outwards' from technology as many constructivists appear to only do. In this perspective metaphors of 'embodied interests' and 'crystallised contingency' are evoked to show the mutual shaping of technology and organisation over time in complex interactions between internal organisational actors, suppliers, vendors, customers, users and other social institutions. A key insight from this position is to reveal how innovation cannot be adequately understood if it is seen as a purely technological phenomenon occurring up to but not beyond the point of first successful adoption (see Chapter 2). Rather, 'post-adoption' innovation and reinnovation become the key dynamic in the mutual shaping of technology and organisation were new technology, new organisational forms, and new production concepts and paradigms become inextricably intertwined.

Whilst debates with other variants of the social shaping perspectives quickly identify potential weaknesses of this approach, for example in relation to the notion that technologies can embody gendered characteristics, the notion of the mutual shaping of technology and organisation does provide a potentially fruitful way of understanding not only how this interaction is shaped, but how it can be reshaped. It is to a preliminary exploration of such a creative enterprise that we now turn. In order to explicate this we begin by outlining an account of socio-technical change in three organisations

The shaping of a manufacturing innovation

The following draws on the experience of a two-year action research project in three Australian companies. In each case, efforts were made to reshape existing social and technical arrangements by introducing team-based cellular manufacturing (TBCM). The action-research basis of the project provided an opportunity to exploit the possibilities for new insights when academic observers engage more directly with organisational performers in actual performance. The project was funded by the Australian Federal government with contributions from the companies themselves.

The team and cellular principles have been identified as the key socio-technical configuration underpinning post-modern organisational forms in both manufacturing and services (Mathews 1994, 1997). The adoption of TBCM creates the possibility of employees operating as autonomous teams and even as 'businesses within a business' responsible not only for boundary management tasks within an organisation but also activities such as sales/marketing, socio-technical design, costing and setting performance measurement criteria (see Figure 8.2). Ultimately such 'businesses within a business' have been seen as the key constituent part of non-hierarchical network organisations and small firm networks (Mathews 1994). In a manufacturing context TBCM involves the movement of machinery into cells according to the particular processes and their sequence that are required to produce parts or families of parts. The 'technical' redesign of production in this way enables the 'social' redesign of work along more 'human-centred' lines (see Chapter 7) so that the tasks performed in the cells can be undertaken by workers operating as multiskilled, semi-autonomous teams. In their most advanced form, team-based cells might have considerable responsibility for interfacing with their environment to the extent that they have direct and high level contact with 'customers' both inside and outside the organisation. Team-based and cellular socio-technical principles are thus radically different to those which result in the traditional layout of machines by function and the organisation and control of work according to 'Taylorist/Fordist' principles and their associated human and organisational dysfunctions (see Chapter 1).

In each company the action researchers defined their role as the

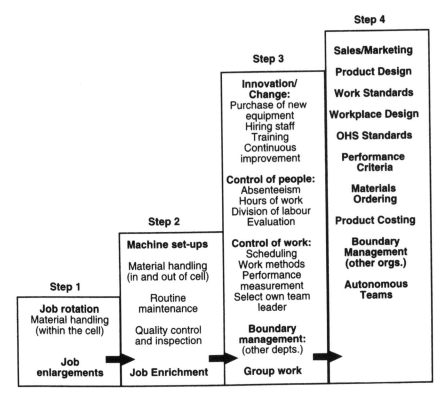

Figure 8.2 Levels of teamworking in cellular manufacture
Source: MITOC 1995.

introduction and promotion of skill-based or human-centred design principles (influenced strongly by European socio-technical projects
conducted in Germany and Scandinavia – see Badham 1994). In each
case a form of 'socio-technology transfer' was attempted whereby
human-centred principles were championed in new or existing manufacturing innovation projects in an effort to encourage company
decision-makers and change agents to think and act in relation to
change in a more creative fashion. Consistent with the 'human-centred'
approach a participative form of project organisation was deployed in
each company. This aimed to draw on a cross-functional spread of
management expertise, permit the action researchers to lobby for a
consideration of more 'human-centred' definitions of problems and solutions, provide forums for senior management involvement, and critically
to involve shop floor operators and their union representatives in decisions which were going to affect their immediate working lives in, they
hoped, fundamental and beneficial ways.

The three case study companies were:

- Kangaroo Whitegoods, part of an international domestic appliance company that manufactured whitegoods and floor care products and which had engaged in small-scale experiments with quality management and just-in-time techniques with mixed success. This included plans to introduce cellular manufacture into a process-based jobbing press shop where equipment was laid out according to function and operator jobs were low skilled and restricted to a narrow range of tasks. However the plans had been left 'on the drawing board' due to concerns about industrial relations problems that might be provoked. In this case the action researchers began by collaborating in a job redesign exercise which spelt out various options concerning the reorganisation of work around these existing plans to introduce cells.

- *Wombat Plastics*, a division of the Australian operation of an international motor company, which supplied plastics components for car assembly to the adjacent factory of its parent organisation. The division had a recent history of experimenting with work teams, participative management techniques and quality improvement programmes that had attracted external industry recognition and awards and a national reputation for its innovative plant manager. The action researchers began by collaborating with company personnel in developing a set of evaluation criteria. These were then used to assess options for introducing a cellular assembly process for the instrument panel ('dashboard') of a new car which was due to be introduced.

- *Koala Irrigation*, a manufacturer of plastic irrigation systems which had already established a programme of cellular production and team-based working that had attracted Federal government support under a programme designed to encourage and disseminate 'best practice'. In this case the action researchers sought to add to the already well developed philosophy on the development of team-based working by extending the existing cellular assembly set-up with particular emphasis on further developing team-based working and associated changes in management organisation.

The fate of these efforts in the three cases will now be outlined.[1]

Kangaroo Whitegoods

At first blush *Kangaroo* appeared the least promising of the three company sites for the implementation of TBCM. The chequered recent history of manufacturing innovation at the plant partly reflected a problematic industrial relations climate. The factory had no history of major investments in the training of shop floor staff where the multicultural workforce was largely poorly educated and many possessed low levels of English literacy. At the same time manufacturing engineering, although receptive to new ideas, was resistant to outside influence and doubts existed as to the extent of senior management commitment to radical changes in production methods.

The implementation programme began with the formation of a project team which included the action researchers, and company personnel from various functional areas with a stake in the outcome. These included the press shop supervisor, and subsequently the prospective team leader of the first cell planned to be introduced. By the end of the project only one, rather than the envisaged five, cells had been implemented in the press shop. The training of the initial cell team members was only completed after a considerable delay following the arrival new manufacturing manager; and a number of critical industrial relations issues concerning the classification of cell team members and the team leader remained unresolved. The degree of autonomy given to the cell team was limited and tasks remained low skill, although the amount of responsibility and range of tasks varied significantly from that previously enjoyed under the functional layout by press operators.

A follow-up visit nearly two years later revealed that, contrary to expectation, the TBCM programme had however been sustained. Fears for the change programme following a company take-over had proved unfounded, a new senior management team was supportive, and the originally hostile press shop supervisor had emerged as full 'owner' and 'champion' of the concept of team-based working in the shop. However, the objectives of the TBCM programme were now more limited – only two cells were fully operational and only one more was planned. In addition several detailed problems still remained, for example in relation to the skill classification of cell team leaders.

Wombat Plastics

In contrast to *Kangaroo* the *Wombat* project appeared to be set in much more fertile ground given the plant's reputation, described in one external report, as a 'veritable laboratory of workplace innovation'. However, at the start of the project the extent of team working and other manufacturing innovations at the plant turned out to be as much rhetoric as reality. In addition the impetus of support for the project from the plant's senior management was lost at an early stage when the plant manager who had previously championed the project retired on health grounds. Efforts to enrol the support of a new plant manager, a technically orientated individual with a more mechanistic view of production, inevitably proved difficult and ultimately unsuccessful. In consequence, as the project got underway, there was an absence of clear cut directives from senior level to engineering management as to the importance of the action researcher's role or brief. The researchers had the status of 'outsiders' whose purpose was never fully realised or understood by company personnel.

The project began with intensive efforts over a short period of time on the part of a cross-functional design team, that included the researchers, to develop plans to cellularise the instrument panel line. The short timescale was a consequence of the broader timetable governing the introduction of the new car. As this deadline approached compromise proposals were put forward which would allow a degree of cellularisation of the old assembly-line. However, these proposals were disregarded by the plant engineering manager with little or no discussion. He then announced his own largely conventional solution to the problem which had secretly been prepared by another team of company engineers working in parallel. Soon after, this solution was aborted by the plant manager because of resource constraints, time pressures arising from the new model launch, and broader developments in the business involving a planned sale of the plant to another solution. In the wake of these events, after a period of uncertainty and inactivity, the efforts of the action researchers were directed by the plant manager to minor evaluation projects concerned with productivity improvement. Subsequently, however, the company was to adapt the TBCM concept – but without the involvement of the action researchers – and deploy it in the assembly process for the instrument panels of 'carry over' models (versions of the existing model that were not being immediately replaced). Ironically, this was a suggestion made by the researchers when plans to cellularise the existing instrument panel assembly-line were scrapped but was at the time, or so they thought, ignored.

Koala Irrigation

The relatively lengthy experience of implementing TBCM at *Koala* also suggested a fertile environment within which to extend and develop 'human-centred' design principles. In this case, a broad-based team embracing both key managers at head office, and different levels of management within the plant, had already succeeded in generating an impressive programme of innovation. This had involved the introduction of a cellular layout in the assembly area and the formation and training of three cell teams. The process was highly participative, cell team members for example being involved in the detailed design and configuration of their work stations. During the action research phase further innovation was attempted, in particular extending team-based working to an intended seven cells, the introduction of a 'cluster' management structure where managers (now 'coordinators') would 'coach' the cell teams, and improving productivity and performance measurement.

However, as key members of the management team moved to other postings in the company and changing contextual factors such as market conditions, alterations in head office product strategy, and other corporate changes – which culminated with the prospective sale of the company – took place, it became evident that too much change was being attempted on too many fronts. As a result, the pace of change slowed, became deflected from its intended course and, for a while, stalled completely. The contributions of the action researchers were submerged within this complex dynamic. The outcome as viewed on a follow-up visit some two years after the conclusion of the action research was that, despite several years of experience, only three of the planned seven cell teams could be said to be fully self-managing and functioning autonomously. In addition many unresolved and unforeseen problems remained, whilst new ones were emerging. For example, frictions between the predominantly female members of the teams and male 'trade' workers allocated to them had grown as pressures to operate more as a team increased. At the same time, the need for training to be constantly updated and repeated to ensure skill retention on the shop floor was becoming evident, placing a further constraint on the capacity of the factory to extend team-based practices to new areas of the workforce.

'Reading' the three cases

As was pointed out in the Introduction, the relevance of metaphor to a concern with exploring more creative modes of thinking and acting in relation to technology and organisation derives from the generative and liberative potential associated with this mode of analysis. In particular, Morgan (see 1997: 351–3) argues that an ability to go beyond the inevitably limiting boundaries of individual metaphors leads to more creative results. In our context this requires seeking to exploit the strengths of some of the metaphors used to understand the technology–organisation relationship whilst also attempting to avoid some of their weaknesses. To do this a willingness to move from one 'metaphorical frame' to another is required as is a preparedness to 'mix metaphors'. As Morgan puts it,

> When you realise that your theories and insights are metaphorical, you have to approach the process in an open-ended way. You have to recognize your limitations and find ways of going beyond them. This results in a style of thinking that is always open and evolving, and extremely well-suited for dealing with the complexity of organisational life.
>
> (Morgan 1997: 353)

As noted in the previous chapter, attempts to reshape the technology–organisation relationship frequently fail or fail to meet planned objectives. A common observation is that images of the organisation as a 'machine' or 'information processing system', where the logic of technological development is seen as the basis for guiding change and shaping its outcomes, are extremely difficult to dislodge. As Orlikowski and Cash (1994) note, new technologies frequently provoke responses based on existing ways of thinking and acting. Typically, organisational decision-makers find it difficult to re-think and imagine alternative ways of shaping the organisation–technology relationship. Even where change is seen in terms of a more 'organismic' metaphor that encourages attention being given to communicating with and involving the 'user' there are still difficulties, for example, in terms of the tendency to see political behaviour and resistance as 'irrational' and as entirely 'negative' in their consequences.

Elements of this type of interpretation can readily be applied to explain the degrees of failure experienced in the three cases. For example, at *Wombat* and *Kangaroo* line managers and production engineering personnel were driven by the requirement to maintain the output of the production system. At *Wombat*, in particular, the assembly process was part of a tightly integrated mass production system where stoppages of production and down-time had 'knock-on' effects which were felt on the parent company's production lines almost immediately. Such linkages were emphasised by the operation of just-in-time production systems, for example between the instrument panel assembly-line and the main assembly-line of the parent company. At *Wombat* too the production schedule for the introduction of the new model was also a major consideration. Innovation of any type, it seemed, was tightly constrained by the existing and ongoing requirements of the production system itself and also constraints already 'built in' by prior decisions concerning the design of the new panel. In such circumstances it is perhaps easy to see why even a modest variant of team-based cellular manufacturing might to be so difficult to implement. Similar observations can be made concerning *Kangaroo*, and it is noteworthy here that the success that was achieved occurred not in the assembly area but in the press shop which was easier to 'de-couple' from the immediate requirements of the production system.

In contrast, the acceptance of socio-technical principles at *Koala Irrigation* suggests an interpretation which points to the advantages to be gained from viewing the social elements of a production system as inherently reliable, rather than unreliable. In this case the management objective was to seek forms of job design and work organisation that would permit employees, as far as possible, to be self-organising and able to learn from and improve the work process, in the belief that this was the best route to secure productive efficiency of a kind needed to enable the factory to compete. However, maintaining this objective was difficult in the face of short-term exigencies and corporate uncertainties. For example, long running battle throughout was the problem of a mechanistic performance measurement system imposed by headquarters. This increasingly failed to record the tangible, but more difficult to measure, benefits of teamworking, for example, in terms of increased product quality and continuous improvement activities which improved production methods and working practices.

The experiences of the three cases can also be understood in terms of the idea of organisations as political and cultural systems. In each company, the ultimate fate of the change project showed considerable variation from what was intended and from what might have been predicted on the basis of either a strictly technical or socio-technical understanding of TBCM. From the politics process perspective, the problems encountered in turning the possibilities of TBCM into actual technical and organisational outcomes are not fully explained by the notion of 'barriers to innovation' (e.g. 'inertial pressures' such as fixed organisation structures and skill distributions amongst the work force, adherence by managers to outmoded assumptions and values, barriers to change posed by trade unions and industrial relations structures which meant it was difficult for the organisations concerned to 'think beyond' their existing knowledge base and path dependencies). Rather, process and outcomes are seen to hinge more on the radical and pervasive nature of socio-technical changes of this type. These introduce uncertainty in terms of objectives and likely outcomes whilst impinging upon a broad range of stakeholder interests. As a result change is highly vulnerable to political disturbance and disruption.

Taking this line of argument it can be seen how in each case the success or otherwise of each project was decisively influenced by how far change agents were able to intervene in political and cultural systems to manage this vulnerability. In the case of *Kangaroo*, for example, that even such a limited outcome was achieved, owed a considerable amount to the capacity of key company change agents and the action researchers to secure support for the change from key groups, and in particular to their ability to win-over potential or actual sources of resistance at key points. For instance, union support was secured in part through a prescient intervention prior to the start of the project by one of the project champions in the company. This occurred during the negotiation of a new enterprise agreement for the factory and resulted in enabling clauses being inserted that permitted a relaxation of job demarcations to allow team-based working. Subsequently, considerable effort was also made by members of the implementation team in order to gain the support of the multicultural press shop workforce, for example by providing remedial English literacy classes and by seeking to present training materials without recourse to formal 'classroom' methods. Later in the project another decisive effort was made to enrol the new manufacturing manager, who was initially cautious and unsupportive, and had blocked the training programme. The eventual full support of this individual was ultimately critical as was the belated 'conversion' of the press shop supervisor to the ideas behind the introduction of TBCM.

At *Wombat*, the action researchers were never able to establish a coalition of interests with key company personnel and were unable to exert any significant influence over the process or outcomes of change. In contrast, at *Koala* the momentum already established meant that the change programme was largely legitimated in the eyes of both managers and employees at the plant, and, for a time at least, corporate headquarters as well. As time passed legitimacy problems became more evident in relations between the plant and corporate headquarters, an area where the change agents had no real brief or capacity to intervene. That change was sustained and revived had much to do with the commitment of two plant engineers who rose to become plant manager and deputy respectively. Their vision and continued belief in socio-technical principles were the key factor in defending the project in difficult times and advancing it when conditions were more favourable.

However, whilst more revealing, it can still be argued that the political perspective takes too much of the 'technical' and 'organisational' component of the changes in the three organisations as given. For example, whilst showing how the 'effects' of TBCM were chosen and negotiated in each case, insufficient is said concerning the shaping of the 'technical' content of change itself. If the organisational outcomes of change were a product of choice and negotiation, the social shaping perspective would claim that these 'technical' aspects were as well. In fact, in each case the scope for 'interpretative flexibility' of TBCM can be demonstrated. There were, for example, considerable debates and disagreements within the organisations and with and between the action researchers as to what constituted a 'cell' and what constituted a 'team'. What was the most appropriate form of technical and social organisation to suit the particular conditions and exigencies faced at each factory was by no means self-evident. The concept of TBCM was thus itself contested and negotiated and ultimately different variants of the idea were settled upon, or not settled upon, in each case. Given this, the process of change could be understood and further explored in terms of the ideas of 'closure' and 'stabilisation', or the activities of change agents viewed as attempts to build networks of heterogeneous human and non-human actors. Moreover, the degree of consensus over TBCM, for example whether it was 'successful' or whether teams were actually now at a point where they could be regarded as working autonomously, seemed to be interpreted differently by different actors, differently to different audiences, and differently in both cases over time. Seen as a 'text' TBCM was continually being rewritten and reread.

Another angle still is to see the experiences of the three organisations as highlighting the importance of post-adoption innovation or 'innofusion' in the social shaping of technology and organisation. In fact TBCM as a manufacturing technique has similar properties to configurational technologies which require considerable adaptation and customisation to local circumstances before they can be regarded as working systems. In each company the finally implemented form of TBCM was shaped in each application by user requirements and the specifics of the circumstances in which it was to be deployed (for example, a simple assembly process at *Koala*, a tightly integrated mass production system at *Wombat*, a low skill set of heavy manual activities in a press shop at *Kangaroo*). Moreover, the knowledge gained from the project, both by the company and the researchers, has subsequently diffused by a variety of means (e.g. movement of company personnel to new jobs, the official reports of the research team to the Federal government funding body, practitioner orientated 'deliverables', the consulting, training, teaching of the action researchers – and so on) to different organisational and other contexts. In a small way, this knowledge learnt from the specific experiences of the three organisations could potentially provide the basis for re-innovation in new organisational circumstances where attempts to adopt TBCM are being made. Indeed, by taking a wider view and contextualising such experiences along with much broader and more generalisable data and research findings on this type of manufacturing innovation, it would in principle be possible to build a picture of the evolution of TBCM. This might show how some innovations in the concept (mutations) contribute to economic variety (innovative and more competitive organisational forms) whilst others have not. For example, take Clark's (1997) approach outlined in Chapter 7. What each organisation was attempting to do was to identify the 'contingent specificity' of TBCM in order embed it in the specific socio-cultural context of each factory and firm. The success of these efforts within the particular 'socio-economic selection environment' faced by each organisation over time would then be seen as determining the extent to which the innovation of TBCM is effectively appropriated. Such appropriation would involve both a shaping and reshaping of the initial innovation and the development of the organisational learning necessary to embody this in the firm's knowledge-base. This would require effective interaction with both suppliers and other third parties, as well as between differing coalitions within the user organisation, over the key 'decision episodes' which shape the process and outcomes of change.

Finally, the broader historical, structural and systemic features of the context and environments of the three organisations might be considered. This would focus attention on the extent to which the outcomes of change represent a trend towards increased control of, or autonomy for, employees through team-based work. Similarly, factors such as the structure of labour and product markets, national culture, gender and ethnic composition of the workforce, industrial relations and training systems, government policy, union organisation and power, employer strategies and organisation, would need to be revealed to fully explain the content, process and outcome of change in the three cases. In particular, the following questions might be asked: Which groups were included and which excluded from the change process? Was the resultant team working in the companies really something which 'empowered' and involved employees as the researchers intended and the companies claimed? On the other hand, was this more rhetoric concealing another reality where workers – many from ethnic minorities and/or female – were subjected to more pervasive forms of control in the form of sophisticated methods of surveillance and the self-disciplining effects of working as part of a team? How participative were the projects in practice and were employees and their representatives capable and able to exert a real influence on the process?

Shaping socio-technical configurations: the micro-politics of change

The insights offered by different metaphors, as illustrated in these three cases, show how different readings of organisational situations and events are possible. Moreover, as should be evident, such accounts are not mutually exclusive and in many ways provide complementary rather than competing interpretations. In fact, Morgan (1986, 1997) argues that the generative potential of metaphor rests in large part on the potential for producing multiple accounts of the same situation. This is particularly pertinent in relation to issues of technological and related organisational change. However, critics have suggested that, even if this was a more prevalent phenomenon, it is not enough to be able to 'imagine' alternatives (see e.g. McCourt 1997). New ways of seeing and thinking have to be translated into new ways of acting and creating new forms of organisation in practice. As Palmer and Dunford note, 'being able to see a situation in a new light may alert one to a whole range of new possibilities but, without the appropriate support and resources to successfully implement these new ideas, the situation may remain substantially unaltered' (Palmer and Dunford 1996: 145).

This draws our attention once again to the micro-politics involved in implementing change and generating post-adoption innovation (see Chapters 4 and 7). In particular it raises the question of the changing role of change agents as they seek to shape and reshape technology and organisation in a more creative fashion. Indeed, their own involvement in the TBCM case studies outlined above suggested to the action researchers that there was a need for more adequate models and guidance on these points than that available in conventional project management and socio-technical change literatures. This was required both to help change agents 'read' the specific features of the content, process and context of change in a particular organisational situation, and to provide a basis for insight and intervention in change processes which were obviously 'vulnerable' and apparently increasingly political in character. Indeed, more generally, it appears that attempts to shift to post-modern organisational forms highlights the political nature of change in a way that has not been so evident in the past. If this is correct, there will be an increasing need for change agents to become competent in a broader range of both perceptual and political behaviour attempts to introduce potentially transformative socio-technical changes are to stand a greater chance of success (Badham and Buchanan 1996; Buchanan and Badham 1998).

Such a model of the change process starts from the observation that the crucial features of both the technical *and* organisational outcomes of change can increasingly be regarded as the result of incremental local/internal customisation and adaptation of generic systems and models – albeit shaped and constrained by broader conditions and influences (Badham 1995; Badham *et al.* 1997; McLoughlin *et al.* 1998). These activities can be described as *configurational processes* carried out in the context of existing *configurations* of technological, organisational and human resources bounded by broader internal and external environmental contexts. Configurational processes have the effect of sustaining or transforming the manner in which material resources are turned into outputs and in so doing the nature of existing configurations of technological, organisational and human resources is either maintained or changed. These processes are enacted by configurational entrepreneurs, a potentially diverse and shifting combination of change initiators, sponsors and drivers who may come from within or outside of the adopting organisation (see Figure 8.3).

Configurations and configurational processes can be seen as linked by what have been termed 'technological frames' (Bijker 1995a; also Orlikowski and Cash 1994; McLoughlin *et al.* 1998). Frames, as was noted in passing in Chapter 5, provide the shared assumptions, knowledge and expectations through which 'relevant groups' give meaning to an existing or emerging socio-technical configuration. On the one hand a frame enables 'thinking and action' or configurational activity on the part of a relevant group but, on the other, by defining what constitutes a socio-technical problem and an acceptable solution to it, it acts as a constraint. The more developed a frame the more such constraints are felt, the more closure in respect of openness to alternative interpretations and arguments exists, the more as a belief system it is stabilised, and the more 'hard' or 'obdurate' the socio-technical configurations which the frame gives rise to appear. Thus, constituent elements of a socio-technical configuration such as the capabilities and characteristics of the technology used, the physical layout, the operational characterstics of a plant, or the skill requirements, job design, and work organisation of operators, take on meanings for members of the relevant groups which suggest a rigidity and indivisibility that appear to 'determine' social relationships.

Political and power dimensions underpin the formation and reproduction of technological frames. Following Giddens (1979), Bijker suggests that technological frames are a product of the 'transformative capacity' of actors or groups to 'harness the agency of others' in order to accomplish a particular goal or end. Moreover, such agents, following the argument of ANT (see Chapter 5), are both human and technical since technologies can be instrumental in the realisation of particular goals. Power is exercised

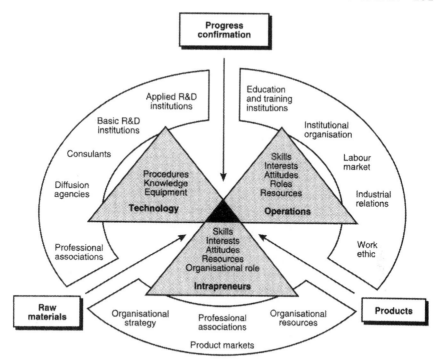

Figure 8.3 Innovation as a configurational process
Source: Badham *et al.* 1997: 158.

through a 'technological frame' in two ways. First, through 'semiotic power' that is manifested to 'the extent that meanings become fixed or reified in certain forms, which then articulate particular facts, artefacts, agents, practices, and relations,...the fixity of power' (Bijker 1995a: 263). Second, through 'micro-political power' which refers to the 'variety of practices' that 'transforms and structures the actions of actors, thereby constituting a particular form of power' (Bijker 1995a: 263). Semiotic power and micro-political power are thus opposite sides of the same coin: 'micro-politics result in a specific semiotic structure, while the semiotic power in turn influences the micro-politics structures' (Bijker 1995a: 263).

The closure of a frame can be seen as a process whereby micro-political processes begin to establish semiotic power by diminishing the interpretative flexibility of a socio-technical configuration and thereby fixing its meaning. Stabilisation furthers this process whereby subsequent interactions result in more elements becoming 'fixed' into the semiotic structure as micro-political practices enlist more individuals into a relevant social group, enrol new relevant groups and elaborate the meaning of the configuration. As a consequence, the dominant technological frame 'constrains the actions of its members and thus exerts power through the fixity of meaning' (semiotic power) and 'enables its members by providing problem-solving strategies, theories and testing practices' (micro-political power) (Bijker 1995a: 263–4). By both enabling and constraining micro-political activity frames can be seen to exert a 'disciplining power' since they govern the way in which thinking and action take place. Technologies themselves can also act to 'discipline' the 'interactions of actors' by providing 'obligatory passage points' and also as 'embodiments' of the interests of particular groups, provided such interests are seen as 'temporarily stabilised outcomes of interaction' which 'partly occurs in the form of artefacts' (Bijker 1995a: 266).

These arguments serve to suggest that technological innovation should be seen as a configurational process which occurs in the context of existing socio-technical configurations and broader historical, contextual and structural factors (the following extrapolates from Bijker 1995a: 276–9). Innovation can thus be thought of as a process where either none, one, or two or more 'technological frames' may be dominant. In the case of there being no one dominant frame, there will be many different potential innovations and the success of processes of enrolment will be key in explaining the emergence of an ultimately dominant technological frame (a situation most likely to be approximated in a greenfield site venture). In the second case, where one frame is dominant, actors with a high degree of inclusion in the frame will tend to generate conventional innovations but those who are more marginal – such as younger engineers – may be able to spot 'presumptive anomalies' where systems might fail under future conditions or that radically different systems might perform better. If one accepts the dominance of Taylorist/Fordist thinking in many contemporary organisations then this could be regarded as a typical situation. In the third case, technological frames will be competing in a manner similar to Hughes' (1987) notion of a 'battle of the systems' and the tendency will be to seek innovations which can be accommodated within each of the competing frames. Arguably an organisation seeking to shift from a Fordist to post-Fordist production strategy is likely to be characterised by such dynamics and will face the problem of the resultant innovations in technology and organisation turning out to be recognisably conventional.

Returning to the three case studies it is possible to see how the last two of these scenarios can be applied. At *Wombat* one socio-technical frame was dominant and this produced a socio-technical configuration strongly influenced by industrial engineering and Taylorist/Fordist beliefs about the 'best way' to organise production. In this case senior engineering and plant personnel were only able to accept a view of the problem of instrument panel assembly which prioritised issues of ensuring continuity of production and product quality. By the same token they were far more likely to be persuaded by a proposal which rested on tight labour control and machine-pacing and gave only minimal discretion to operators. By virtue of their relatively low inclusion in the frame younger engineers on the project team were able to flirt with the more 'human-centred' approach proposed by the action researchers. This saw the goals of continuity of production and product quality as better served by also prioritising worker discretion and autonomy. However, this interest in and support for such design solutions – which involved inserting buffers and the like between the proposed cell team and the main production line – was short-lived. Given prevailing systems of motivation and reward, these actors had little choice but to eventually accept counter arguments generated from within the dominant 'Fordist' frame. In this way the exemplary status of Fordist socio-technical design principles was maintained and the apparent obduracy of the Fordist configuration of production line technology and work design reinforced.

In the case of *Kangaroo* the basic assumptions, expectations and knowledge embodied in the dominant technological frame (whose essential elements were summarised concisely by one company engineer as 'cost reduction, overhead recovery, great pay back, no investment and fuck all training'!) also resulted in a socio-technical configuration based on conventional Taylorist/Fordist functional layout and job design criteria. However, the closure and stabilisation of this frame was less complete and more open to challenge, at least internally, from alternative problem definition/resolution arguments. The company had, at the instigation of an innovative manufacturing director, experimented with 'lean production' concepts such as just-in-time and operator responsibility for quality and he, with a junior engineer with a relatively low inclusion in the dominant frame, became receptive to 'human-centred' concepts. Subsequently, the micro-political activities of the junior engineer – in combination with other company change agents and some of the action researchers – ensured that the 'interpretative flexibility' of TBCM was maintained sufficiently for alternative work design principles to be implemented. In particular, symbolic appeals were made to key constituencies – notably a new engineering manager, but also press shop operators, the press shop supervisor, human resource management and trade unions – in order to enrol them to the project and into an emergent frame of alternative production practices in the factory. That the resultant outcomes appear modest from a human-centred perspective reflects the inevitable conservatism in innovation that occurs as interests are amalgamated in this way (see Bijker 1995a).

At *Koala* a rather different case of change being dominated by one technological frame was experienced. Here socio-technical principles were already strongly embedded and articulated in the belief system of key actors in the factory. Whilst the action researchers might thus be seen as 'pushing on an open door' they in fact experienced considerable difficulty in having their role accepted by key company personnel as of any significance in the changes that occurred. One possible way of understanding this is to say that key factory personnel already had a high level of inclusion in the 'socio-technical' technological frame as configured at the plant. On the one hand this meant their thoughts and actions were constrained by a relatively unambiguous concept of what TBCM was but, on the other, there were many uncertainties at the level of detail as to how these principles could be implemented, operated and developed over time (a case of the more that was known the less it was realised was known). The action researchers, on the other hand, had a relatively low inclusion in the dominant frame at the plant although they were well versed in the general models of human-centred system design and TBCM. Paradoxically, the degree of 'interpretative flexibility' of TBCM at the plant had been reduced by closure to an extent that it had begun to stabilise and had achieved an obduracy and hardness. This made attempts to render it malleable by the action researchers sometimes appear naïve and politically inept in the eyes of key plant personnel (for example by attempting as occurred on one occasion to 'deconstruct it' through a politically radical analysis, and on another in terms of attempting to define alternatives to existing performance measurement systems). The general view reported by factory personnel after the project had finished was that the action researchers had learnt far more from them than plant personnel ever did from the supposed external 'experts'.

Concluding comment

The core argument of this volume has been that creative approaches to technological change and its organisational outcomes increasingly rest on the collective creation of intuitive and serviceable metaphors to make sense of and learn from experiences in the workplace, organisation and beyond. However, both generating new images of the relationship between technology and organisation and translating these into practice raise fundamental questions concerning the nature of the process of technological innovation and organisational change, in particular its micro-political nature. The argument offered in this final chapter has been that advances in both the thinking and action of organisational observers and organisational performers can be enhanced by a willingness to 'mix metaphors' in the search for new ways of making sense of and enacting contemporary technological and organisational complexity. Indeed one profitable way in which the challenge of developing new ways of thinking about, viewing and ultimately responding creatively in seeking to reshape technology and organisation is precisely a willingness to blur the distinction between observer and performer.

Notes

1 At the end of the action research stage a summative study was undertaken to produce case studies of the three projects. These were supplemented in late 1996 by a follow-up site visit to two of the companies and interviews with company and other personnel involved in the original project at the third. For a full account of the case studies see McLoughlin *et al.* (1997).

References

Abernathy, W.J. and Utterback, J.M. 1978. 'Patterns of industrial innovation', *Technology Review*, June–July, 41–7.

Adler, P.S. and Borys, B. 1996. 'Two types of bureaucracy: enabling and constraining', *Administrative Science Quarterly*, 41, 61–89.

Adler, P.S. and Cole, R.E. 1993. 'Designed for learning: a tale of two auto plants', *Sloan Management Review*, Spring, 85–94.

Aldrich, H. 1979. *Organisations and Environments*, Englewood Cliffs, NJ: Prentice-Hall.

Allen, P.M. 1988. 'Evolution, innovation and economics', in Dosi, G., Freeman, C., Nelson, R., Silverberg, G. and Soete, L. (eds) *Technical Change and Economic Theory*, London: Pinter, 95–119.

Amin, A. 1994. 'Post-Fordism: models, fantasies and phantoms of transition', *Post-Fordism: A Reader*, Oxford: Blackwell, 1–39.

Atkins, P. 1994. 'Against', *The Times Higher*, 30 September, 17.

Attewell, P. 1996. 'Technology diffusion and organisational learning', in Moingeon, B. and Edmonson, A. (eds) *Organisational Learning and Competitive Advantage*, London: Sage, 203–29.

Badham, R. 1993. 'Systems, networks and configurations: inside the implementation process', Editorial for special issue of *International Journal of Human Factors in Manufacturing*, 3 (1), 3–13.

—— 1994. 'From socio-economic to socially orientated innovation policy', in Aichholzer, G. and Schienstock, G. (eds) *Technology Policy: Towards an Integration of Social and Ecological Concerns*, Berlin: De Gruyter, 25–66.

—— 1995. 'Managing socio-technical change: a configuration approach to technology implementation', in Benders, J., de Haan, J. and Bennett, D. (eds) *The Symbiosis of Work and Technology*, London: Taylor & Francis, 77–94.

Badham, R. and Buchanan, D.A. 1996. 'Power assisted steering: the new princes of socio-technical change', *Occasional Paper 33*, Leicester Business School.

Badham, R. and Jürgens, U. 1998. 'Images of good work and the politics of team work', *Economic and Industrial Democracy*, 19 (1), 33–58.

Badham, R. and Mathews, J. 1989. 'The new production systems debate', *Labour and Industry*, 2 (2), 194–246.

Badham, R. and Naschold, F. 1994. 'New technology policy concepts: some reflections on technology and work humanisation in West Germany', in Aichholzer,

G. and Schienstock, G. (eds) *Technology Policy: Towards an Integration of Social and Ecological Concerns*, Berlin: De Gruyter, 125–60.

Badham, R., Couchman, P. and McLoughlin, I. 1997. 'Implementing vulnerable socio-technical change projects', in McLoughlin, I. and Harris, M. (eds) *Innovation, Organisational Change and Technology*, London: ITB Press, 146–69.

Bailey, J. 1983. *Job Design and Work Organisation*, London: Prentice-Hall.

Baldry, C. 1988. *Computers, Jobs and Skills: The Industrial Relations of Technological Change*, London: Plenum Press.

Barker, J. and Downing, H. 1985. 'Word processing and the transformation of patriarchal relations of control in the office', in MacKenzie, D. and Wajcman, J. (eds) *The Social Control of Technology*, Milton Keynes: Open University Press, 147–64.

Barnatt, C. 1995a. *Cyberbusiness: Mindsets for a Wired Age*, Chichester: Wiley.

—— 1995b. 'Office space, cyberspace and virtual organisation', *Journal of General Management*, 20 (4), 78–92.

Batstone, E., Gourlay, S., Levie, H. and Moore, R. 1988. *New Technology and The Process of Labour Regulation*, Oxford: Clarendon Press.

Beechey, V. 1982. 'The sexual division of labour and the labour process', in Wood, S. (ed.) *The Degradation of Work?: Skill, Deskilling and the Labour Process*, London: Hutchinson, 54–73.

Bell, D. 1973. *The Coming of the Post-Industrial Society*, New York: Basic Books.

—— 1980. 'The social framework of the information society', in Forester, T. (ed.) *The Microelectronics Revolution*, Oxford: Blackwell, 500–49.

Benders, J., de Haan, J. and Bennett, D. 1995. 'Symbiotic approaches: contents and issues', in Benders, J., de Haan, J. and Bennett, D. (eds) *The Symbiosis of Work and Technology*, London: Taylor & Francis, 1–12.

Berggren, C. 1993. *The Volvo Experience: Alternatives to Lean Production in the Swedish Auto Industry*, London: Macmillan.

Bessant, J. 1991. *Managing Advanced Manufacturing Technology*, Oxford: NCC/Blackwell.

Bijker, W. 1994. 'Do not despair: there is life after constructivism', *Science, Technology and Human Values*, 18 (1), 113–38.

—— 1995a. *Of Bicycles, Bakelites and Bulbs: Toward a Theory of Socio-technical Change*, Cambridge, MA: MIT Press.

—— 1995b. 'Sociohistorical technology studies', in Jasanoff, S., Markle, G.E., Peterson, J.C. and Pinch, T.J. (eds) *Handbook of Science and Technology Studies*, New York: Sage, 229–56.

Bijker, W.E. and Law, J. 1992. 'Do technologies have trajectories?', in Bijker, W.E. and Law, J. (eds) *Shaping Technology/Building Society: Studies in Socio-technical Change*, Cambridge, MA: MIT Press, 17–20.

Bijker, W.E., Hughes, T.P. and Pinch, T. 1987. 'General introduction', in Bijker, W.E., Hughes, T.P. and Pinch, T.J. (eds) *The Social Construction of Technological Systems: New Directions in the Sociology of History and Technology*, Cambridge, MA: MIT Press, 1–6.

Birchall, D. and Lyons, D. 1995. *Creating Tomorrow's Organisation*, London: Pitman.

Black, M. 1993. 'More about metaphors', in Ortony, A. (ed.) *Metaphor and Thought* (2nd edn), Chicago, IL: University of Chicago Press, 19–41.

Blackler, F. 1994. 'Post(-)modern organizations: understanding how CSCW affects organizations', *Journal of Information Technology*, 9, 129–36.

Blauner, R. 1964. *Alienation and Freedom*, Chicago, IL: Chicago University Press.

Bloomfield, B., Coombs, R., Cooper, D. and Rea, D. 1992. 'Machines and manoeuvres: responsibility accounting and the construction of hospital information systems', *Accounting, Management and Information Technology*, 2 (4), 197–219.

Bloor, D. 1973. 'Wittgenstein and Mannheim on the sociology of mathematics', *Studies in History and Philosophy of Science*, 4, 173–91.

Boddy, D. and Gunson, N. 1996. *Organizations in the Network Age*, London: Routledge.

Bødker, S. and Greenbaum, J. 1993. 'Design of information systems: things versus people', in Green, E., Owen, J. and Pain, D. *Gendered by Design? Information Technology and Office Systems*, London: Taylor & Francis, 130–60.

Boisot, M.H. 1996. *Information Space: A Framework for Learning in Organisations, Institutions and Culture*, London: Routledge.

Braverman, H. 1974. *Labor and Monopoly Capital: The Degradation of Work in the Twentieth Century*, New York: Monthly Review Press.

Brigham, M. and Corbett, M. 1996. 'Trust and the virtual organisation: handy cyberias', in Jackson, P. and Van der Weilen, J. (eds) *New Perspectives on Telework – From Telecommuting to the Virtual Organisation*, Report on workshop held at Brunel University, West London: 31 July–2 August, 45–59.

—— 1997. 'E-mail, power and the constitution of organisational reality', *New Technology Work and Employment*, 12 (1), 25–35.

Brödner, P. 1990, *The Shape of Future Technology*, London: Springer-Verlag.

Buchanan, D.A. 1989. 'Principles and practice in work design: current trends; future prospects', in Sisson, K. (ed) *Personnel Management in Britain*, Oxford: Blackwell, 78–100.

—— 1994. 'Theories of change', Loughborough University Business School Research Series, *Paper No. 5*, March.

Buchanan, D.A. and Badham, R., 1999. *Winning the Turf Game: Power, Politics and Organisational Change*, London: Sage.

Buchanan, D.A. and Boddy, D. 1983. *Organisations in the Computer Age: Technological Imperatives and Strategic Choice*, Aldershot: Gower.

—— 1992. *The Expertise of the Change Agent: Public Performance and Back Stage Activity*, Hemel Hempstead: Prentice-Hall.

Buchanan D.A. and Storey, J. 1997. 'Role taking and role switching in organizational change: the four pluralities', in McLoughlin, I. and Harris, M. (eds) *Innovation, Organisational Change and Technology*, London: ITB Press, 127–45.

Burawoy, M. 1979. *Manufacturing Consent: Changes in the Labour Process under Monopoly Capitalism*, Chicago, IL: University of Chicago Press.

Burnes, B. 1989. *New Technology in Context: The Selection, Installation and Use of Numerically Controlled Machine Tools*, Avebury, Gower.

Burns, T. and Stalker, G.R. 1961. *The Management of Innovation*, London: Tavistock.

Burrell, G. 1996. 'Normal science, paradigms, metaphors, discourses and genealogies of analysis', in Clegg, S.R., Hardy, C. and Nord, W.R. (eds) *Handbook of Organization Studies*, London: Sage, 642–58.

Callon, M. 1986. 'The sociology of an actor-network: the case of the electric vehicle', in Callon, M., Law, J. and Rip, A. (eds) *Mapping the Dynamics of Science and Technology: Sociology of Science in the Real World*, Basingstoke: Macmillan, 19–34.

—— 1987. 'Society in the making', in Bijker, W.E., Hughes, T.P. and Pinch, T.J. (eds) *The Social Construction of Technological Systems: New Directions in the Sociology of History and Technology*, Cambridge, MA: MIT Press, 83–106.

—— 1991. 'Techno-economic networks and irreversability', in Law, J. (ed.) *A Sociology of Monsters: Essays on Power, Technology and Domination*, London: Routledge, 132–61.

Callon, M., Law, J. and Rip, A. 1986. *Mapping the Dynamics of Science and Technology*, London: Macmillan, 19–34.

Campbell, A. 1996. 'Creating the virtual organisation and managing the distributed workforce', in Jackson, P. and Van der Weilen, J. (eds) *New Perspectives on Telework – From Telecommuting to the Virtual Organisation*, Report on workshop held at Brunel University, West London: 31 July–2 August, 79–89.

Castells, M. (1996) *The Information Age: Economy, Society and Culture, vol 1: The Rise of the Network Society*, Oxford: Blackwell.

Child, J. 1972. 'Organisation structure, environment and performance: the role of strategic choice', *Sociology*, 6 (1), 1–22.

—— 1997. 'Strategic choice in the analysis of action, structure, organizations and environment: retrospect and prospect', *Organization Studies*, 18 (1), 43–76.

Child, J. and Loveridge, R. 1990. *Information Technology in European Services: Towards a Microelectronic Future*, Oxford: Blackwell.

Child, J. and Smith, C. 1987. 'The context and process of organisational transformation – Cadbury limited in its sector', *Journal of Management Studies*, 24, 565–93.

Clark, J. 1995. *Managing Innovation and Change: People, Technology and Strategy*, London: Sage.

Clark, J., McLoughlin, I.P., Rose, H. and King, J. 1988. *The Process of Technological Change: New Technology and Social Choice in the Workplace*, Cambridge: Cambridge University Press.

Clark, P. 1997. 'Appropriating administrative innovations: decision episode framework', in Clausen, C. and Williams, R. (eds) *The Social Shaping of Computer-Aided Production Management and Computer-Integrated Manufacture*, Proceedings of COST A4 Workshop, Luxembourg: European Commission, 29–48.

Clark, P. and Newell, S. 1993. 'Societal embedding of production and inventory control systems: American and Japanese influences on adaptive implementation in Britain', *International Journal of Human Factors in Manufacturing*, 3 (1), 69–81.

Clark, P. and Staunton, N. 1989. *Innovation in Technology and Organisation*, London: Routledge.

Clausen, C. 1997. 'The social shaping of IT and the company social constitution', Paper presented at the COST A4 workshop, Social Issues about Information

Technology: Organisational Models, Decision Processes, San Sebastian: University of the Basque Country, 3–5 July 1997.

Clausen, C. and Langaa Jensen, P. 1993. 'Action-oriented approaches to technology assessment and working life in Scandinavia', *Technology Analysis and Strategic Management*, 5 (2), 83–97.

Clausen, C. and Nielsen, T. 1997. 'Working environment and technological change', in Neilsen, T. and Clausen, C. (eds) *Working Environment and Technological Development – Positions and Perspectives*, Working Paper No. 3, Roskilde University/Aalborg University/DTU.

Clausen, C. and Williams, R. 1997. 'The social shaping of computer-aided production management and computer aided manufacture', in Clausen, C. and Williams, R. (eds) *The Social Shaping of Computer-Aided Production Management and Computer-Integrated Manufacture*, Proceedings of COST A4 Workshop, Luxembourg: European Commission, 1–28.

Clegg, C., Waterson, P. and Carey, N. 1994. 'Computer supported collaborative working: lessons from elsewhere', *Journal of Information Technology*, 9, 85–98.

Clegg, S.R. 1989. *Frameworks of Power*, London: Sage.

—— 1990. *Modern Organisations in a Post Modern World*, London: Sage.

Clegg, S.R. and Gray, J.T. 1996. 'Metaphors in organisational research: of embedded embryos, paradigms and powerful people', in Grant, D. and Oswick, C. (eds) *Metaphor and Organisation*, London: Sage, 74–93.

Cockburn, C. 1983. *Brothers: Male Dominance and Technological Change*, London: Pluto.

—— 1985. *Machinery of Dominance: Women, Men and Technical Know-how*, London: Pluto.

—— 1993. 'Do artifacts have gender? Feminism and the domestication of technical artifacts', in collection of papers for the CRICT workshop on 'European Theoretical Perspectives on New Technology: Feminism, Constructivism and Utility', London: CRICT, Brunel University.

Cockburn, C. and Ormrod, S. 1993. *Gender and Technology in the Making*, London: Sage.

Collins, H.M. 1994. 'For', *The Times Higher*, 30 September, 16.

Collins, H.M. and Pinch, T.J. 1982. *Frames of Meaning: The Social Construction of Extraordinary Science*, London: Routledge and Kegan Paul.

—— 1995. *The Golem: What Everyone Should Know about Science*, Cambridge: Cambridge University Press.

Collins, H.M. and Yearley, S. 1992a. 'Epistimological chicken', in Pickering, A. (ed.) *Science as Practice and Culture*, Chicago, IL: University of Chicago Press, 301–26.

—— 1992b. 'Journey into space', in Pickering, A. (ed.) *Science as Practice and Culture*, Chicago, IL: University of Chicago Press, 369–81.

Cooley, M. 1980a. *Architect or Bee? The Human/Technology Relationship*, Slough: Langley Technical Services.

Cooley, M. 1980b. 'The designer in the 1980s: the deskiller deskilled', *Design Studies*, 1, 197–201.

Coombs, R., Richards, A., Saviotti, P., and Walsh, V. 1996. 'Introduction: technological collaboration and networks of alliances in the innovation process', in

Coombs, R., Richards, A., Saviotti, P. and Walsh, V. (eds) *Technological Collaboration: The Dynamics of Co-operation in Industrial Innovation*, Cheltenham: Edward Elgar, 1–17.

Coombs, R., Saviotti, P. and Walsh, V. 1987. *Economics and Technological Change*, London: Macmillan.

—— 1992. 'Technology and the firm: the convergence of economic and sociological approaches', in Coombs, R., Saviotti, P. and Walsh, V. (eds) *Technological Change and Company Strategies*, London: Academic Press, 1–24.

Coriat, B. 1991. 'Technical flexibility and mass production', in Benko, G. and Dunford, M. (eds) *Industrial Change and Regional Development*, London: Belhaven, 130–60.

Cotgrove, S. and Box, S. 1970. *Science, Industry and Society*, London: George, Allen & Unwin.

Crompton, R. and Jones, G. 1984. *White Collar Proletariat: Deskilling and Gender in Clerical Work*, London: Macmillan.

Daft, R.L. and Lengel, R.H. 1986. 'Organisational information requirements, media richness and structural design', *Management Science*, 32 (5): 554–71.

Dankbar, B. 1988. 'New production concepts, management strategies and the quality of work', *Work, Employment and Society*, 2 (1), 25–50.

Davidow, W.H. and Malone, M.S. 1992. *The Virtual Corporation*, New York: Harper Business.

Dawkins, R. 1994 'The moon is *not* a calabash', *The Times Higher*, 30 September, 17.

Dawson, P. 1994. *Organizational Change: A Processual Perspective*, London: Paul Chapman Publishers.

—— 1996. *Technology and Quality: Change in the Workplace*, London: ITB Press.

Dawson, S. and Wedderburn, D. 1980. 'Introduction: Joan Woodward and the development of organisation theory', in Woodward, J., *Industrial Organisation: Theory and Practice*, 2nd edn, Oxford, Oxford University Press, xii–xxxvi.

Dodgson, M. 1996. 'Learning, trust and inter-firm technological linkages: some theoretical associations', in Coombs, R., Richards, A., Saviotti, P. and Walsh, V. (eds) *Technological Collaboration: The Dynamics of Cooperation in Industrial Innovation*, Cheltenham: Edward Elgar, 54–75.

Donaldson, L. 1996. *For Positivist Organizational Theory*, London: Sage.

Dosi, G. 1982. 'Technical paradigms and technological trajectories – a suggested interpretation of the determinants and directions of technological change', *Research Policy*, 11 (3), 147–62.

Dosi, G., Freeman, C., Nelson, R., Silverberg, G. and Soete, L. (eds). 1988. *Technical Change and Economic Theory*, London: Pinter.

Døving, E. 1996. 'In the image of man: organisational action, competence and learning', in Grant, D. and Oswick, C. (eds) *Metaphor and Organisation*, London: Sage, 185–99.

Dunford, R. and Palmer, I. 1996. 'Metaphors in popular management discourse: the case of corporate restructuring', in Grant, D. and Oswick, C. (eds) *Metaphor and Organisation*, London: Sage, 95–109.

Edge, D. 1995. 'The social shaping of technology', in Heap, N., Thomas, R., Einon, G., Mason, R. and Mackay, H. (eds) *Information Technology and Society: A Reader*, London: Sage, 14–32.

Edwards, R. 1979. *Contested Terrain: The Transformation of Work in the Twentieth Century*, London: Heinemann.

Einjatten, F. van 1993. *The Paradigm that Changed the Workplace*, Stockholm: Arbetslivcentrum.

Elger, T. 1990. 'Technical innovation and work re-organisation in British manufacturing in the 1980s: continuity, intensification or transformation?', *Work, Employment and Society*, Special Issues, 67–101.

Emery, F. 1978. *The Emergence of a New Paradigm of Work*, Canberra: Centre for Continuing Education.

Eveland, J.D. and Tornatzky, L. 1990. 'The deployment of technology', in Eveland, J.D. and Tornatzky, L. (eds) *The Process of Technological Innovation*, New York: Lexington Books, 130–60.

Faulkner, W. and Arnold, E. (eds) 1985. *Smothered by Invention*, London: Pluto.

Fleck, J. 1987. 'Innofusion or diffusation: the nature of technological development in robotics', *Working Paper 87/9*, Edinburgh: Department of Business Studies, Edinburgh University.

—— 1993. 'Configurations: crystallising contingency', *International Journal of Human Factors in Manufacturing*, 3 (1), 15–36.

Fleck, J. and Howells, J. 1997. 'Defining technology and the paradox of technological determinism', *Working Paper*, Uxbridge: Department of Management Studies, Brunel University.

Forest, J.E. 1991. 'Models of the process of technological innovation', *Technology Analysis and Strategic Management*, 3 (4), 439–53.

Forester, T. (ed.) 1980. *The Microelectronics Revolution*, Oxford: Blackwell.

—— 1985. *The Information Technology Revolution*, Oxford: Blackwell.

—— 1987. *High-Tech Society*, Oxford: Blackwell.

—— 1989a. 'Editor's introduction: making sense of IT', in Forester, T. (ed.) *Computers in the Human Context: Information Technology, Productivity and People*, Oxford: Blackwell, 1–15.

—— (ed.) 1989b. *Computers in the Human Context: Information Technology, Productivity and People*, Oxford: Blackwell.

Foucault, M. 1977. *Discipline and Punish: The Birth of the Prison*, New York: Vintage.

Freeman, C. 1982. *The Economics of Industrial Innovation* (2nd edn), London: Pinter.

—— 1988. 'Introduction', in Dosi, G., Freeman, C., Nelson, R., Silverberg, G. and Soete, L. (eds) *Technical Change and Economic Theory*, London: Pinter, 1–8.

—— 1991. 'Networks of innovators: a synthesis of research issues', *Research Policy*, 20, 499–514.

—— 1994. 'The diffusion of information and communication technology in the world economy in the 1990s', in Mansell, R. (ed.) *Communication and Information Technologies*, London: ASLIB, 8–41.

—— 1996. 'The factory of the future and the productivity paradox', in Dutton, H. (ed.) *Information and Communication Technologies: Visions and Realities*, Oxford: Oxford University Press, 19–36.

Freeman, C. and Perez, C. 1988. 'Structural crises of adjustment: business cycles and investment behaviour', in Dosi, G., Freeman, C., Nelson, R., Silverberg, G., and Soete., L. (eds) *Technical Change and Economic Theory*, London: Pinter, 38–66.

Freeman, C. and Soete, L. 1997. *The Economics of Industrial Innovation* (3rd edn), London: Pinter.

Friedman, A. 1977. *Industry and Labour*, London: Macmillan.

—— 1990. 'Managerial activities, techniques and technology: towards a complex theory of the labour process', in Knights, D. and Wilmott, H. (eds) *Labour Process Theory*, London: Macmillan, 177–208.

Friedman, A. and Cornford, D. 1989. *Computer Systems Development: History, Organisation and Implementation*, Chichester: Wiley.

Fulk, J. 1993. 'Social construction of communication technology', *Academy of Management Journal*, 36 (5), 921–50.

Galbraith, J. 1973. *Designing Complex Organisations*, Reading, MA: Addison-Wesley Press.

Gallie, D. 1978. *In Search of the New Working Class*, Cambridge: Cambridge University Press.

Garahan, P. and Stewart, P. 1992. *The Nissan Enigma: Flexibility at Work in the Local Economy*, London: Mansell.

Gattiker, U.E. 1990. *Technology Management in Organisations*, London: Sage.

Giddens, A. 1979. *Central Problems in Social Theory: Action, Structure and Contradiction in Social Analysis*, London: Macmillan.

—— 1984. *The Constitution of Society: Outline of the Theory of Structure*, Cambridge: Polity Press.

Gill, R. 1994. 'Beyond Technological Determinism and Social Determinism: Theorising Gender-Technology Relations', *Discussion paper No. 49*, Uxbridge: CRICT, Brunel University.

Grant, D. and Oswick, C. 1996. 'Getting the measure of metaphors', Introduction to Grant, D. and Oswick, C. (eds) *Metaphor and Organisation*, London: Sage, 1–20.

Grenier, R. and Mates, G. 1995. *Going Virtual: Moving Your Organisation into the 21st Century*, New York: Prentice-Hall.

Grint, K. and Gill, R. 1985. 'The gender-technology relation: an introduction', in Grint, K. and Gill, R. (eds) *The Gender-Technology Relation: Contemporary Theory and Research*, London: Taylor & Francis, 1–28.

Grint, K. and Woolgar, S. 1992. 'Computers, guns, and roses: what's social about being shot?', *Science, Technology and Human Values*, 17 (3) Summer, 366–80.

—— 1995. 'On some failures of nerve in constructivist and feminist analyses of technology', in Grint, K. and Gill, R. (eds) *The Gender-Technology Relation: Contemporary Theory and Research*, London: Taylor & Francis, 48–76.

—— 1997. *The Machine at Work*, Oxford: Polity Press

Hall, S. and Jaques, M. 1989. *New Times: The Changing Face of Politics in the 1990s*, London: Lawrence & Wishart.

Hammer, M. and Champy, J. 1993. *Re-engineering the Corporation: A Manifesto for a Business Revolution*, New York: HarperCollins.

Handy, C. 1995. 'Trust and the virtual organisation', *Harvard Business Review*, May–June, 40–50.

Hannan, M.T. and Freeman, J.H. 1977. 'The population ecology of organisations', *American Journal of Sociology*, 82, 924–64.

Harris, M. 1998. 'Rethinking the virtual organisation', in Jackson, P.J. and Van der Wielen, J. (eds) *Teleworking: International Perspectives: From Telecommuting to the Virtual Organisation*, London: Routledge, 74–92.

Harvey, D. 1989. *The Condition of Post-modernity*, Oxford: Blackwell.

Hatch, M.J. 1997. *Organisation Theory: Modern Symbolic and Post Modern Perspectives*, Oxford: Oxford University Press.

Hildebrandt, E. and Seltz, R. 1989. *Wandel betrieblicher Sozialverfassung durch systemische Kontrolle*, Berlin: Edition Sigma.

Hill, S. 1988. *The Tragedy of Technology*, Sydney: Pluto Press.

Hill, S., Harris, M. and Martin, R. 1997. 'Flexible technologies, markets and the firm: strategic choice and FMS', in McLoughlin, I.P. and Harris, M. (eds) *Innovation, Organisational Change and Technology*, London: ITB Press, 61–86.

Huczynski, A. and Buchanan, D.A. 1991. *Organisational Behaviour* (2nd edn), London: Prentice-Hall.

Hughes, T.P. 1983. *Networks of Power: Electrification in Western Society, 1880–1930*, Baltimore, MD: Johns Hopkins University Press.

—— 1987. 'The evolution of large technological systems', in Bijker, W.E., Hughes, T.P. and Pinch, T.J. (eds) *The Social Construction of Technological Systems*, Cambridge, MA: MIT Press, 51–82.

Hyman, R. 1991. '*Plus ça change?* The theory of production and the production of theory', in Pollert, A. (ed.) *Farewell to Flexibility*, Oxford: Blackwell, 259–83.

Inkpen, A.C. 1996. 'Creating knowledge through collaboration', *California Management Review*, 39 (1), 123–40.

Jackson, P. 1996. 'The virtual society and the end of organisation', *Working Paper*, Uxbridge: Department of Management Studies, Brunel University.

—— 1997. 'Information systems and metaphor: innovation and the 3 Rs of representation', in McLoughlin, I.P. and Harris, M. (eds) *Innovation, Organisational Change and Technology*, London: ITB Press, 186–206.

Jackson, P.J. and Van der Wielen, J. 1998. 'Introduction: actors, approaches and agendas – from telecommuting to the virtual organisation', in Jackson, P.J. and Van der Wielen, J. (eds) *Teleworking: International Perspectives – From Telecommuting to the Virtual Organisation*, London: Routledge, 1–18.

Jones, B. 1982. Distribution or redistribution of engineering skills? The case of numerical control', in Wood, S. (ed.) *The Degradation of Work?: Skill, Deskilling and the Labour Process*, London: Hutchinson, 179–200.

—— 1997. *Forcing the Factory of the Future: Cybernation and Societal Institutions*, Cambridge: Cambridge University Press.

Jürgens, U., Malsch, T. and K. Dohse, 1993. *Breaking from Taylorism: Changing Forms of Work in the Automobile Industry*, Cambridge: Cambridge University Press.

Kerr, C., Dunlop, J.T., Harbison, F.H. and Myers, C.A. 1960. *Industrialism and Industrial Man*, London: Heinemann.

Kidd, P. 1994. *Agile Manufacturing: Forging New Frontiers*, London: Addison-Wesley.

Kling, R. 1991a. 'Computerisation and social transformations', *Science, Technology and Human Values*, 16 (3) Summer, 342–67.

—— 1991b. 'Reply to Woolgar and Grint: a preview', *Science, Technology and Human Values*, 16 (3) Summer, 379–81.

—— 1992a. 'Audiences, narratives, and human values in social studies of technology', *Science, Technology and Human Values*, 17 (3) Summer, 349–65.

—— 1992b. 'When gunfire shatters bone: reducing socio-technical systems to social relationships', *Science, Technology and Human Values*, 17 (3) Summer, 381–5.

Knights, D. and Murray, F. 1994. *Managers Divided: Organisational Politics and Information Technology Management*, Chichester: Wiley.

Knights, D. and Wilmott, H. (eds) 1986. *Gender and the Labour Process*, Aldershot: Gower.

—— 1988. *New Technology and the Labour Process*, London: Macmillan.

Knights, D. Wilmott, H. and Collinson, D. 1985. *Job Redesign: Critical Perspectives on the Labour Process*, Aldershot: Gower.

Koch, C. 1997a. 'Production management systems: bricks or clay in the hands of social actors?', in Clausen, C. and Williams, R. (eds) *The Social Shaping of Computer-Aided Production Management and Computer-Integrated Manufacture*, Proceedings of COST A4 Workshop, Luxembourg: European Commission, 131–52.

—— 1997b. 'Social and technological development in context', in Neilsen, T. and Clausen, C. (eds) *Working Environment and Technological Development – Positions and Perspectives*, Working Paper No. 3, Roskilde University/Aalborg University/DTU.

Kohn, M. 1997. 'Technofile', *Independent on Sunday*, 5th January, 34.

Kumar, K. 1995. *From Post-Industrial to Post-Modern Society: New Theories of the Contemporary World*, Oxford: Blackwell.

Lane, C. 1989. *Management and Labour in Europe*, London: Edward Elgar.

Langrish, J., Gibbons, M., Evans, P. and Jevons, F. 1972. *Wealth from Knowledge*, London: Macmillan.

Lash, S. and Urry, J. 1987. *The End of Organised Capitalism*, Cambridge: Polity Press.

Latour, B. 1987. *Science in Action: How to Follow Scientists and Engineers Through Society*, Milton Keynes: Open University Press.

—— 1991. 'Technology is society made durable', in Law, J. (ed.) *A Sociology of Monsters: Essays on Power, Technology and Domination*, London: Routledge, 103–31.

—— 1996. 'On actor-network theory: a few clarifications', *Soziale Welt*, 47, 369–81.

Law, J. 1987. 'Technology and heterogeneous engineering', in Bijker, W.E., Hughes, T.P. and Pinch, T.J. (eds) *The Social Construction of Technological Systems*, Cambridge, MA: MIT Press, 111–34.

Lewin, K. 1951. *Field Theory in Social Science*, New York: Harper & Row.

Littler, C.R. 1982. *The Development of the Labour Process in Capitalist Societies*, London: Heinemann.

Lukes, S. 1974. *Power: A Radical View*, London: Macmillan.

Lyon, D. 1994. *The Electronic Eye: The Rise of the Surveillance Society*, Oxford: Polity Press.

McCarthy, J. 1994. 'The state-of-the-art of CSCW: SCCW systems, co-operative work and organization', *Journal of Information Technology*, 9, 73–83.

McCourt, W. (1997) 'Using metaphors to understand organisations: a critique of Gareth Morgan's approach', *Organization Studies*, 18(3): 511–23

Mackay, H. 1995. 'Theorising the IT/society relationship', in Heap, N., Thomas, R., Einon, G., Mason, R. and Mackay, H. (eds) *Information Technology and Society: A Reader*. London: Sage, 41–53.

Mackay, H. and Gillespie, G. 1992. 'Extending the social shaping of technology approach: ideology and appropriation', *Social Studies of Science*, 11, 685–716.

MacKenzie, D. 1996. *Knowing Machines: Essays on Technological Change*, Cambridge, MA: MIT Press, 49–65.

MacKenzie, D. and Wajcman, J. 1985. 'Introductory essay', in MacKenzie, D. and Wajcman, J. (eds) *The Social Shaping of Technology*, Milton Keynes: Open University Press, 2–25.

McLoughlin, I.P. 1997. 'Babies, bathwater, guns and roses', in McLoughlin, I.P. and Harris, M. (eds) *Innovation, Organisational Change and Technology*, London: ITB Press, 207–21.

McLoughlin, I. and Clark, J. 1994. *Technological Change at Work* (2nd edn), Buckingham: Open University Press.

McLoughlin, I.P. and Harris, M. (eds) 1997. *Innovation, Organisational Change and Technology*, London: ITB Press.

McLoughlin, I.P., Badham, R. and Couchman, P. 1997. *Case Studies in the Introduction of Team-based Cellular Manufacturing in Australia*, Wollongong: Wollongong University Press.

—— 1998. 'Implementing vulnerable socio-technical change: three cases from Australia', in Karwowski, W. and Goonetilleke, R. *Manufacturing Agility and Hybrid Automation – II*, 93–96.

Majchrzak, A. 1988. *The Human Side of Factory Automation*, New York: Josey-Bass.

—— 1997. 'What to do when you can't have it all: toward a theory of socio-technical dependencies', *Human Relations*, 50 (5), 535–65.

March, J.G. and Simon, H.A. 1958. *Organisations*, New York: Wiley.

Marx, G.T. 1988. *Undercover: Police Surveillance in America*, Berkeley, CA: University of California Press.

Masuda, Y. 1985. 'Computopia', in Forester, T. (ed.) *The Information Technology Revolution*, Oxford: Blackwell, 620–34.

Mathews, J. 1989a. *Tools of Change: New Technology and the Democratisation of Work*, Sydney: Pluto Press Australia.

—— 1989b. *Age of Democracy: The Politics of Post-Fordism*, Melbourne: Oxford University Press.

—— 1994. *Catching the Wave: Workplace Reform in Australia*, Sydney: Allen & Unwin.

—— 1997. 'Introduction', to the special issue *Human Relations*, 50 (5), 487–97.

Misa, T.J. 1994. 'Retrieving socio-technical change from technological determinism', in Smith, M.R. and Marx, L. (eds) *Does Technology Drive History? The Dilemma of Technological Determinism*, Cambridge, MA: MIT Press.

MITOC, 1995. 'Job design and teamwork', *TBCM Pamphlet No. 4*, Wollongong: Management of Integrated Technology and Organisation Centre, Wollongong University.

Molina, A. 1994. 'The generation of large scale capability building initiatives – extending the socio-technical constituencies perspective', in Mansell, R. (ed.) *Communication and Information Technologies*, London: ASLIB.

Morath, F. 1997. 'From telework to virtual work: creating a hyper-learning organisation', in Jackson, P. and Van der Weilen, J. (eds) *Proceedings of Second International Workshop on Telework, Building Action on Ideas*, Amsterdam, 2–5 September, 45–63.

Morgan, G. 1986. *Images of Organisation*, London: Sage.

—— 1993. *Imaginisation: The Art of Creative Management*, London: Sage.

—— 1996. 'An after word: is there anything more to say about metaphor?', in Grant, D. and Oswick, C. (eds) *Metaphor and Organisation*, London: Sage, 227–40.

—— 1997. *Images of Organisation* (2nd edn), London: Sage.

Nelson, R. and Winter, S. 1982. *An Evolutionary Theory of Economic Change*, Boston, MA: Harvard University Press.

Noble, D. 1979. 'Social choice in machine-design: the case of automatically controlled machine tools', in Zimbalist, A. (ed.) *Case Studies on the Labor Process*, New York: Monthly Review Press, 18–50.

Nohria, N. 1992. 'Introduction: is a network perspective a useful way of studying organisations?', in Nohria, N. (ed.) *Networks and Organisations*, Harvard, MA: Harvard Business School Press, 1–22.

Nohria, N. and Eccles, R.G. 1992. 'Face-to-face: making network organisations work', in Nohria, N. and Eccles, R.G. *Networks and Organisations*, Harvard, MA: Harvard Business School Press, 288–308.

Nonaka, I. and Takuchi, H. 1994. *The Knowledge-Creating Company*, Oxford: Oxford University Press.

Open University T362 Course Team. 1986a. 'Design and innovation: an introduction', *T362 Design and Innovation Units 1–2*, Milton Keynes: Open University Press.

—— 1986b. 'Some conclusions'. *T362 Design and Innovation Units ?-?*, Milton Keynes: Open University Press.

Orlikowski, W.J. 1992. 'The duality of technology: rethinking the concept of technology in organisations', *Organisational Science*, 3 (3), 398–427.

Orlikowski, W.J. and Cash, D.J. 1994. 'Technological frames: making sense of information technology in organisations', *ACM Transactions on Information Systems*, 12 (2), 174–207.

Orlikowski, W.J. and Hofman, D.J. 1997. 'An improvisational model for change management: the case of groupware technologies', *Sloan Management Review*, Winter, 11–21.

Orwell, G. 1954. *Nineteen Eighty Four*, Harmondsworth: Penguin.

Palmer, I. and Dunford, P. 1996. 'Interrogating reframing: evaluating metaphor-based analysis of organisations', in Clegg, S. and Palmer, G. (eds) *The Politics of Management Knowledge*, London: Sage.

Parayil, G. 1990. 'Book review', *Science, Technology and Human Values*, 15 (1), 124–5.

Pavitt, K. 1984. 'Sectoral patterns of technical change: towards a taxonomy and a theory', *Research Policy*, 13, 83–94.

—— 1987. 'Commentary on chapter 3', in Pettigrew, A. (ed.) *The Management of Strategic Change*, Oxford: Blackwell, 123–7.

—— 1990. 'Strategic management in the innovating firm', in Mansfield, R. (ed.) *The Management of Strategic Change*, London: Routledge.

Perrow, C. 1967. 'A framework for comparative analysis of organizations', *American Sociological Review*, 32 (2), 194–208.

—— 1983. 'The organisational context of human factors engineering', *Administrative Science Quarterly*, 28, 521–41.

Pettigrew, A.M. 1973. *The Politics of Organisational Decision-making*, London: Tavistock.

—— 1977. 'Strategy formulation as a political process', *International Studies of Management and Organisation*, 7 (2), 78–87.

—— 1985. *The Awakening Giant: Continuity and Change in Imperial Chemical Industries*, Oxford: Blackwell.

—— 1987. 'Context and action in the transformation of the firm', *Journal of Management Studies*, 24 (6), 649–70.

—— 1990. 'Is corporate culture manageable?', in Wilson, D. and Rosenfeld, R. (eds) *Managing Organizations: Text, Readings and Cases*, London: McGraw-Hill, 266–72.

Pettigrew, A. and Whip, R. 1991. *Managing Change for Competitive Success*, Oxford: Blackwell.

Pettigrew A.M., Ferlie, E. and McKee, L. 1992. *Shaping Strategic Change*, London: Sage.

Pettigrew A.M., McKee, L. and Ferlie, E. 1988. 'Understanding change in the NHS', *Public Administration*, 66 (3), 297–317.

Pfeffer, J. and Salancik, G.R. 1978. *The External Control of Organisations: A Resource Dependence Perspective*, New York: Harper & Row.

Pinch, T.J. and Bijker, W.B. 1987. 'The social construction of facts and artifacts: or how the sociology of science and the sociology of technology might benefit each other', in Bijker, W.E., Hughes, T.P. and Pinch, T.J. (eds) *The Social Construction of Technological Systems: New Directions in the Sociology of History and Technology*, Cambridge, MA: MIT Press, 17–50.

Piore, M.J. and Sabel, C.F. 1984. *The Second Industrial Divide: Possibilities for Prosperity*, New York: Basic Books.

Pollert, A. 1991. 'The orthodoxy of flexibility', in Pollert, A. (ed.) *Farewell to Flexibility?*, Oxford: Blackwell, 3–31.

Preece, D. 1995. *Organisations and Technical Change*, London: ITB Press.

Pugh, D.S. and Hickson, D.J. 1976. *Organisation Structure in its Context: The Aston Programme I*, Farnborough: Saxon House.

Quinn, J.B. 1992. *The Intelligent Enterprise*, New York: Basic Books.

Reed, M. 1985. *Redirections in Organisational Analysis*, London: Tavistock.

—— 1992. *The Sociology of Organisations* Brighton: Harvester Wheatsheaf.

Reeves, T.K. and Woodward, J. 1970. 'The study of managerial control', in Woodward, J. (ed.) *Industrial Organisation: Behaviour and Control*, London: Oxford University Press, 37–56.

Ritzer, G. 1996. *The McDonaldisation of Society*, London: Sage.

Roberts, K.H. and Grabowski, M. 1996. 'Organisations, technology and structuring', in Clegg, S.R., Hardy, C. and Nord, W.R. (eds) *Handbook of Organization Studies*, London: Sage, 408–23.

Roethlisberger, F.J. and Dickson, W.J. 1964. *Management and the Worker* (1st edn 1939), New York: Wiley.

Rose, M. 1988. *Industrial Behaviour: Research and Control*, London: Penguin.

Rosenberg, N. 1982. *Inside the Black Box: Technology and Economics*, Cambridge: Cambridge University Press.

Rosenbrock, H.H. 1985. 'Engineers and the work that people do', in Littler, C.R. (ed.) *The Experience of Work*, Aldershot: Gower, 161–71.

Rothschild, J. (ed.) 1983. *Machina Ex Dea: Feminist Perspectives on Technology*, New York: Pergamon.

Rothwell, R. 1992. 'Successful industrial innovation: critical factors for the 1990s', *R&D Management*, 22 (3), 221–39.

Rothwell, R. and Zegfeld, W. 1985. *Reindustrialisation and Technology*, London: Longman.

Rule, J. 1973. *Private Lives, Public Surveillance*, London: Allen-Lane.

Russell, S. 1991. 'Interests and the shaping of technology: an unresolved debate reappears', *Department of Science and Technology Studies Working Paper No 4*, Wollongong: University of Wollongong.

Sabel, C.F. 1982. *Work and Politics: The Division of Labour in Industry*, Cambridge: Cambridge University Press.

Sætnan, A.R. 1991. ' "Rigid politics and technological flexibility": the anatomy of a failed hospital innovation', *Science, Technology, and Human Values*, 16 (4), 419–47.

Salaman, G. and Littler, C. 1984. *Class at Work*, London: Batsford.

Salzman, H. and Rosenthal, S. (1994) *Software by Design: Shaping Technology and the Workplace*, New York: Oxford University Press.

Saviotti, P.P. 1996. *Technological Evolution, Variety and Economy*, Cheltenham: Edward Elgar.

Saviotti, P.P. and Metcalfe, J.S. (eds) 1991. *Evolutionary Theories of Economic and Technological Change*, Reading: Harwood.

Sayles, L.R. 1958. *The Behaviour of Industrial Workgroups*, New York: Wiley.

Scarbrough, H. and Corbett, M.J. 1992. *Technology and Organisation: Power, Meaning and Design*, London: Routledge.

Schon, D.A. 1983. *The Reflective Practitioner: How Professionals Think in Action*, New York: Basic Books.

Schumann, M. 1998. 'New concepts of production and productivity', *Economic and Industrial Democracy*, 19, 17–32.

Schumpeter, J.A. 1934. *The Theory of Economic Development*, Cambridge, MA: Harvard University Press.

—— 1939. *Business Cycles*, New York: McGraw-Hill.

—— 1942. *Capitalism, Socialism and Democracy*, London: Allen & Unwin.

Sitter, L.U. de., Hertog, F den. and Dankbaar, B. 1997. 'From complex organizations with simple jobs to simple organizations with complex jobs', *Human Relations*, 50 (5), 497–533.

Smith, C. 1989. 'Flexible specialisation, automation and mass production', *Work, Employment and Society*, 3 (2), 203–20.

Soete, L. 1996. *Technological Evolution, Variety and the Economy*, London: Edward Elgar.

Stonier, T. 1983. *The Wealth of Information: A Profile of the Post-industrial Economy*, London: Methuen.

Storey, J. 1994. 'New wave manufacturing strategies: an introduction', in Storey, J. (ed.) *New Wave Manufacturing Strategies: Organisational and Human Resource Management Dimensions*, London: Paul Chapman, 1–21.

Strauss, G., Schatzman, L., Ehrlich, D., Bucher, R. and Sabshim, M. 1973. 'The hospital and its negotiated order', in Salaman, G. and Thompson, K. (eds) *People and Organisations*, London: Longman, 303–20 (first published in Friedson, E. (ed.) 1963. *The Hospital in Modern Society*, London: Macmillan, 147–69).

Thompson, J. 1967. *Organisations in Action*, New York: McGraw-Hill.

Thompson, P. 1989. *The Nature of Work* (2nd edn), London: Macmillan.

Thompson, P. and McHugh, D. 1995. *Work Organisations: A Critical Introduction* (2nd edn), London: Macmillan Business.

Tidd, J., Bessant, J. and Pavitt, K. 1997. *Managing Innovation: Integrating Technological, Market and Organisational Change*, London: Wiley.

Tierney, M. and Williams, R. 1990. 'Issues in the black-boxing of technologies', *Working Paper No. 22*, Edinburgh: PICT, Edinburgh University.

Tinker, T. 1986. 'Metaphor and reification', *Journal of Management Studies*, 23, 363–84.

Toffler, A. 1981. *The Third Wave*, New York: Bantam Books.

Tomaney, J. 1994. 'A new paradigm of work organisation and technology?', in Amin, A. (ed.) *Post-Fordism: A Reader*, Oxford: Blackwell, 157–94.

Trist, E., Higgin, G.W., Murray, H. and Pollock, A.B. 1963. *Organisational Choice: The Loss, Rediscovery and Transformation of a Work Tradition*, London: Tavistock.

Tsoukas, H. 1993. 'Analogical reasoning and knowledge generation in organisational theory', *Organisation Studies*, 14 (3), 323–46.

Upton, D.M. and McAfee, A. 1996. 'The real virtual factory', *Harvard Business Review*, July–August, 123–33.

Useem, M. and Kochan, T.A. 1992. 'Creating the learning organisation', in Kochan, T.A. and Useem, M. (eds) *Transforming Organisations*, Oxford: Oxford University Press, 391–406.

Wajcman, J. 1991. *Feminism Confronts Technology*, Oxford: Blackwell.

Walker, C.R. and Guest, R.H. 1952. *The Man on the Assembly Line*, Cambridge MA: Harvard University Press.

Walsham, G. 1993. *Interpreting Information Systems*, Chichester: Wiley.

Webster, J. 1990. 'The shaping of software systems in manufacturing: issues in the generation and implementation of network technologies in British industries', *Working Paper No. 17*, Edinburgh: PICT, Edinburgh University.

—— 1993. 'Chicken or egg? The interaction between manufacturing technologies and paradigms of work organisation', *International Journal of Human Factors in Manufacturing*, 3 (1), 53–68.

—— 1996. *Shaping Women's Work: Gender, Employment and Information Technology*, London: Longman.

Weick, K.E. 1990. 'Technology as equivoque: sense making in new technologies', in Goodman, P.S., Sproull, L.S. and associates (eds) *Technology and Organizations*, 1–44.

Westrum, R. 1987. *Technologies and Society: The Shaping of People and Things*, Belmont, CA: Wadsworth.

Whittington, R. 1988. 'Environmental structure and theories of strategic choice', *Journal of Management Studies*, 25, 521–36.

Wiener, N. 1968. *The Human Use of Human Beings: Cybernetics and Society*, London: Sphere Books.

Wilkinson, B. 1983. *The Shop Floor Politics of New Technology*, London: Heinemann.

Willcocks, L. and Grint, K. 1997. 'Re-inventing the organisation? Towards a critique of business process re-engineering', in McLoughlin, I.P. and Harris, M. (eds) *Innovation, Organisational Change and Technology*, London: ITB Press, 87–110.

Willcocks, L., Currie, W. and Mason, D. 1996. *Information Systems at Work: People, Politics and Technology*, London: McGraw-Hill.

Williams, R. 1997a. 'Universal solutions or local contingencies? Tensions and contradictions in the mutual shaping of technology and work organisation', in McLoughlin, I.P. and Harris, M. (eds) *Innovation, Organisational Change and Technology*, London: ITB Press, 170–85.

—— 1997b. 'The social shaping of a failed technology? Mismatch and tension between the supply and use of computer-aided production management', in Clausen, C. and Williams, R. (eds) *The Social Shaping of Computer-Aided Production Management and Computer-Integrated Manufacture*, Proceedings of COST A4 Workshop, Luxembourg: European Commission, 109–30.

Williams, R. and Edge, D. 1992a. 'The social shaping of technology: research concepts and findings in Great Britain', in Dierkes, M. and Hoffmann, U. (eds) *New Technology at the Outset: Social Forces in the Shaping of Technological Innovations*, Frankfurt and New York: Campus and Westview, 31–61.

—— 1992b. 'Social shaping reviewed: research concepts and findings in the UK', *Working Paper No. 41*, Edinburgh: PICT, Edinburgh University.

Williams, R. and Russell, S. 1987. 'Opening the black box and closing it behind you: on micro-sociology in the social analysis of technology', *Working Paper No. 3*, Edinburgh: PICT, Edinburgh University.

Willman, P. 1997. 'Appropriability of technology and internal organisation', in McLoughlin, I.P. and Harris, M. (eds) *Innovation, Organisational Change and Technology*, London: ITB Press, 42–60.

Wilmott, H. 1995. 'A reply to Zuboff', Paper presented at IFIP WG8.2 conference on *Information Technology and Changes in Organisational Work*, Cambridge University, December.

Winner, L. 1977. *Autonomous Technology*, Cambridge, MA: MIT Press.

—— 1980. 'Do artifacts have politics?', *Daedalus*, 109, 121–36. Extract repr. in MacKenzie, D. and Wajcman, J. (eds), 1985. *The Social Shaping of Technology*, Milton Keynes: Open University Press, 26–38.

Winnigrad, T. and Adler, P. (eds) 1997. *Usability: Turning Technology into Tools*, New York: Oxford University Press.

Womack, J.P., Jones, D.T. and Roos, D. 1990. *The Machine That Changed the World*, Oxford: Maxwell Macmillan International.

Wood, S. 1989. *The Transformation of Work?*, London: Unwin Hyman.

Woodward, J. (ed.) 1970. *Industrial Organisation: Behaviour and Control*, London: Oxford University Press.

—— 1980. *Industrial Organisation: Theory and Practice* (2nd edn), Oxford: Oxford University Press.

Woolgar, S. 1991a. 'The turn to technology in social studies of science', *Science, Technology and Human Values*, 16 (1), 20–50.

—— 1991b. 'Configuring the user: the case of usability trials', in Law, J. (ed.) *A Sociology of Monsters: Essays on Power, Technology and Domination*, London: Routledge, 58–99.

—— 1992. 'Putting the social into software or why no systems designer should be without social science', in *Software Systems Practice: Social Science Perspectives*, Uxbridge: CRICT, Brunel University.

—— 1994. 'Rethinking requirements analysis: some implications of recent research into producer–consumer relationships in IT development, in Jirotk, M. and Goguen, J.A. (eds) *Requirements Engineering: Social and Technical Issues*, London: Academic Press, 201–16.

—— 1997. 'A new theory of innovation?', *Third Annual 3M Innovation Lecture*, Brunel University, 11 June.

Woolgar, S. and Grint, K. 1991. 'Computers and the transformation of social analysis', *Science, Technology and Human Values*, 16 (3) Summer, 368–78.

Zimbalist, A. (ed.) 1979. *Case Studies on the Labour Process*, New York: Monthly Review Press.

Zuboff, S. 1988. *In the Age of the Smart Machine*, Harvard, MA: Harvard Business School Press.

—— 1996. *The Emperor's New Information Economy*, in Orlikowski, W., Walsham, G., Jones, M.R., DeGross, J.I. (eds), London: Chapman & Hall. ch. 4: 13–17.

Index